Robert Redfield and the Development of American Anthropology

Robert Redfield in Tepoztlán, Mexico (1926).
Used by permission of *University of Chicago Magazine*.

Robert Redfield and the Development of American Anthropology

Clifford Wilcox

LEXINGTON BOOKS

A division of
ROWMAN & LITTLEFIELD PUBLISHERS, INC.
Lanham • Boulder • New York • Toronto • Plymouth, UK

LEXINGTON BOOKS

A division of Rowman & Littlefield Publishers, Inc.
A wholly owned subsidary of The Rowman & Littlefield Publishing Group, Inc.
4501 Forbes Boulevard, Suite 200
Lanham, MD 20706

Estover Road
Plymouth PL6 7PY
United Kingdom

British Library Cataloguing in Publication Information Available

The hardback edition of this book was previously catalogued by the Library of Congress
as follows:

Wilcox, Clifford, 1956–
     Robert Redfield and the development of American anthropology / Clifford Wilcox.
        p. cm.
     Includes bibliographical references and index.
     1. Redfield, Robert, 1897– 2. Anthropologists—United States—Biography.
Anthropology—United States—History. 2. Chicago school of sociology—History. I.
Title.

GN21.R43W55 2004
301'.092—dc22
[B]   2004044182
ISBN-13: 978-0-7391-0728-7 (cloth : alk. paper)
ISBN-10: 0-7391-0728-3 (cloth : alk. paper)
ISBN-13: 978-0-7391-1777-4 (pbk : alk paper)
ISBN-10: 0-7391-1777-7 (pbk : alk paper)

Printed in the United States of America

♾™ The paper used in this publication meets the minimum requirements of American
National Standard for Information Sciences—Permanence of Paper for Printed Library
Materials, ANSI/NISO Z39.48–1992.

To my mother, Elinor A. Wilcox,

who believed in this project

but did not live to see it completed.

Contents

Acknowledgments

In the course of conducting this study, I have accumulated numerous debts. Although space considerations prevent me from acknowledging all who contributed to this project, I would like to express my gratitude to those who assisted me most directly. First, I would like to thank David A. Hollinger, who kindled my interest in the history of the social sciences and first assisted me in defining my study of Robert Redfield and the modernizationist project. James Turner lent further definition to my efforts to investigate the development of the social sciences in mid-twentieth century America. Most important, Richard Cándida Smith, John S. Gilkeson, Jr., and Howard Brick assisted me immeasurably in both the conceptualization and writing of this book. Not only did they read and reread numerous drafts, but also they provided me with invaluable encouragement and help, particularly in regard to its publication. I also want to acknowledge the assistance and guidance of my editors at Lexington Books, Jason Hallman and Hedi Hong.

This work had its beginnings as a dissertation completed at the University of Michigan. Several people graciously assisted me in researching and writing this dissertation, freely giving their time to discuss Redfield and mid-century Chicago sociology and anthropology with me and reading and criticizing drafts of individual chapters or the dissertation in its entirety. I gratefully acknowledge the following individuals for their willingness to read and comment upon my work: Lawrence S. Berlin, Fred W. Beuttler, Robert T. Blackburn, Nicholas B. Dirks, Milton Eder, Charles M. Leslie, Fred H. Matthews, and Terrence J. McDonald. I would also like to thank the many archivists who assisted me in this project: Daniel Meyer and Debra Levine of the Regenstein Library at the University of Chicago, Monica Blank and Thomas Rosenbaum of the Rockefeller Archive Center, Alan Divak of the Ford Foundation Archives, and Elizabeth Sandager of the Peabody Museum of Archaeology and Anthropology at Harvard University.

I want to express my gratitude, furthermore, to the numerous colleagues and former students of Robert Redfield who kindly shared with me their memories of Redfield. A complete list of these persons appears in the bibliography. Robert Redfield's children, Lisa Redfield Peattie, Joanna Redfield Gutmann, and James M. Redfield, also proved extremely helpful. They not only gave generously of their time to discuss their father, but also responded readily to my multiple requests for information.

I am happy to acknowledge the support I received from the Andrew W. Mellon Foundation, the Rackham Graduate School of the University of Michigan, and the Department of History at the University of Michigan. These agencies provided me the resources necessary to allow me to pursue without interruption the research for and writing of the dissertation that served as the basis for this book.

I also want to thank my family for their unflagging support. Fred Wilcox and Marcea and Richard Azimov have stood behind me from the beginning of this project, and I am sincerely grateful for the way they have believed in me. Above all, my thanks go to my wife Michelle B. Azimov, who not only took time away from her already overcrowded schedule to read every word of this manuscript, but also encouraged and assisted me and believed in this project from its very inception.

Finally, I would like to acknowledge the following copyright owners and literary executors who have granted me permission to quote from their works:

Passages from the Ford Foundation's University of Chicago Comparative Civilizations Project Papers are quoted with the permission of the Ford Foundation Archives.

A letter by Robert E. Park to Robert Redfield, 23 January 1932, in the Robert Redfield Papers, Special Collections, Joseph Regenstein Library, University of Chicago, is quoted with the permission of James M. Redfield.

Passages from Robert E. Park, "The City: Suggestions for the Investigation of Human Behavior in the Urban Environment," in *The City*, edited by Robert E. Park, Ernest W. Burgess, and Roderick D. McKenzie (1925), is quoted with permission of the publisher, the University of Chicago Press.

A letter by Donald Culross Peattie to Robert Redfield, 25 December 1918, in the Robert Redfield Papers, Addenda, Special Collections, Joseph Regenstein Library, University of Chicago, is quoted with the permission of Noel Peattie.

Passages from Robert Redfield's letters and papers in the Robert Redfield Papers, Robert Redfield Papers Addenda, Robert Maynard Hutchins Papers, John U. Nef Papers, Sol Tax Papers, and President's Papers, University of Chicago, Special Collections, Joseph Regenstein Library, University of Chicago, are quoted with the permission of James M. Redfield. Also, photographs of Robert Redfield were provided by Special Collections, Joseph Regenstein Library, University of Chicago, and are published with the permission of James M. Redfield.

Passages from Robert Redfield, *Tepoztlán, A Mexican Village* (1930), are quoted with permission of the publisher, the University of Chicago Press.

Passages from Robert Redfield, *The Folk Culture of Yucatan* (1941), are quoted with permission of the publisher, the University of Chicago Press.

Passages from Robert Redfield, *A Village That Chose Progress: Chan Kom Revisited* (1950), are quoted with permission of the publisher, the University of Chicago Press.

Passages from Robert Redfield, *The Primitive World and Its Transformations* (1953), are quoted with permission of the publisher, Cornell University Press.

Passages from Robert Redfield, *The Little Community* (1955), are quoted with permission of the publisher, the University of Chicago Press.

Passages from Robert Redfield, *Peasant Society and Culture* (1956), are quoted with permission of the publisher, the University of Chicago Press.

Passages from Robert Redfield, *The Papers of Robert Redfield: Human Nature and the Study of Society,* vol. 1 (1962), edited by Margaret Park Redfield, are quoted with permission of the publisher, the University of Chicago Press.

Passages from Robert Redfield, *The Papers of Robert Redfield: The Social Uses of Social Science,* vol. 2 (1963), edited by Margaret Park Redfield, are quoted with permission of the publisher, the University of Chicago Press.

Passages from Robert Redfield and Milton Singer, "The Cultural Role of Cities," in *Economic Development and Cultural Change* 3 (October 1954): 53-73, are quoted with the permission of the publisher, the University of Chicago Press.

Passages from the records of the Laura Spelman Rockefeller Memorial are quoted with the permission of the Rockefeller Archive Center.

Passages from the Anne Roe interview with Robert Redfield (1950) are quoted with the permission of the American Philosophical Society Library.

Passages from Sol Tax's letters in the Sol Tax Papers, Special Collections, Joseph Regenstein Library, University of Chicago, are quoted with the permission of Susan Tax Freeman and Marianna Tax Choldin.

Passages from Leslie White's papers in the Leslie A. White Papers, Bentley Historical Library, University of Michigan, are quoted with the permission of the Bentley Historical Library.

Introduction

Although American anthropology emerged as a serious intellectual pursuit in the mid-nineteenth century, it was not until the twentieth century that it became an academic discipline. For its first fifty years, the field was dominated by learned amateurs—physicians, lawyers, businessmen, and the like—and museums, rather than universities, served as the primary institutional setting for anthropological activities. American anthropology underwent a sea change, however, in the late nineteenth century. Franz Boas, more than any other single figure, presided over this transformation. In 1889, he joined the faculty of Clark University and created the first anthropology teaching program in the United States; three years later, he awarded the first American Ph.D. He then moved in 1896 to Columbia University, and in 1899 became Columbia's first professor of anthropology. Under his leadership, the department quickly emerged as the premier anthropology program in the United States, and Boas's students dominated the discipline for the first three decades of the twentieth century.

Much of the turn-of-the-century change in American anthropology can be attributed to the general processes of professionalization and specialization, which were transforming almost all scholarly fields during the late nineteenth and early twentieth centuries. Nevertheless, Boas exerted a powerful personal influence over the professionalization project in anthropology. Specifically, he attacked the speculative "armchair" approach that was common in nineteenth-century anthropology. Rather than conducting on-site field investigations, most anthropologists relied upon traveler's accounts and often embellished their accounts with hypothetical or "conjectural" history.

Most troubling to Boas was the predominance of evolutionary thinking among anthropologists. Nineteenth-century anthropologists in both the United States and Britain engaged in extensive evolutionary speculation and propounded elaborate schemes of human social evolution. Invariably, white European civilization appeared in these accounts as the apex of civilization, and peoples of color from the rest of the world were portrayed as occupying lower rungs on the figurative ladder of civilization. Boas rejected this ethnocentric perspective. Not only did he reject the notion that the way of life of one people could be judged as superior or inferior to another, but also he rejected the notion that observed differences in civilization reflected racial distinctions. Differences in

1

ways of life, he argued, reflected historical contingency, not the genetic or racial heritage of a people. He regarded such evolutionary thinking as one of the worst manifestations of the amateur approach that had characterized American anthropology for most of its existence, and he argued that anthropologists needed to distance themselves from such speculative theorizing and pursue instead empirical historical investigation. In short, Boas equated speculative "armchair anthropology" with amateurism; the professional approach rested, by contrast, upon scientific field investigation. Boas's efforts to professionalize American anthropology and to replace ethnocentric evolutionary theorizing with empirical historical investigation were thus mutually reinforcing aims—indeed, they were but opposite sides of the same coin.

By the first few decades of the twentieth century, the Boasian program came to represent the mainstream of American anthropological practice. Evolutionary thinking all but disappeared from the discipline, and Boas's approach to anthropological fieldwork became the standard model of study up till the 1920s. Boas advocated that anthropologists focus their efforts upon study of North American Indian tribes; he stressed, furthermore, that researchers produce historical accounts of these tribes based upon personal observation. Under his direction, anthropologists attempted to produce ethnographic descriptions of as many of these Indian tribes as possible before modern civilization obliterated their distinctive ways of life. Boas believed that after a sufficient body of scientific historical accounts had been completed, anthropologists would be able to derive certain generalizations about cultural process. Nevertheless, Boas directed his students to focus primarily on completion of empirical studies and not the search for generalizations.[1]

During the mid- to late 1920s, however, a new generation of anthropologists began to chafe against Boas's strictures. Young anthropologists began to refer to his historical studies pejoratively as "salvage anthropology." The rapidly accumulating body of historical studies had led to few important generalizations, and the young critics began to regard the Boasian approach as antiquarian. Boas had discouraged theoretical efforts in anthropology because they had been based upon ethnocentric assumptions and unsound speculations. Yet critics of the 1920s and 1930s charged that Boas's empirical approach had grown arid for lack of sufficient theoretical reach.[2]

University of Chicago anthropologist Robert Redfield (1897-1958) was one of the first to challenge Boas's approach. During the mid-1920s, Redfield launched an investigation designed to reawaken the generalizing impulse in American anthropology. Redfield argued that Boas had gone too far in banishing evolutionary notions from anthropology. Whereas he agreed with Boas's desire to rid the discipline of racist assumptions, he did not accept the need to quash evolutionary thinking altogether. The evolutionary conception—purged of its racist ideology—could be used, Redfield asserted, to provide necessary theoretical dimension to anthropology. Redfield focused his challenge especially on the limitations of Boas's historical or "salvage anthropology" approach. In a typical salvage anthropology study, an investigator often had to ignore changes that were disrupting the traditional way of life of a particular Indian tribe. Salvage anthropology aimed at producing an "ethnographic photograph" of the way of life long characteristic of a people, and an anthropologist often had to rely upon memories of older members of the tribe to construct an image of that particular way of life. Redfield proposed, however, that changes occurring among these peoples should not be ignored or glossed over. Indeed, he argued, these changes should constitute the focal point of anthropological investigation.[3]

Constant change had come to be recognized during the early decades of the twentieth century as one of the most characteristic features of modern life. Numerous social scientists during these years attempted to examine the process of change itself to gain a better understanding of contemporary life. Redfield was inspired by early examples of these studies, especially those conducted by sociologists at the University of Chicago, and he believed anthropology could serve as a powerful technique for pursuing such investigations. Because change was occurring at a particularly rapid rate among the so-called primitive peoples who lived on the margins of civilized society, Redfield proposed that studies of these peoples offered an ideal setting for studying change "as it happens." By conducting a number of these studies and evaluating the results comparatively, he argued, generalizations about social change, or social evolution, could then be achieved.

Redfield was not the only anthropologist during the 1920s to return to consideration of social process and change. Several other British and American anthropologists, including Bronislaw Malinowski, A. R. Radcliffe-Brown, Melville Herskovits, Ralph Linton, George Murdock, and Ralph Beals, also concerned themselves with examination of social dynamics. The efforts of these individuals and others working in similar directions during the interwar years resulted in the emergence of social anthropology—a major initiative within the discipline characterized by its effort to join the generalizing scientific approach of sociology with the more descriptive approach of anthropology.[4] Over the course of his thirty-year career, Redfield served as one of the primary theorists of the new social anthropology movement, and his work exercised a powerful influence within both sociology and anthropology from the 1930s to the 1960s.

Redfield earned his doctorate in sociology and anthropology at the University of Chicago in 1928. His intellectual agenda derived primarily from two factors: (1) the "culture versus civilization" debate of the 1920s and (2) the influence of his father-in-law, Robert E. Park, one of the leading figures in the "Chicago School" of urban sociology. Following World War I, artists and intellectuals on both sides of the Atlantic engaged in a searching debate over the nature of progress and the relationship between culture and civilization in human societies. To some extent, this debate reflected postwar disillusion. The savagery and brutality of the war, perpetrated by nations that just prior to the war had prided themselves on their advanced level of civilization, revealed them to be people capable of unspeakable barbarism. The Great War called into question the pieties associated with Western civilization and the march of progress. The debate reached beyond the aftermath of the war, however, and inquired searchingly into the very nature of civilization, which came to be seen by many in the 1920s as a chilling influence within human society characterized by a deadening over-formalization that posed particular danger to local cultures. Formative voices in this discourse included T. S. Eliot, F. Scott Fitzgerald, Oswald Spengler, Lewis Mumford, Edward Sapir, and Walter Lippmann. Redfield had been profoundly affected by the war—at age seventeen he left college for a year to drive ambulances in France—and as a serious student of literature he followed the debate over culture and civilization with great interest. The conception of civilization as inherently dangerous to local cultures stuck with him, furthermore, and haunted his thinking for most of his career.

Robert E. Park provided the second formative influence in Redfield's intellectual development. Redfield's own father died shortly after Redfield married Park's daughter Margaret, and Robert Park quickly came to fill a fatherlike role in Redfield's life. Redfield had followed in his own father's footsteps and earned a law degree. But after practicing for a little over two years, Redfield found little in the law that interested him. Park perceived this discontent and urged Redfield to return to the university to pursue a Ph.D. in social science. Park served as his unofficial graduate mentor, moreover, and through frequent conversations with him, both verbal and written, helped Redfield shape his intellectual agenda for the first fifteen years of his career. Park guided Redfield toward the use of anthropology to study problems typically considered by sociology. Specifically, Park helped Redfield craft a methodology by which anthropology could be used to study the processes of social change. From 1915 to 1925, Park had exercised profound influence over the development of Chicago sociology and had guided the majority of student research into consideration of the basic processes of social change through analyses of specific urban areas experiencing rapid transition, such as immigrant communities within the city of Chicago. Park urged Redfield, however, to look beyond Chicago and to use anthropological studies of villages that lay just at the transforming edge of industrialized civilization.

Redfield followed Park's urging first in his dissertation research, conducted in the village of Tepoztlán, Mexico, and later in a decade-long investigation on the Yucatan peninsula. Redfield completed his dissertation in 1928 and published it in 1930, unmodified except for the introduction, as *Tepoztlán, A Mexican Village: A Study of Folk Life*. Both popular and scholarly critics responded enthusiastically to *Tepoztlán*, and it served to gain Redfield national renown as one of the most promising of the second generation of academic American anthropologists. He displayed striking originality in his account of this small village that lay forty-five miles outside the metropolis of Mexico City. Contrary to other anthropologists of this period, his work did not portray village life in a timeless state, in what has come to be known as the "ethnographic present." Other anthropologists wrote about primitive villagers, Redfield observed, as if they existed outside of time. He wanted, on the contrary, to write these people back into time, indeed, to show that their seemingly static way of life was being subtly transformed by forces from without. Tepoztecans, in his depiction, were an "intermediate" or "folk" people who were caught in the middle of the "general type of change whereby primitive man becomes civilized man, the rustic becomes the urbanite."[5]

Yet Redfield's explanation of the specific processes of change that were transforming the village of Tepoztlán fell short of his expectations and, starting in the early 1930s, he launched a much more ambitious series of comparative community studies conducted in villages and towns on the Yucatan peninsula to examine the processes of modernization. Redfield published the conclusions of this study in 1941 as *The Folk Culture of Yucatan.*[6] Here he elaborated his notion of the "folk-urban continuum," an ideal-type dichotomy that he derived largely from the work of Henry Sumner Maine, Émile Durkheim, and Ferdinand Tönnies. Redfield's dichotomy was essentially a linear model that emphasized the harmony and sense of shared meaning in the preurban community and the breakdown of this community in the face of urbanization. One of the central contributions of Redfield's Mexican and Yucatan studies was the influence they exerted on the development of modernization theory. Redfield was arguably the first to use the word "modernization" in the specialized sense that it came to acquire in post–World War II social science, and he proved highly original in the modernization project through his grounding of his empirical studies of change in nineteenth-century European social theory.[7] By the 1950s, American social scientists, particularly the modernizationists, came to draw heavily upon European social theory, mediated largely through the work of Talcott Parsons. But prior to Parsons, Redfield provided the primary theoretical and empirical model for modernization studies.[8]

With his Tepoztlán study, Redfield became one of the first to apply anthropological methods to the study of semicivilized rather than primitive peoples. He viewed the peasants of Tepoztlán as a transitional type—they stood, in his perspective, "intermediate between the tribe and the modern city."[9] His interest in such transitional types stimulated the growth of peasant studies, today one of the largest subfields within anthropology. Redfield holds a lasting significance in peasant studies because he was the first to theorize the profound implications the study of peasants held for anthropology. By the mid-1920s, the standard anthropological study provided a description of an isolated primitive tribe. The primary purpose of such a study was to document the cultural system of the tribe and to describe how its cultural system fit together to form a unique cultural whole or cultural universe. This cultural whole represented, moreover, a system of functionally interrelated parts. Redfield's insight lay in his recognition that although the same anthropological techniques used for the study of primitive isolated villages could be applied to peasants, peasant communities could not be conceptualized in the same manner as primitive communities. Specifically, the peasant village could not be viewed as a self-contained cultural universe. The peasant village was not self-sufficient, and it did not represent a cultural whole; it was dependent instead upon the more civilized world lying beyond its borders. It was attached through economic, political, and cultural linkages to nearby cities. Thus, Redfield argued, anthropologists could not search for the cultural unity of the peasant village—that unity could be perceived only at the level of the civilization to which the village was attached.

Civilizations are complex and ill-defined entities, however, and are not easily studied from the perspective of any single discipline. But over the course of several years, Redfield became convinced that despite conceptual difficulties, scholars needed to turn their attention toward understanding the cultural unities of civilizations. Accordingly, he devoted the latter half of his career to developing a scholarly approach for the study of civilizations. Redfield envisioned this approach as being an interdisciplinary effort between humanists and social scientists. Characterization of a civilization appeared to him to be best approached initially through study of its smallest units; these units, in his view, were the peasant villages on the peripheries of civilizations. Because anthropologists were most skilled in studying small villages, Redfield expected them to take the leading role in civilizations study. Anthropologists would first study the local oral traditions of villages; they would then enlist assistance from other scholars, such as historians, sociologists, literary critics, and philosophers, to study the more powerful written traditions which impinged upon villages. Redfield referred to this approach as the "social anthropology of civilizations." He formalized study of civilizations through this method, moreover, by establishing at the University of Chicago an interdisciplinary venture in civilizations studies. Generously funded by the Ford Foundation, this project drew together nationally prominent scholars from several disciplines and facilitated a concerted effort to bring scholarly attention to the comparative study of world civilizations throughout the decade of the 1950s.

Redfield's turn toward the study of civilizations catalyzed profound reconsiderations of his earlier work, specifically his folk-urban typology. Throughout the years in which he conducted his studies in Tepoztlán and the Yucatan, Redfield had conceived of civilization as the antithesis of culture. Yet in the 1950s, when he began serious consideration of the dynamics of civilizations, particularly of the relationships between various entities within civilizations, Redfield came to view culture and civilization as coexistent and dialectically linked to one another. Rather than seeing a strict distinction between Gemeinschaft and Gesellschaft, as he had posited in *The Folk Culture of Yucatan*, Redfield offered in *The Little Community* (1955) a revised view of cultural dynamics which held that Gemeinschaft and Gesellschaft were both present in societies and while capable of modifying one another did not exist in a simple zero-sum relationship. In Redfield's final conception, therefore, modernization did not consist of a unidirectional irreversible transition from tradition to modernity. Instead, the urban influence at times modified or replaced folk elements in a community, but at other times the urban influence was simply additive, producing a mosaic of folk and urban elements within the same community.[10]

In addition to his theoretical work regarding the dynamics of social change, Redfield also devoted much effort to examining the philosophical principles and methodologies of social science. Beginning in the mid-1940s, Redfield joined with several other American sociologists and anthropologists in questioning the directions and ultimate purposes of social science. Prominent among those involved in this discourse were Ruth Benedict, Alfred Kroeber, Clyde Kluckhohn, and Gunnar Myrdal. Their discussion focused primarily upon the relative merits of qualitative versus quantitative and objective versus subjective methodologies, the place of values in social science and, most important, the role of social scientists vis-á-vis contemporary political and cultural issues. In many ways the dialogue over the aims of social science conducted by Redfield and his colleagues closely resembled the discourse described by Mark C. Smith conducted by economists, sociologists, and political scientists during the 1920s and the 1930s.[11] Post–World War II concerns certainly colored the later dialogue, but the two discussions shared many basic concerns and reflected an important continuing theme within American social science. The issues raised in the postwar discussion of the practices and purposes of social science resonated deeply with Redfield, and he lectured and wrote on these topics extensively from the late 1940s through the 1950s, focusing particularly on them in *The Primitive World* (1953) and *The Little Community* (1955). Redfield had begun his career viewing anthropology as analogous to natural science, in which practice consisted of objective fact-gathering, analysis, and deductive generalization. But after spending several years conducting ethnographic fieldwork, Redfield found that the nomothetic law-seeking approach failed to embrace much of the data he gathered through his field experience. And by the close of his career, Redfield regarded anthropology as a discipline that lay between art and science, a discipline that belonged to both the humanities and social sciences.

Taken as a whole, Redfield's primary contribution as an anthropologist lay in the realm of theory-making. His ideas provoked great debate from the 1940s through the early 1960s, and he attracted strongly partisan followers as well as equally partisan detractors. This work seeks to understand both the development of Redfield's ideas, especially the contexts in which he worked and the questions that drove his investigations, and the nature and degree of influence Redfield exercised upon others through his teaching and writing. This study relies upon close readings of virtually all Redfield's published works. Extensive use is made, moreover, of Redfield's unpublished writings, including letters and article and book manuscripts. Numerous interviews conducted with Redfield's children, students, and colleagues are also used as sources of information on more personal aspects of Redfield's life.

Redfield's works represented contributions to more than the mere disciplinary histories of anthropology and sociology. Redfield participated in a broad intellectual conversation that extended well beyond the confines of academia.

His explorations of social change touched upon several larger issues that seriously engaged many during the mid-1920s through the 1960s. In particular, his inquiries into the nature and process of social change carried distinct ideological connotations. In his studies of social change in Mexican villages, Redfield was aware that the United States was the most important source of the dramatic (and disruptive) change he observed in the villages. His interest was primarily in determining a theory of change; however, he was also concerned with developing an understanding of the nature of the change the United States, and the industrialized West in general, was imposing on all the people that lay at its margins. In a sense, Redfield was attempting to come to terms with the power the West had to change the rest of the world. His questions reflect an intense interest in self-knowledge: Who as Americans are we? How does our existence impinge, furthermore, on others who live beyond the margins of our society? Revisiting Redfield's work allows us not only to explore the early development of modernization theory, but also prompts us to rethink the questions that drove his work, particularly regarding the roles and responsibilities of the United States vis-á-vis global development.

Notes

1. This account of Boas's influence within American anthropology relies heavily upon the treatments of Boas by George W. Stocking, Jr., and Marvin Harris. See George W. Stocking, Jr., *Race, Culture, and Evolution: Essays in the History of Anthropology* (New York: Free Press, 1968), 110-307; Stocking, "Boas, Franz," in *Dictionary of American Biography*, Supplement III, ed. Edward T. James (New York: Charles Scribner's Sons, 1973); Stocking, "Introduction: The Basic Assumptions of Boasian Anthropology," in *The Shaping of American Anthropology, 1883-1911: A Franz Boas Reader*, ed. George W. Stocking, Jr. (New York: Basic Books, 1974), 1-20; and Marvin Harris, *The Rise of Anthropological Theory: A History of Theories of Culture* (New York: Thomas Y. Crowell Company, 1968), 250-289 .

2. On the reaction against Boasian anthropology in the 1920s and 1930s, see Elvin Hatch, *Culture and Morality: The Relativity of Anthropological Values* (New York: Columbia University Press, 1983), 105-106.

3. For a particularly sharp attack against Boas's antievolutionary strictures by one of his own students, see Alexander Lesser's "Evolution in Social Anthropology," *Southwestern Journal of Anthropology* 8 (Summer 1952): 136-146. Lesser originally presented this paper to the 1939 annual meeting of the American Anthropological Association as "The Present Status of Evolution in Social Anthropology." This paper is included in *History, Evolution, and the Concept of Culture: Selected Papers of Alexander Lesser*, ed. Sidney W. Mintz (Cambridge: Cambridge University Press, 1985), 78-91. Redfield's challenge to the Boasian antievolutionary program appeared in the introduction to his doctoral dissertation,"A Plan for the Study of Tepoztlán, Morelos," University of Chicago, 1928.

4. On the development of American anthropology during the 1920s and 1930s, see George W. Stocking, Jr., "Ideas and Institutions in American Anthropology: Thoughts toward a History of the Interwar Years," in *The Ethnographer's Magic and Other Essays in the History of Anthropology* (Madison: University of Wisconsin Press, 1992), 114-177.

5. Robert Redfield, *Tepoztlán, A Mexican Village: A Study of Folk Life* (Chicago: University of Chicago Press, 1930), 14.

6. Robert Redfield, *The Folk Culture of Yucatan* (Chicago: University of Chicago Press, 1941).

7. Redfield's first use of the term "modernization" appears on page 4 of his 1930 *Tepoztlán*.

8. Several recent works address Redfield's role in the development of modernization theory. See Howard Brick, *Age of Contradiction: American Thought and Culture in the 1960s* (New York: Twayne Publishers, 1998; reprint, Ithaca: N.Y.: Cornell University Press, 2000), 44-52; Dwight Hoover, "The Long Ordeal of Modernization Theory," *Prospects* 11 (1986): 407-451; Jordan Kleiman, "Modernization," in *A Companion to American Thought*, ed. Richard W. Fox and James T. Kloppenberg (Cambridge, Mass.: Blackwell, 1995); Werner Sollors, "Anthropological and Sociological Tendencies in American Literature of the 1930s and 1940s: Richard Wright, Zora Neale Hurston, and American Culture," in *Looking Inward, Looking Outward: From the 1930s through the 1940s,* European Contributions to American Studies 18, ed. Steve Ickringill (Amsterdam:

VU University Press, 1990), 22-75; and Carla Cappetti, *Writing Chicago: Modernism, Ethnography, and the Novel* (New York: Columbia University Press, 1993).

9. Redfield, *Tepoztlán*, 217.

10. Robert Redfield, *The Little Community: Viewpoints for the Study of a Human Whole* (Chicago: University of Chicago Press, 1955).

11. Mark C. Smith, *Social Science in the Crucible: The American Debate over Objectivity and Purpose, 1918-1941* (Durham, N.C.: Duke University Press, 1994).

Chapter 1

Robert Redfield and the Modernist Vision in American Social Science

Robert Redfield was born in 1897 in Chicago, Illinois. His mother, Bertha Dreier Redfield, was the daughter of the Danish consul in Chicago; his father, Robert Redfield, Sr., was descended from English settlers who had come to America during the seventeenth century. Redfield's father was a self-made man of means, and Redfield grew up in a relatively privileged environment. His family owned property in a rural area northwest of Chicago, and until he was in high school, Redfield spent almost six months per year at the family's country home. The Redfields only moved to their Chicago apartment for the late fall and winter. This unusual pattern of residency prevented Redfield from attending conventional school for his grammar school years. He was educated during these years exclusively through private tutors, usually students from the University of Chicago. When Redfield turned thirteen, he entered the University of Chicago Laboratory School, which had been founded in 1896 by John Dewey. While at the Laboratory School, Redfield regularly made the honor's list—even securing a few votes in the yearbook as the senior class's "biggest grind." He also participated actively in extracurricular events, serving on the board of the school's literary magazine, *The Midway*, and as an officer of the science club. Upon graduating in the spring of 1915, he elected to attend the University of Chicago.[1]

Forging a Direction: Redfield's Early Years

When Robert Redfield entered college at the University of Chicago in the autumn of 1915, he had no declared interest in social science. From his youth, he had been interested in literature and biology, and he chose to pursue these fields in college. He was a good student, but during his first few years in college, he did not demonstrate a strong sense of direction. He alternated between wanting to become a poet and a biologist. His father, a powerful Chicago lawyer, gave no support to either aspiration. Instead, he urged Redfield to follow his lead and study law. Redfield's father was a domineering figure, and Redfield spent as much effort in his college years trying to throw off his father's influence as he did pursuing academic work.[2]

Redfield made his critical break during his second year in college. Without consulting his family, Redfield dropped out of Chicago in the spring of 1917 and enlisted in the American Field Service to drive an ambulance in France. He then spent the summer and early fall on the front lines of the war in France. Malcolm Cowley called the ambulance service "college-extension courses for a generation of writers," and Redfield joined scores of other would-be writers, including Dos Passos, Hemingway, E. E. Cummings, and Dashiell Hammett, on the battlefields of Europe. This wartime service proved to be a crucial coming-of-age experience for Redfield. Not only did he become much more worldly and philosophically mature through his time in France, but also he developed a much stronger sense of his own independence. Redfield well expressed the underlying purpose of his enlistment when he closed his first letter to his father with the phrase "And know that I can take care of myself."[3]

On a deeper level, however, Redfield found his experience at the front lines profoundly troubling. He was haunted by the destruction and death he had witnessed, and he found himself "very much confused and disorganized" upon returning home. Instead of reenrolling in college at Chicago, Redfield followed his family to Washington, D.C., where his father had accepted a job with the federal government to assist in the war preparedness effort. The war had left Redfield with his motivation "completely askew," and for several months—first in Washington and then back in Chicago—he drifted somewhat aimlessly from job to job. At the beginning of 1919, though, he enrolled at Harvard in an attempt to recover his academic direction. In an interview he gave in 1950, Redfield minimized his efforts at Harvard.[4] However, a letter written by Donald Culross Peattie, his closest high school friend, early intellectual mentor, and later his brother-in-law, indicates that Redfield had approached his work at Harvard with serious expectations. Peattie's comments in his letter of 25 December 1918 offer a glimpse of how Redfield's intimates—and by inference, Redfield himself—perceived his intellectual intentions at Harvard:

> I want to speak about your entering Harvard. I think it is fine. . . . I think it perhaps the thing of all things for you to do. You see, I have always wanted you to be a scientist. I think you will become, at least a scholarly one and one who truly loves his work and sees it with great breadth, and with your superb brain and your acquisitive intellectuality, you could, if you wanted to go through the dull parts, perfectly well become a very great name in science. All this sounds like extravagance in words. But it springs from my deepest beliefs in you. Of course, I want you to be a poet more than a scientist. But if you become a great scientist, you will *certainly* become a great poet. Other people wouldn't, but you will.[5]

Yet Redfield did not last even a full term at Harvard. Apparently, he was extremely lonely in Cambridge and quickly decided that he wanted to leave Harvard. After Redfield had only been in Cambridge for a few weeks, Peattie observed that Redfield's letters to his family were "most pathetic and lost and woozy," and he expressed regret about Redfield's response to Harvard. Thus in the spring of 1919, Redfield returned home once again and continued to struggle for a direction. For a brief period, he took a job as a reporter on the Chicago *Tribune* but found himself unsuited to the hard-edged world of journalism. In despair, his father urged him to go to law school and offered to pay for him to do so. Redfield accepted his father's offer and entered the University of Chicago law school in April 1919.[6] Redfield had still not completed his bachelor's degree at the time he began law school; Chicago allowed him to apply some of his law school credits toward his undergraduate degree, though, and he received a bachelor's of philosophy degree from the College at the University of Chicago on 15 June 1920.[7]

At the same time he was making the decision to go to law school, Redfield found himself falling in love with Margaret (Greta) Park, daughter of University of Chicago sociologist Robert E. Park. Redfield, called Bob by his family and friends, had known Greta since his first years in college. They had corresponded while he was in France, and they came to know each other well during the fall of 1917 and winter of 1918 when both were in Washington, D.C.—Bob because of his father's war-related work and Greta because she was helping her father conduct a Carnegie Foundation-sponsored study on immigration. Their romance did not begin, however, until after Redfield returned to Chicago from Harvard. During the spring months of 1919, Greta and Bob fell deeply in love; in June of the following year, two days after Bob graduated from the College, they married.[8]

Bob's father provided them money to take a long honeymoon, and the two spent the entire summer after their wedding hiking and camping in the American southwest. Greta provided the inspiration for the camping vacation. Previously, Bob had done little camping. But Greta had grown up taking camping trips with her family, and she persuaded Bob to go for the idea. In a sense, their honeymoon reflected a pattern that characterized much of their marriage. Greta was an adventurous and imaginative woman, and she often propelled Bob forward into avenues that he had not yet experienced. Greta also brought stability to Bob. Upon returning to Chicago in September of 1920, Bob resumed his studies at the law school, and he pursued this course without interruption until he graduated with a J.D. degree in December 1921.[9]

While Bob was in his last year of law school, his father died suddenly. This left a huge void in Bob's life, a void that eventually came to be filled by Greta's father, Robert Park. After graduating from law school, Bob took a position with his father's law firm Tolman, Sexton, and Chandler (formerly Tolman, Redfield, and Sexton) in downtown Chicago. The firm did much of their business with the city of Chicago, and Redfield took over work dealing with the municipal sewer department. This position turned out to be highly routine; he spent most of his time examining records "to see if specifications had been met." After practicing law for two years, during which time he came to know "more about manhole covers than anyone in the city of Chicago," he found himself highly dissatisfied with his work and in a "state of great restlessness." At this point his father-in-law intervened. Robert Park had been convinced for some time that Redfield was wasting his talent practicing law, and he had talked with Redfield at length about his own work in sociology and encouraged him to consider taking up a more intellectually fulfilling career. To jar Redfield out of the rut he seemed to be in, Park gave Bob and Greta a thousand dollars to take a trip to Mexico in the fall of 1923 to experience firsthand the heady atmosphere of postrevolutionary social reconstruction.[10]

This trip proved to be the major turning point in Redfield's life. Robert Park had taught at Chicago a young Mexican intellectual, Elena Landazuri, and she had become a close personal friend of the Park family. After studying at Chicago, Landazuri had returned to Mexico and had established the Mexican branch of the YWCA. She was also active in promoting social reforms, for which she came to be called the "Jane Addams of Mexico." Landazuri served as hostess and guide to Bob and Greta in Mexico; she not only allowed Bob and Greta to stay with her and assisted them in traveling to a number of Indian villages in Mexico, but she also introduced them to several important figures in the postrevolutionary Mexican intelligentsia.[11]

Bob's encounter with the Mexican villages affected him on both aesthetic and philosophical levels. On the aesthetic level, he fell in love with the small traditional village. He was particularly gripped by the sense of shared meaning and harmony that seemed to pervade the village. On the philosophical level, the village provoked in Redfield a profound realization of the world that had been lost. The village did not represent a haven to which modern humanity could retreat by choice. Rather, it represented the lingering form of a once widespread way of life, a way of life rapidly being destroyed by the onrush of Western civilization. The Mexican villages—poised on the threshold of change—thus awakened in Redfield a sense of the threat and challenge of modernity.[12]

Complementing Redfield's experiences in the villages were his encounters with several Mexican intellectuals. Through Elena Landazuri, Bob and Greta met many social and intellectual activists helping to shape the new Mexico. Most important among these encounters was their meeting of anthropologist Manuel Gamio. Gamio, who had been trained by Franz Boas at Columbia University, had come during the early 1920s to wield a powerful influence over the Indian policy of Mexican government. Indians composed almost half the population of Mexico, and intellectuals, such as Gamio, who had taken positions in the postrevolutionary government were anxious to implement a humane and enlightened approach for dealing with the Indians—especially for bringing to the Indians a share of material benefits and educational opportunities won through the revolution.

Redfield saw in Gamio a man who was able to combine a close personal knowledge of the Indian villages—a knowledge both scientific and aesthetic—with an activist social agenda. Gamio understood the pressure that the modern industrialized West was exerting upon Mexico's myriad of traditional villages. But he was actively engaged in devising and implementing policies to ease the transition of the villagers into modernity. In his role as enlightened social engineer, Gamio provided a compelling example to Redfield for a way to combine scientific study with social activism. Gamio's example offered Redfield, in other words, a career that seemed richer both personally and intellectually compared to what he had experienced in his law practice.[13]

Over the weeks during the fall of 1923 when they were in Mexico, Greta and Bob wrote home to Park enthusiastic letters about their experiences. Park responded by urging both of them, if possible, to become professional social scientists so that they could devote their careers to the study of traditional and semi-modern villages. The University of Chicago was renovating its anthropology program, Park told them, and he encouraged Bob, in particular, to enroll immediately at Chicago and commit himself to an academic career. Bob's experiences in Mexico had put him in a ready frame of mind to consider changes. Despite difficult circumstances—Greta had been pregnant when they left for Mexico and was due to deliver in early 1924—Redfield decided that he indeed wanted to change career directions. Upon returning to Chicago in December, therefore, he proceeded to resign from his father's law practice, "an untangling of some delicacy," he later admitted, and enroll in the Chicago graduate program in sociology and anthropology. His father had left Greta and him enough money to see them through a few years of graduate study. Thus in January 1924, Redfield commenced his preparation to become a social scientist, a calling that occupied him fully until his death in 1958.[14]

The Culture-Civilization Discourse of the 1920s

Two primary streams of thought influenced Redfield during his formative intellectual period: the "culture versus civilization" discourse of the 1920s and the ideas associated with the "Chicago School" of sociology. During the 1920s, artists and intellectuals on both sides of the Atlantic subjected the notions of culture and civilization to searching analysis. The terms culture and civilization have a long and entwined history. They emerged during the late eighteenth century and since that time have undergone extensive development in Scottish, French, German, and to a lesser extent Anglo-American thought. Although the meanings of both terms have shifted dramatically over the last two centuries, two distinct themes can be discerned in their usage. The primary conception has held that civilization is a form of culture. Within this conception are three possible relationships: (1) civilization and culture are synonyms; (2) civilization differs from culture based upon complexity and scale of organization; and (3) civilization differs from culture in a qualitative fashion, specifically when evaluated according to a fixed concept of progress. The second widely used conception of the terms culture and civilization holds the two concepts to be diametrically opposed. Culture, in this view, refers to the realm of values, myth, religion, art, and literature in human societies; civilization refers, by contrast, to the technical and organizational aspects of societies. German thinkers, in particular, have since the Enlightenment largely viewed culture and civilization as oppositional terms. On the contrary, during the eighteenth and nineteenth centuries, British and American thinkers treated culture and civilization as synonyms, associating them both with the notions of cultivation and progress.[15]

Yet in the early years of the twentieth century, the Anglo-American conception of the terms culture and civilization shifted, and the two words that had long been used as synonyms came to be used by many as antonyms. This semantic shift stemmed from a much larger transition in British and American society, namely the rebellion by artists, intellectuals, and social iconoclasts against the Victorian worldview. Although this rebellion began during the first decade of the twentieth century, World War I served as the watershed event and provided the primary stimulus to the dissenters. In the Victorian worldview, Western civilization stood at the apex of world cultural development, and its trajectory defined progress. But the unparalleled brutality and savagery of World War I belied the Victorians' easy belief in cultural sophistication and moral superiority. Following the war, critics not only challenged the claims of superiority made for Western civilization, but they also challenged the very terms of debate established by the Victorians. Specifically, rebels attacked the Victorians' belletristic notion of culture, which held culture to be "the best that has been thought and known," a highly self-congratulatory view that privileged Victorian society above all others, and embraced instead the view, advanced largely by Boasian anthropologists, that held all cultures to be functionally and morally equivalent. The rebels also rejected the Victorian belief in the inevitability of progress and, borrowing heavily from late nineteenth-century German social theory, adopted a view of cultural dynamics that recognized progress as well as decline in the trajectory of Western civilization.[16]

Loss of the belief in progress resulted for many, however, in a profound sense of disorientation, and one of the leading questions for the postwar generation thus became "Where are we going?" A broad discourse driven by novelists, poets, philosophers, social scientists, artists, historians, and cultural critics emerged during the 1920s to explore the issues surrounding cultural direction and, essentially, the fate of Western civilization. Although writers who entered into this culture-civilization discourse echoed a commonly felt postwar despair, their larger concern dealt with the sense that Western civilization had entered an irreversible decline. In this view, life in the West during the first decades of the twentieth century had been emptied of meaning and was marked most distinctly by its emotional and spiritual sterility.[17]

One of the first expressions of concern over the state of American civilization appeared through the efforts of the cultural critic Harold Stearns. In the fall of 1921, Stearns organized a symposium of intellectuals to develop a critique of American society and culture. Meeting every two weeks over the course of several months, Stearns and his colleagues conducted an extensive review of American life. Stearns then edited and published a collection of the essays under the title *Civilization in the United States: An Inquiry by Thirty Americans*

(1922). Included in this collection were essays on "The City" by Lewis Mumford, "Politics" by H. L. Mencken, "The Literary Life" by Van Wyck Brooks, "The Intellectual Life" by Harold Stearns, "The Theater" by George Jean Nathan, "Sex" by Elsie Clews Parsons, "The Alien" by Frederic C. Howe, and "Racial Minorities" by Geroid Tanquary Robinson. Stearns identified three primary themes that were central to all the essays. First, America was rife with hypocrisy—rather than living according to deeply held convictions, most Americans lived by a moral code that "resolves itself into the one cardinal heresy of being found out, with the chief sanction enforcing it, the fear of what people might say." Second, despite shrill claims made by many Americans during the 1920s, American civilization was not Anglo-Saxon but derived instead from a rich and complex mixture of peoples. Third, and most pressing, America suffered from "emotional and aesthetic starvation." Americans stood on the verge of cultural collapse, Stearns charged, with "no heritages or traditions to which to cling except those that have already withered in our hands and turned to dust." The disaffected contributors to Stearns's volume hoped that by speaking the "truth about American civilization" they could do their share to make a "real civilization possible."[18]

In the same year that Stearns published *Civilization in the United States*, T. S. Eliot published a searching exploration of the decline of culture in the face of civilization, a work that was to become one of the most famous indictments of Western civilization ever written. In his groundbreaking poem *The Waste Land* (1922), T. S. Eliot offered a sweeping view of the "waste" of contemporary Western civilization. Centered in the "Unreal City" of contemporary London, *The Waste Land* portrays the agony and terror that resulted from humanity's loss of the ability to believe in religious truths during the modern era. The sterile knowledge of science had robbed mythic truths of their values, and modern men and women were left wandering in search of meaning in a drought-stricken land where "there is no water" but only rock. Huddled together in their cities, linked only by the secular commercial connections, modern humanity is trapped in a pattern of inevitable decline. And in the same way that ancient civilizations had all disintegrated from within and then fallen to small tribes of barbarian invaders, so too, Eliot portends, would Western civilization fall:

> Who are those hooded hordes swarming
> Over endless plains, stumbling in cracked earth
> Ringed by the flat horizon only
> What is the city over the mountains
> Cracks and reforms and bursts in the violet air
> Falling towers
> Jerusalem Athens Alexandria
> Vienna London
> Unreal

Probably no single literary work of the 1920s better captured the haunting sense of emptiness and the belief that modern civilization was on the verge of collapse, particularly for those who were young during this era, than *The Waste Land*. Writing in 1931, Edmund Wilson said of this work that "it enchanted and devastated a whole generation."[19]

Another principal voice in the 1920s debate over culture versus civilization was Oswald Spengler. In *The Decline of the West*, published in Germany in 1918 (volume 1) and 1922 (volume 2), Spengler advanced a philosophy of history that created a great stir among American intellectuals during the 1920s. The leading "little magazines" of the period published in-depth critical reviews and popularizations of the *Decline*, and in 1924, two years prior to publication of the English translation of the first volume, the *Dial* published in full Kenneth Burke's translation of the provocative introductory chapter to the volume.[20] Spengler offered an organic theory of society to explain the dynamics of the rise and fall of civilizations that held strong appeal for intellectuals who had grown wary of the history-as-progress point of view that had enjoyed such wide acceptance during the nineteenth century. Using the organic analogy of a plant, Spengler posited that civilizations passed through three phases in their life cycle: growth, maturity, and decay. He identified seven distinct civilizations that had emerged over the course of human history: Chinese, Babylonian, Egyptian, Indian, Greco-Roman, Mayan, and Western. Significantly, Spengler observed, these civilizations had all passed through similar life cycles. The early phases of birth, growth, and maturity for these societies could be described as the period of Culture. Yet as maturity in the organic world inevitably gives way to decay and then death, each Culture gives way to Civilization. Civilization thus stands as the "inevitable *destiny*" of Culture. Civilization does not represent a pinnacle, however, but rather a death rattle. Whereas Culture is characterized by spontaneity and spirituality, by life lived close to the soil, Civilization is characterized by artificiality and disbelief, by life lived not on the land but in the "petrifying world-city." Indeed, it is the very rise of the city that marked the turning point of a Culture. For as the world-city emerges, it impoverishes the hinterlands, it divides the once undifferentiated domain of a Culture into the asymmetric distinction of "world-city and province."

> In place of a world there is a *city, a point*, in which the whole life of a broad region is collecting while the rest dries up. In place of a true type people, born of and grown on the soil, there is a new sort of nomad, cohering unstably in fluid masses, the parasitical city dweller. . . . The world-city means cosmopolitanism in place of "home," cold matter-of-fact in place of reverence for tradition and age, scientific irreligion as a fossil representative of the older religion of the heart.[21]

Like T. S. Eliot, Spengler exercised his greatest influence among younger intellectuals. F. Scott Fitzgerald was one of the many young intellectuals of the 1920s who was deeply influenced by both Spengler and Eliot, and his 1925 work *The Great Gatsby* stands as a signal text within the 1920s culture-civilization discourse. *Gatsby* operates on several levels simultaneously. Although the dominant theme is the corruption of the American dream by materialism, a closely related subtext is the exhaustion of American civilization. Fitzgerald echoes Spengler's theory of cultural dynamics in his depiction of American declension. America had arisen, in Fitzgerald's vision, out of the soil of a new continent and had been nurtured in a myriad of villages and towns that grew up in the wake of the westward-moving frontier. This endless land that stretched out for Americans did not merely represent opportunity. It also represented purity and innocence, and the life of the villages was genuine, sustaining Gemeinschaft culture. By the end of the nineteenth century, the frontier had reached its limits, and Americans seeking opportunity could no longer move west but were forced to return to the East. Yet the East they returned to was not the same as it had been when the Dutch sailors had first cast their eyes upon the "fresh, green breast of the new world." By the twentieth century, giant cities had devoured the East, and the land that had once sustained life and culture had become, in a phrase that strongly evokes *The Waste Land*, a "valley of ashes." Following Spengler, Fitzgerald saw the city as the sterile culmination of cultural development. As the city came to dominate the land, its values displaced the folkways of the village. Culture gave way to civilization as money, sophistication, and disbelief replaced character, faith, and honesty as the constituent values of society. Fitzgerald thus articulated in *The Great Gatsby* a vision of America torn between two worlds—the world of the Gemeinschaft past, characterized by innocence and sincerity, and the world of the Gesellschaft future, characterized by sophistication and artifice.[22]

Although humanists devoted much attention to the culture-civilization issue during the 1920s, social scientists, especially anthropologists, also played an important role in the debate. Edward Sapir, one of the first students to earn a doctorate in anthropology under Franz Boas at Columbia University, led the way in venturing beyond academia to join the public debate over the nature of culture in America. In 1919, Sapir published in the *Dial* "Civilization and Culture," the first version of what was to become a foundational article in the culture-civilization discourse. In "Civilization and Culture," Sapir defined civilization as the "ever increasing degree of sophistication of our society and our individual lives." This conception, which saw civilization as providing the structure and mechanics of society, drew largely upon the nineteenth-century German social theorists. Culture stood in distinction to civilization, in Sapir's scheme, and represented the values and moral organization of society. He focused, especially, on the nature of "genuine" culture, which he contrasted to "spurious" culture. Clarifying that he was not drawing a distinction between "high" or "low" cultures, Sapir argued that "genuine" culture was "inherently harmonious, balanced, self-satisfactory" and all activities in such a culture were charged with spiritual meaning. A "spurious" culture, by contrast, was "superficial, discordant, and empty." Sapir spent most of "Civilization and Culture" engaged in a thoroughgoing critique of American culture. Specifically, he found contemporary America, obsessed with Frederick Taylor-inspired notions of efficiency, to be tightly organized but essentially unfulfilling and empty. He compared a telephone operator, "who, for economic reasons, lends her capacities during the greater part of the living day, to the manipulation of a technical routine that has an eventually high efficiency value but that answers to no spiritual needs of her own" to an American Indian who "solves the economic problem with salmon-spear and rabbit-snare" and pronounced that even though the Indian may be seen to be "operating on a relatively low level of civilization," he represented "an incomparably higher solution than our telephone girl." He further attacked the materialistic and fragmentary nature of contemporary American life, observing that Americans spent their lives trapped as "dray horses" in sterile routines of work or, when not working, as "listless consumers of goods." The net result of American culture, Sapir concluded, was that "our spiritual selves go hungry, for the most part, pretty much all the time."[23]

That Sapir, a professional anthropologist, would publish this critique of American society and culture in the *Dial*, one of the leading American literary magazines of the 1920s and the very journal that three years later would publish *The Waste Land*, clearly illustrates how the anthropological and literary critiques of American life intersected during the 1920s. Sapir later went on to publish expanded versions of "Civilization and Culture" as "Culture, Genuine and Spurious" first in the *Dalhousie Review* (1922) and then in final form in the *American Journal of Sociology* (1924).[24] The *American Journal of Sociology* version proved to be a seminal article in American social science and was particularly influential in transferring the anthropological conception of culture to American sociologists. Sapir also exercised a powerful influence on younger anthropologists in the 1920s. He was a mentor and confidant to both Margaret Mead and Ruth Benedict and, upon moving to the University of Chicago in 1923, Sapir became an important mentor to Redfield, serving as both teacher and member of his dissertation committee.[25]

At the end of the decade, Walter Lippmann published a capstone text that eloquently summarized the 1920s culture-civilization discourse. In *A Preface to Morals* (1929), Lippmann offered a penetrating analysis of the modern condition at the close of the 1920s. As Lippmann surveyed American society in 1929, all essential moorings of tradition, religion, sense of progress, and social order had been lost. The "acids of modernity" had eroded religious faiths and traditional beliefs, Lippmann argued, and modern humanity stood stripped of all supportive belief systems. Yet such change had come at great cost. "The modern man who has ceased to believe . . . hangs, as it were, between heaven and earth, and is at rest nowhere." Most agonizing, modern humanity was losing the sense of identity, purpose, and certainty that once sprang from being a part of a people and a place. "In the modern world it is this very feeling of certainty itself which is dissolving. It is dissolving not merely for an educated minority but for everyone who comes within the orbit of modernity." Lippmann spent the first third of the book describing the "dissolution of the ancestral order" and the next two-thirds constructing a system by which the alienated and disbelieving soul might cope with the chilly modern order. He offered his modern readers not despair but a lean and ascetic secular humanism. In spite of its severe tone, Lippmann's *A Preface to Morals* resonated strongly with the public, and the book quickly became a bestseller. No book offered a better analysis for the "middlebrow" reader of the 1920s of the psychological and philosophical consequences associated with the modern worldview.[26]

Redfield read deeply in the culture-civilization literature of the 1920s, and he maintained a close familiarity with this literature over the course of his career by making many of its central texts required reading for his students. The dialectical relationship between culture and civilization came to serve, moreover, as the primary framework for his thinking. And by the early 1930s, Redfield became through his own publications an important participant in the culture-civilization discourse.

Chicago Sociology and the Notion of Social Change

The second primary influence upon Redfield's intellectual development stemmed from the "Chicago School" of sociology, a body of thought that provided the theoretical grounding for virtually all of Redfield's work. When Redfield entered graduate school in January 1924, anthropology and sociology at Chicago constituted a single department. Although this joint arrangement resulted in part merely from administrative convenience, it exercised important intellectual consequences upon those who worked in the department. Throughout the twenties, students could choose to concentrate in either sociology or anthropology, but all were required to take several courses in common. Redfield, more than most of his colleagues, chose to pursue both fields with almost equal intensity. He formally identified himself as an anthropologist, but his conceptual outlook was always much closer to that of a sociologist than a conventionally trained anthropologist.[27]

From the inception of the joint department in 1892, sociology clearly played the dominant role. Indeed, only a single anthropologist held a position within the department from the 1890s through the early 1920s. Sociology at Chicago came to be recognized as a nationally important program almost as soon as its founding chairman, Albion Small, organized the department. But it was not until around 1915, under the leadership of W. I. Thomas, that "Chicago sociology" came to be recognized as a distinct school. Thomas established the linkage between theory and research that distinguished Chicago sociology through the 1910s and 1920s.[28] Although Thomas first advanced his approach to empirical sociology in his programmatic article, "Race Psychology: Standpoint and Questionnaire, with Particular Reference to the Immigrant and the Negro" (1912), he exercised his greatest influence through his monumental *The Polish Peasant in Europe and America* (1918-1919), which he cowrote with Florian Znaniecki.[29]

Unfortunately, just as Thomas was publishing the multivolume text of the *Polish Peasant*, the University of Chicago dismissed him from its faculty for alleged violation of the Mann Act.

Despite his physical departure from Chicago, Thomas exerted a defining influence upon Chicago sociology that held sway throughout the 1920s. Thomas's influence operated on two distinct levels. First, Thomas provided in *The Polish Peasant* an example of how to do empirical sociology. Thomas viewed social processes as arising from the interplay between objective and subjective factors, and he stressed the necessity of using "personal documents," such as letters, diaries, and life histories, to explore subjective aspects of human experience. Second, Thomas offered a powerful theoretical framework for conceptualizing social change. The central element in his theoretical system was the notion of social organization. Social organization represented the "socially systematized schemes of behavior imposed as rules upon individuals." Social change involved the "disorganization" of this system of social control. Typically, this disorganization arose as external factors, such as market forces, new forms of communication, or war, impinged upon a society and disrupted the consensus between societal norms ("values") and subjective orientations toward those norms ("attitudes"). In *The Polish Peasant*, Thomas and Znaniecki depicted the decline of social organization in turn-of-the-century Polish peasant society as market relations from Germany and immigration transformed Polish village society. They explored the course of this disorganization both in Polish society at home and among Polish immigrants in America. *The Polish Peasant* was the first study to combine theory and empirical analysis on such a scale, and it represented a landmark in American sociology. It not only offered a general theory of social change, but also served as a model for the ethnographic participant-observer methodology that came to characterize Chicago sociology during the twenties and thirties.[30]

After Thomas left Chicago, Robert E. Park asserted leadership in the Department of Sociology, a role he exercised throughout the 1920s. Contrary to Thomas, Park conducted little empirical research; he contributed largely as a theorist. Park first expressed his theoretical conception of sociology in his article "The City: Suggestions for the Investigation of Human Behavior in the Urban Environment" (1915). Here Park not only presented a series of questions about urban social phenomena, but also a detailed discussion of how investigators could connect their empirical observations of the city with sociological theory. This article served as a research agenda for Chicago sociology graduate students throughout the twenties. Park's major contribution lay, however, in his *Introduction to the Science of Sociology* (1921), which he wrote with the assistance of his colleague Ernest Burgess. The *Introduction* offered a systematic exposition of the principles of theoretical sociology, a conceptualization that defined the Chicago approach for an entire generation.

Park organized "The City" and the *Introduction* around a small cluster of major ideas. One of the most important of these ideas was the notion that the fundamental dynamic in human society was the transition from small intimate human communities held together through the tight bonds of kinship to larger societies held together through the looser bonds of mutual interest. The notion of this shift was implicit in Thomas's work, but Park—drawing heavily from his Berlin mentor Georg Simmel as well as Émile Durkheim and Henry Sumner Maine—raised discussion of this issue to the explicit level. The concern with this "great transformation" between familial village society and cosmopolitan urban society stands at the center of virtually all Park's major writings. Park often referred to these two models of social organization by different terms, including secular versus sacred society, culture versus civilization, and moral versus technical order. But these terms were largely synonymous in Park's usage and all related to the basic dichotomy Park had derived from nineteenth-century Continental social theorists.[31]

Park and Thomas invested much effort in defining sociology as a science, a law-seeking discipline capable of producing theoretical generalizations about the functioning of society. Despite their emphasis upon theory, though, they expected their science of sociology to have practical applications. Most particularly, they expected sociology to offer a means for dealing with the forces that were transforming the United States so rapidly during the late nineteenth and early twentieth centuries. Massive immigration, explosive industrialization and urbanization, and rising conflict between capital and labor had produced a sense of crisis during the early decades of the twentieth century over the increasing pace and intensity of social change. Political reformers, journalists, and academics had all weighed in with various solutions to address the problems associated with the economic, industrial, and sociocultural transformations sweeping across early twentieth-century America. Indeed, much of the rhetoric of the muckrakers and Progressive Era reformers can be seen as part of the effort to confront the general problem of rapid social change.

Thomas and Park distanced themselves, however, from the approach Progressive Era theorists and reformers took toward the problem of social change. Progressive reformers had taken a moralistic rather than scientific approach to social problems and had attempted to stabilize society through legislation, through "ordering and forbidding."[32] Thomas and Park and their Chicago colleagues rejected the moralistic approach to social reform because they believed it glossed over fundamental aspects of human nature and, consequently, was destined to fail. "Until recent years," Park and Burgess argued, "what we are now calling the human factor has been notoriously neglected in most social experiments. We have been seeking to reform human nature while at the same time we refused to reckon with it." Progressive reformers had thus assumed that they could "bring about social changes" merely by decree, "that is by 'arousing' public opinion and formulating legislation."[33] The Chicago sociologists, by contrast, advocated an approach to the management of social change that did not expect social control to rest upon first effecting changes in basic human nature. Instead, they believed that scientific study of society could yield an understanding of the principles of human nature that would allow for the establishment of "rational" controls. In short, they believed sociology could provide sufficient understanding of human nature and social dynamics to serve as the basis for a secular morality.[34]

Nineteenth-century evolutionary notions lay at the base of Thomas's and Park's thinking. They regarded competition as the inevitable condition of all forms of life and saw no exceptions for human societies. Competition manifested itself in the contemporary world, they proposed, through wars, migrations, nation-building, and endless quests by different groups for territory and markets. Thomas and Park conformed to Eric Goldman's definition of "Reform Darwinists," however, because both viewed human agency to be a powerful force for modifying the direction of evolutionary change. In keeping with their Darwinian vision, both regarded flux or change as the fundamental reality of human existence. Yet they believed humanity, through concerted effort, could influence the direction of this change and thus assert some control over its own destiny.

Probably no single thinker influenced Park and Thomas more in their conceptualization of evolutionary change than John Dewey. Park had studied under Dewey as an undergraduate at Michigan, and Thomas worked with him as a graduate student at Chicago. It was Dewey who inspired Park and Thomas to focus their inquiries upon process, especially upon the nature of change in the contemporary world. Moreover, it was Dewey who provided them with the conceptualization of sociology as a discipline useful not merely for studying the social world, but also for shaping and modifying that world. Dewey's pragmatic vision revealed to them, in other words, a reflexive aspect of sociological practice. Through Dewey's work, they derived the notion that empirical study could provide knowledge about the social world that could be used to construct contingent "truths." Sociological science thus became in the Deweyan conception a way to negotiate the ever-changing social world; it offered a potential source of stability in the face of contemporary uncertainty.[35]

Thomas and Park viewed social change as a discrete process that could be described in general terms. Instead of regarding social change as an infinitely variable contingent stream of events that occurred over the course of human history, they believed certain elements repeated in different times and places. It was the task of sociology, they believed, to view historical and contemporary change comparatively to determine which elements repeated. Such comparative analysis promised to provide a general theory of the process of social change. This empirically determined model of change would far surpass the many schemes of change proposed by nineteenth-century social theorists: rather than being simply descriptive, their model would be predictive. A predictive model would lend itself, moreover, to measures taken to control the pace and direction of contemporary social, cultural, and economic development.[36]

During the 1920s, Park and his colleague Ernest Burgess directed several dozen Chicago graduate students in the empirical study of social change. Virtually all these students focused their investigations upon the city, specifically the city of Chicago. With the publication of his 1915 article "The City: Suggestions for the Investigation of Human Behavior in the Urban Environment," Park had led the way within American sociology in defining the value of urban studies. In a memorable phrase, Park defined the city as the sociologist's laboratory, claiming that it was in the city that "human nature and social processes could be most conveniently studied." Park expanded upon his urban studies ideas in a series of papers he published over the course of the 1920s. "The city was a peculiarly advantageous place in which to study institutions and social life," he proposed, because it was "under the conditions of urban life" that institutions grew most rapidly. "They grow under our very eyes, and the processes by which they grow are open to observation and so, eventually, to experimentation." The city, in short, was the "source and center of social change"; by focusing their observations upon the city, moreover, sociologists were "in a position to investigate the process of civilization, as it were, under a microscope."[37]

Ernest Burgess also contributed meaningfully to the definition of Chicago urban studies. His most important contribution was his "zonal hypothesis." In "The Growth of the City: An Introduction to a Research Project" (1925), Burgess proposed that the basic outline of the city of Chicago could be represented by a map that designated distinct socioeconomic zones within the city. These zones formed a pattern of concentric rings. The business district occupied the central zone or core of the city; the next zone, which Burgess labeled the "zone in transition," included industrial and slum regions and served as a first-settlement location for many immigrant groups; the third ring included working-class homes outside the slum district; the next ring was composed of residential homes; the final zone included the ring of commuters' homes that surrounded the city. Burgess argued that a pattern of succession could be observed in the city in which residents from the inner zones continuously pushed outward from the less-desirable core and invaded the outer zones. Burgess's sociogeographic representation of the city, coupled with his description of social process within the city, came to exercise great influence in urban studies. Burgess and Park were most interested in the region of the city designated as the "zone in transition." This was the area of the city experiencing most rapid succession (characterized by social disorganization), and this was the area to which they dispatched their students to observe most closely in their studies of social change.[38]

Although Park defined the focus of Chicago sociologists during the 1910s and 1920s upon the study of the city, he was aware that the city exerted effects that far transcended its own borders. Through mass communications, rapid transportation, and trade, the city extended its influence far into the hinterland. By the early twentieth century, Park argued, "every metropolitan city" had become "a local center of a world-economy, and of a civilization in which local and tribal cultures now in a process of fusion will presently disappear altogether." The metropolises of the world were reaching out inevitably, in Park's vision, to transform their hinterlands. The zone of transition in such a vision thus

became the traditional towns and villages located at the closest reach, or the periphery, of the city's lines of influence.[39]

Park's interest in studying social changed stemmed from one overriding concern: the desire to come to terms with modernity. The hallmark of modernity in
his perspective was the metropolis. This new urban order had set in motion profound shifts within the character of human relationships and in the nature of
social existence. Modernity implied the loss of certainty:

> The older order, based as it was on custom and tradition was absolute and sa-
> cred. It had, besides, something of the character of nature itself; it had grown
> up, and men took it as they found it, like the climate and the weather, as part of
> the natural order of things. The new social order, on the other hand, is more or
> less of an artificial creation, an artifact. It is neither absolute nor sacred, but
> pragmatic and experimental.[40]

The transition from a traditional order to a new "artificial" order involved, however, profound dislocation. Park frequently commented on the cruelty and
wastefulness of this transition, and he noted with regret how the course of modernity had left cities filled with "human junk"—persons who had simply been
left behind by the rapid pace of change.

Park and his Chicago colleagues adopted a very specific approach for dealing with modernity: knowledge. Positing that change was inevitable, they attempted to discover some sense of order in that change that might enable them
to assert control over human destiny. As Park observed:

> Natural science came into existence in an effort of many to obtain control over
> external and physical nature. Social science is now seeking, by the same meth-
> ods of disinterested observation and research, to give man control over him-
> self.[41]

The Chicago sociologists were not, as Dorothy Ross claims, attempting to out-
wit or deny history. Instead, they were trying to work with history; rather than
trying to *escape* history, they were attempting to insert themselves *within* history. As confirmed pragmatists, they believed humans were not mere subjects
within the evolutionary process but active participants capable of influencing the
direction of their own evolution. By sending their students out to walk the city,
to observe and examine change "as it happened," the Chicago sociologists were
attempting to use empirical inquiry as a means to construct knowledge that
would enable them to achieve some level of control over experience. The process of inquiry—or the scientific method—represented for them, therefore, a
source of stability in the face of uncertainty and inevitable change.[42]

In their efforts to construct a scientific theory of social change, the pre–
World War II Chicago sociologists stand as precursors of what came to be
known a generation later as modernization theory. Robert Redfield grounded

himself thoroughly in the theories and methods of the Chicago sociologists. But he attempted in his research and writings to push beyond their formulations. Specifically, he aimed to develop a methodology by which he might identify and measure key indicators of social change. Such research, he assumed, would yield a general theory of directional change—a theory, in short, of how societies became modern. Redfield pursued this course of research over his entire career, and he came to serve as a key bridge figure linking the Chicago sociologists of the 1920s and 1930s with the post–World War II modernizationists.

A Robert Park Apprenticeship

The 1920s are generally regarded as the high moment of the "first school" of Chicago sociology. During this decade, the department was distinguished by the strength of its faculty and students; the department also enjoyed unprecedented financial support from the Laura Spelman Rockefeller Memorial. Over the course of the twenties, the Memorial provided the department more than a million dollars to support field research by graduate students and professors. A diverse but extremely cohesive group of professors composed the faculty during this period. Five professors—three sociologists and two anthropologists—served as the core of the department through most of the 1920s: Robert E. Park, Ernest W. Burgess, Ellsworth Faris, Fay-Cooper Cole, and Edward Sapir. The cohort of students who studied with these professors included such standouts as Louis Wirth, Herbert Blumer, Everett C. Hughes, Leslie White, and Robert Redfield.[43]

Redfield entered the department in January 1924 and graduated in August 1928. During his years in the department, he studied with almost all the major professors in the program. Since Redfield's main field was anthropology, he studied primarily under Fay-Cooper Cole and Edward Sapir. Redfield took several courses, furthermore, with the sociologists in the department, including William Ogburn's statistics course, Floyd House's "The Study of Society," for which the text was Park and Burgess's *Introduction to the Science of Society*, Robert E. Park's "Races and Nationalities," and Ellsworth Faris's "The Mind of Primitive Man" and "Social Origins." Faris's courses were particularly important for Redfield because they introduced him to the ideas of John Dewey and George Herbert Mead.[44] Finally, complementing Faris's courses in social psychology, Redfield studied Gestalt psychology with the famous German theorist Kurt Koffka, who spent the summer of 1925 teaching at Chicago.[45]

Although Fay-Cooper Cole served as Redfield's formal adviser at Chicago, Robert E. Park also acted as an adviser to Redfield and exercised a profound influence upon his intellectual development. Park not only brought Redfield into social science, but also he continued to guide Redfield through his years in graduate school and all through the 1930s. Park and Redfield talked constantly, and much of their discussion focused upon sociology. During the twenties, the Redfields and Parks lived near each other in Hyde Park and saw each other frequently; by the early 1930s, Park and his wife Clara had begun to spend several months of the year overseas. Redfield and Park maintained an active correspondence, though, and regularly discussed each other's research and various problems in social theory. Park and Redfield picked up their conversation each summer, moreover, when their two families gathered at Park's property in Roaring Brook, Michigan.

Park's influence upon Redfield can be clearly seen in the first article Redfield published, "Anthropology, A Natural Science?" (1926).[46] In this article, which he wrote during his second year of graduate school, Redfield compared and contrasted recent anthropological and sociological literature. He observed that while sociology demonstrated a strong generalizing trend, displayed most explicitly in Frederick J. Teggart's *The Processes of History* (1918) and Park and Burgess's *Introduction to the Science of Sociology*, such a trend was only beginning to appear in anthropology.[47] Redfield welcomed the shift in anthropology away from the historical and toward the generalizing or nomothetic approach, and he cited approvingly Clark Wissler's recently published *Man and Culture* (1923) as an example of this new trend.[48] Particularly in the last chapter of *Man and Culture*, Redfield noted, Wissler "anticipate[d] an explanatory science of cultural phenomena which shall have for its end *control*."[49] Redfield concluded his article by voicing doubt that anthropology would soon become a "nomothetic science of human behavior." Instead, he predicted, "it is probable that for some time [anthropology's] important contribution will remain the collection of a wide variety of invaluable data. Upon these data sociologists and social psychologists are in a large degree dependent."[50]

With this article, Redfield was essentially expressing the conception of anthropology that Park had advanced in the first section of the *Introduction to the Science of Sociology*. Park held that the social sciences existed in a hierarchical relationship. While sociology sat atop this hierarchy and served as the grand generalizing discipline, the other branches of the social sciences concerned themselves more with concrete particular phenomena than with general processes.[51] The other branches of the social sciences functioned, in short, as data gathering operations for the generalizing project of sociology. Park believed that anthropology was particularly suited for collecting data for sociological analysis. In the revised and expanded version of his article "The City" (1925), Park encouraged sociologists to apply anthropological techniques to the study of urban neighborhoods.[52] He personally challenged Redfield, furthermore, to make his career serve as a bridge between these two closely related disciplines. Redfield accepted Park's challenge, and his effort to bridge sociology and anthropology stands as one of the most distinguishing aspects of his career.[53]

Complementing Redfield's interactions with his professors were his relationships with fellow students at Chicago. The texture of student life in the social sciences at Chicago during the 1920s was particularly rich. Students from all branches of the social sciences associated closely with each other. Students talked sociology, anthropology, and political science until all hours at night, and they participated in several Greek-letter dining clubs and formal organizations designed to promote discussion of social scientific issues.[54] Redfield associated with a wide variety of students at Chicago. During his years in graduate school, he shared an office with two sociology students, Louis Wirth and Herbert Blumer, and Harold Lasswell, who was studying political science. He also belonged to one of the most prestigious sociology fraternities, Zeta Phi, and participated actively in its reading club and dinner events. Finally, he regularly attended and occasionally presented at meetings of the Society for Social Research, the organization Robert Park had established to bring graduate students and professors together on a regular basis to discuss and criticize ongoing research.[55]

Clearly most important of Redfield's relationships with other students, though, was his friendship with Everett C. Hughes. Redfield met Hughes during his first semester in the graduate program at Chicago. Hughes was also a first-year student who was working primarily in sociology. Hughes and Redfield quickly became good friends, and they worked together closely through all their graduate school years at Chicago. They took many of the same courses and shared reading, especially in courses requiring heavy reading in non-English sources, in which Redfield read the French sources and Hughes the German. While Bob was pursuing his doctorate, Greta Redfield was also taking an occasional course in the Chicago sociology program. Through these courses, she became friends with a fellow sociology student, Helen McGill, who later married Everett Hughes. The two couples became close friends in graduate school and developed a friendship that endured over a lifetime.[56]

Like all sociology and anthropology graduate students at Chicago during the 1920s, Redfield underwent a long apprenticeship in field research. He began during his second year by conducting a survey of Mexican immigrants in Chicago. Redfield's interest in Mexicans had been awakened by the trip he and Greta took through Mexico in the fall of 1923. Mexican immigration was also a matter of great political importance during the mid-twenties. Anti-immigrant feelings in general were on the rise during the twenties, and public debate over Mexican immigration had become increasingly heated by the middle of the decade. The postwar economic boom had proved short-lived, and immigrants had become an easy target for public discontent. President Coolidge signed the Reed-Johnson Act in 1924, setting in place quotas restricting European immigrants, especially those coming from southern and eastern Europe. Passage of this bill represented a victory for its nativistic backers, but they were not content with limiting only European immigration. To many Americans, Mexicans represented another source of racial danger, of "colored blood." And throughout the 1920s, racist zealots demanded that immigration exclusions be expanded to cover Mexican immigration.[57]

Chicago social scientists had concerned themselves with immigrants since the founding of the university in 1892. From the outset this concern had been expressed in opposition to the hostility toward immigrants that prevailed among much of the American population. Thomas and Znaniecki had constructed the most sophisticated expression of this alternative approach. In *The Polish Peasant*, Thomas and Znaniecki had offered a conceptual model of the experience immigrants underwent when they entered into a new society. Thomas and Znaniecki challenged the common prejudice which held that the troubles immigrants often experienced upon arrival in the United States, such as poverty, crime, and family disintegration, resulted from biological inferiority. Instead, they argued, these conditions resulted from the predictable phenomenon of social disorganization. The shock of the new environment destroyed the social order that had prevailed in the community the immigrants had left. Only through time, effort and especially education, moreover, could a new order be established in the transplanted community. Robert Park had built upon the Thomas and Znaniecki model and proposed that full social reorganization was reestablished only when immigrants fully assimilated into the host society. One goal of Chicago sociologists, therefore, was to provide basic information about the social and cultural backgrounds of immigrants that would assist social workers in their efforts to help immigrants assimilate.[58]

Redfield undertook his study of Mexican immigrants in Chicago with this purpose in mind. Supported by a Local Community Research Committee grant, which was funded in turn by the Laura Spelman Rockefeller Memorial, Redfield plotted the geographic distribution of Mexicans in the city, charted their employment records, and tried to explore personal attitudes and life histories for individual members of the Chicago Mexican immigrant community. Redfield worked on his study of Mexicans in Chicago throughout the 1924-1925 academic year. Although no final report exists presenting the results of his survey—it appears that he did not write one—a good sense of the nature of his study can be obtained from the April 1925 interim report he submitted to the Executive Committee at Chicago that oversaw LCRC projects and from the detailed set of research notes he kept on his work.[59] Fay-Cooper Cole also discussed Redfield's project at the August 1925 SSRC Hanover Conference. Cole reviewed the general outline of Redfield's study and stated that Redfield had eventually concluded his project after eight months of work because the transient nature of the Chicago Mexican community did not lend itself to intimate ethnographic study. The Mexicans in Chicago worked primarily as migrant farmworkers outside the city and only returned to Chicago periodically; the community consequently was in a state of perpetual flux. Redfield determined therefore that in order to study Mexican immigrants in America one must either move about with them or go to Mexico and study a community representative of those from which most of the immigrants had come. Cole concluded his remarks by describing Redfield's plan for such a village study in Mexico and proposed to the SSRC that they fund this study.[60]

During the same period of time, Redfield had applied to the John Simon Guggenheim Foundation for funds to support his research in Mexico. By the spring of 1925, however, it appeared that no such funding would be forthcoming, and Redfield determined to find a teaching job. The savings his father had left him had dwindled, and Redfield realized he could no longer remain as a full-time student and still support his wife and young daughter. Redfield applied to a handful of colleges and universities to teach sociology and anthropology, and he received an offer for a full-time position as an instructor in sociology at the University of Colorado. Redfield accepted the post, and he, Greta, and their daughter Lisa moved to Boulder in the summer of 1925. Redfield proceeded to teach at Colorado four courses per quarter—anthropology, ethnology, archaeology, and sociology—from the fall of 1925 through the spring of 1926.[61]

Fay-Cooper Cole continued to lobby the SSRC, however, for funds to support Redfield's Mexican village study. Before he had left Chicago for Colorado, Redfield had written a proposal for his village study which Cole presented to SSRC officials. Cole tried unsuccessfully from August 1925 through January 1926 to persuade the SSRC's Committee on Human Migration to fund Redfield's research.[62] In the spring of 1926, though, the SSRC's Committee on Research Fellowships decided to award Redfield one of its first fellowships. The SSRC provided Redfield $2,500, which proved sufficient to support Redfield and his family for almost nine months in Mexico.[63]

In November 1926, Bob and Greta and their two children—Lisa, a toddler, and Robert, Jr., an infant who had been born to them in Boulder—took up residence in the village of Tepoztlán, Mexico. Manuel Gamio had encouraged Redfield to study this village for two reasons. First, it was representative of the type of village from which many Mexican immigrants in the United States had come; second, it is located close to Mexico City, and its study would not have required Redfield to expose his family to extreme isolation. Redfield lived with his family in Tepoztlán from November 1926 until February 1927. In early 1927, post-revolutionary strife forced Redfield to relocate his family to Mexico City to stay with Elena Landazuri, and Redfield then worked by himself in Tepoztlán, periodically returning to Mexico City, until July 1927.[64]

When Redfield arrived in Tepoztlán, he had only a general plan for how to conduct his study of the village. In the brief description he submitted to the SSRC, Redfield stated he intended to conduct an "ethnographic study of a typical village community in Mexico." He described his plan to go live in a Mexican village for nine to twelve months where he "would as far as possible enter into the lives of the people and learn the problems which occupy their minds and the ways they have devised for meeting them." He described his plan to write a conventional ethnographic account of life in the village. Redfield also called attention to the social and political relevance of his project by noting that "a description of the life" of "Mexicans in their home communities would facilitate an intensive study of the problems arising out of the growing Mexican immigration into the United States." Redfield sounded in this proposal very much like his mentor Fay-Cooper Cole. Indeed, at the 1925 SSRC Hanover Conference, where he pushed hard to gain support for Redfield's project, Cole spoke at length about the issues facing Mexican immigrants in Chicago and described how he expected ethnographic studies, such as Redfield's, to provide information that would help facilitate the transition of Mexican immigrants into American society.[65]

Yet Redfield also described a second aim in his proposal that went well beyond immigration concerns. "I would like to do more," he asserted, "than produce an ethnographic monograph. I would like to make a study in comparative mentality." The "most significant changes" that the "village Mexican" underwent upon coming to the United States, Redfield proposed, lay in the "extension of rational thinking at the expense of magical thinking." Basing his thought on Robert Park's recently published article "Magic, Mentality, and City Life," Redfield suggested that it was "perhaps possible to select certain indices of magical or rational patterns of thought, and compare these indices in the Mexican village community and in the Mexican communities in American cities." Redfield thus envisioned the "study of comparative mentality" to provide a means to chart social change, especially the transition of people from the traditional village to the modern metropolis. The comparative mentality project clearly reflected Robert Park's influence on Redfield, an influence that grew ever more pronounced over the next several years.[66]

While in Tepoztlán, Redfield struggled to accommodate his two very different objectives within a single study. He was unsure about how exactly to conduct his survey of the village, and he frequently wrote to Robert Park describing his difficulties and asking for advice. He also wrote to Cole, but with Cole he mostly discussed logistical issues, for example, how long the SSRC expected him to stay in Mexico. His correspondence with Park during the months he was in Tepoztlán reveals Redfield's progressive development of a theoretical point of view; through Park's suggestions, Redfield came to focus, especially, upon the social and cultural significance of Tepoztecan calendrical rituals, the cultural geography or human ecology of the village, and the differences between the cosmopolitan and tradition-oriented villagers.[67]

Redfield spent nine months studying Tepoztlán—a long field study for an anthropologist during the 1920s. In July 1927, Redfield brought his study to a close, and he and his family returned to Chicago. Fay-Cooper Cole had arranged to have Redfield appointed as an assistant (equivalent to a position as an instructor or lecturer) in anthropology at Chicago beginning in the fall of 1927.[68] Redfield thus had means to support his family and, at the same time, complete his course work and dissertation at Chicago. For the autumn quarter of 1927 and the winter and spring quarters of 1928, Redfield taught two courses per quarter, took two courses per term himself as a student, and wrote his dissertation.[69] Over the academic year of 1927-1928, Redfield worked to forge a coherent report out of the materials he had collected in Tepoztlán. In the summer of 1928, Redfield accepted a position at Cornell University teaching anthropology and sociology—a course in which he taught the Park and Burgess text. He completed his dissertation while teaching at Cornell and, after receiving his Ph.D. in August, accepted an offer to return to Chicago in the autumn of 1928 as an assistant professor of anthropology.

Notes

1. The best biographical source on Redfield is the interview Anne Roe conducted with him in 1950; see Robert Redfield, Interview by Anne Roe, 1950, transcript, Anne Roe Papers, B/R621, Robert Redfield folder, American Philosophical Society, Philadelphia; additional details have been drawn from *The Correlator* Yearbook, vols. 11 and 12 (Chicago: University of Chicago High School, 1914, 1915), Archival Serials, Special Collections, Joseph Regenstein Library, University of Chicago, Chicago. Also useful are Charles M. Leslie, "Redfield, Robert," in *International Encyclopedia of the Social Sciences*, ed. David L. Sills (New York: Macmillan and Free Press, 1968) and George W. Stocking, Jr., "Redfield, Robert," in *Dictionary of American Biography*, suppl. VI, ed. John A. Garraty (New York: Charles Scribner's Sons, 1980).

2. Redfield, interview by Anne Roe; Lisa Redfield Peattie, interview by author (Boston, 2 August 1994).

3. Redfield, interview by Anne Roe; Robert Redfield, Jr., to Robert Redfield, Sr., 4 June 1917, box 3, folder 3, Robert Redfield Papers Addenda, Special Collections, Joseph Regenstein Library, University of Chicago, Chicago (hereafter cited as RRA-UC). On the connection between World War I ambulance drivers and young American writers in the 1920s, see Malcolm Cowley, *Exile's Return: A Literary Odyssey of the 1920s* (New York: Norton, 1934; revised edition, New York: Viking Press, 1951; reprint, New York: Penguin, 1976), 36-47; see also, Charles A. Fenton, "Ambulance Drivers in France and Italy: 1914-1918," *American Quarterly* 3 (Winter 1951): 326-343.

4. Redfield, interview by Anne Roe; Redfield expressed some of his disorientation upon returning home from the war in a series of poems he published in Harriet Monroe's journal *Poetry*: Robert Redfield, "War Sketches," *Poetry* 12 (August 1918): 242-243.

5. Donald Culross Peattie to Robert Redfield, 25 December 1918, box 1, folder 7, RRA-UC.

6. Redfield, interview by Anne Roe; Donald Culross Peattie to Robert Redfield, 17 March, 1919, box 1, folder 7, RRA-UC.

7. Robert Redfield, official transcript, Registrar's Office, University of Chicago.

8. Redfield, interview by Anne Roe; Margaret Park Redfield to Charles M. Leslie, 16 July 1964, box 3, folder 7a, Margaret Park Redfield Papers, Special Collections, Joseph Regenstein Library, University of Chicago, Chicago; many letters that Bob and Greta exchanged with each other during the years before their marriage are filed in box 2, folder 6, RRA-UC.

9. Redfield, interview by Anne Roe; Lisa Redfield Peattie, interview.

10. Redfield, interview by Anne Roe; Lisa Redfield Peattie, interview.

11. Elena Landazuri to Robert Park family, 16 April 1922, Robert E. Park Papers Addenda, Special Collections, Joseph Regenstein Library, University of Chicago, Chicago (hereafter cited as REPA-UC); on Elena Landazuri, see Anna Macias, *Against All Odds: The Feminist Movement in Mexico to 1940* (Westport, Conn.: Greenwood Press, 1982).

12. The impact of Redfield's encounter with modernity in Mexico can be seen in a literary essay, "Milk, Mexico, and Modern Life," that Redfield wrote upon returning from Mexico. The appearance of this essay suggests that Redfield intended to have it published; however, it never did appear in print (box 5, folder 5, RRA-UC).

13. On Manuel Gamio, see Ramón Eduardo Ruiz, *Mexico: The Challenge of Poverty and Illiteracy* (San Marino, Calif.: Huntington Library, 1963), 129-141, and Henry C. Schmidt, *The Roots of Lo Mexicano: Self and Society in Mexican Thought, 1900-1934* (College Station, Tex.: Texas A&M Press, 1978), 77-84. Redfield discussed the personal influence he derived from Gamio in his interview with Anne Roe and in a letter he wrote to a student (Robert Redfield to Armand Winfield, 3 May 1948, box 42, folder 5, RR-UC).

14. Robert E. Park to Margaret Park Redfield, 16 November 1923, box 2, folder 5, REPA-UC; Redfield, interview by Anne Roe; Redfield to Winfield, 3 May 1948.

15. This summary account of the historical and philosophical development of the terms civilization and culture draws heavily upon the following: Arden R. King, "Civilization," in *A Dictionary of the Social Sciences*, ed. Julius Gould and William L. Kolb (New York: The Free Press of Glencoe, 1964); Raymond Williams, "Culture and Civilization," in *The Encyclopedia of Philosophy*, ed. Paul Edwards (New York: Macmillan and Free Press, 1967); and A. L. Kroeber and Clyde Kluckhohn, *Culture: A Critical Review of Concepts and Definitions* (Cambridge, Mass.: Papers of the Peabody Museum of American Archaeology and Ethnology, Harvard University, vol. 47, no. 1, 1952; reprint, New York: Vintage Books, 1963), 11-73.

16. On the prewar rebellion against Victorian culture and the general cultural dynamics of the 1920s, see Henry F. May, *The End of American Innocence: A Study of the First Years of Our Own Time, 1912-1917* (New York: Alfred A. Knopf, 1959; reprint, Chicago: Quadrangle Books, 1964); Frederick J. Hoffman, *The Twenties: American Writing in the Postwar Decade,* rev. ed. (New York: Free Press, 1962); George W. Stocking, Jr., "The Ethnographic Sensibility of the 1920s and the Dualism of the Anthropological Tradition," in *The Ethnographer's Magic and Other Essays in the History of Anthropology* (Madison: University of Wisconsin Press, 1992), 276-341; and Stanley Coben, *Rebellion against Victorianism: The Impetus for Cultural Change in 1920s America* (New York: Oxford University Press, 1991).

17. Warren I. Susman provides an excellent description of the culture-civilization debate in "Culture and Civilization: The Nineteen-Twenties" in *Culture as History: The Transformation of American Society in the Twentieth Century* (New York: Pantheon, 1984), 105-121, 150-183; John Rundell and Stephen Mennell offer a valuable overview of the historical and philosophical dimensions of the culture-civilization contrast in "Introduction: Civilization, Culture and the Human Self-Image" in John Rundell and Stephen Mennell, ed., *Classical Readings in Culture and Civilization* (London: Routledge, 1998), 1-38; Richard Lehan provides several insightful readings of key 1920s literary texts in *The City in Literature: An Intellectual and Cultural History* (Berkeley: University of California Press, 1998); and George Stocking complements and extends Susman's discussion of culture and civilization in the 1920s in "The Ethnographic Sensibility of the 1920s and the Dualism of the Anthropological Tradition."

18. Harold E. Stearns, ed., *Civilization in the United States: An Inquiry by Thirty Americans* (New York: Harcourt, Brace, and Company, 1922), iii-vii.

19. T. S. Eliot, *The Waste Land* in *The Waste Land and Other Poems* (New York: Harcourt, Brace & World, 1934), 31, 37, 43-44; Edmund Wilson, *Axel's Castle: A Study in the Imaginative Literature of 1870 to 1930* (New York: Charles Scribner's Sons, 1931), 113-114; on Eliot's critique of modern civilization, see Lehan, *The City in Literature*, 128-143.

20. Oswald Spengler, *The Decline of the West,* trans. Charles Francis Atkinson, 2 vols. (New York: Alfred A. Knopf, 1926). One of the most widely read popularizations of Spengler's ideas was W. K. Stewart, "The Decline of Western Culture: Oswald Spengler's 'Downfall of Western Civilization' Explained," *Century* 108 (September 1924): 589-598. Kenneth Burke's translation of Spengler's introductory chapter appeared as "The Downfall of Western Civilization," *Dial* 77 (November 1924): 361-378; *Dial* 77 (December 1924): 482-504; *Dial* 78 (January 1925): 9-26. Lewis Mumford also provides an insightful view of the relevance of Spengler to intellectuals in the 1920s and 1930s in his essay "Spengler's 'The Decline of the West'" in Malcolm Cowley and Bernard Smith, eds., *Books That Changed Our Minds* (New York: Doubleday, Doran 1939; reprint, Freeport, N. Y.: Books for Libraries Press, 1970), 217-235.

21. Spengler, *Decline of the West,* 1: 31-33. Richard Lehan provides a thoughtful analysis of Spengler's thought and influence during the 1920s in *The City in Literature,* 210-215.

22. F. Scott Fitzgerald, *The Great Gatsby* (New York: Charles Scribner's Sons, 1925), 121, 15. Richard Lehan offers a wide-ranging and penetrating analysis of Fitzgerald's role in the culture and civilization discourse in *The City in Literature,* 206-223. On connections between *The Waste Land* and *The Great Gatsby,* see Letha Audhuy, "The *Waste Land* Myth and Symbols in *The Great Gatsby,*" in *F. Scott Fitzgerald's "The Great Gatsby,"* ed. Harold Boom (New York: Chelsea House, 1986), 109-122.

23. Edward Sapir, "Civilization and Culture." *Dial* 67 (20 September 1919): 233-236.

24. Edward Sapir, "Culture, Genuine and Spurious," *Dalhousie Review* 2 (1922): 358-368; "Culture, Genuine and Spurious," *American Journal of Sociology* 29 (January 1924): 401-429.

25. On the importance of Sapir's "Culture, Genuine and Spurious" essay to the culture-civilization discourse, see Richard Handler, "Anti-Romantic Romanticism: Edward Sapir and the Critique of American Individualism," *Anthropological Quarterly* 62 (October 1988): 1-13, and George Stocking, "The Ethnographic Sensibility of the 1920s and the Dualism of the Anthropological Tradition," 288-290; in the same article, Stocking also provides valuable insight into Sapir's personal influence on Margaret Mead, Ruth Benedict, and Robert Redfield.

26. Walter Lippmann, *A Preface to Morals* (New York: Macmillan, 1929), 9, 19; on the reception of *A Preface to Morals,* see Ronald Steel, *Walter Lippmann and the American Century* (New York: Vintage Books, 1981), 262-263.

27. On the general nature of the Chicago Department of Sociology and Anthropology during the 1920s, see Robert E. L. Faris, *Chicago Sociology, 1920-1932* (San Francisco: Chandler, 1967; reprint, Chicago: University of Chicago Press, 1970); George W. Stocking, Jr., *Anthropology at Chicago: Tradition, Discipline, Department* (Chicago: Joseph Regenstein Library of the University of Chicago, 1979), and Martin Bulmer, *The Chicago School of Sociology: Institutionalization, Diversity, and the Rise of Sociological Research* (Chicago: University of Chicago Press, 1984).

28. On Thomas's definitive role in Chicago sociology, see Bulmer, *The Chicago School of Sociology,* 36-63, and Lester R. Kurtz, *Evaluating Chicago Sociology: A Guide to the Literature with an Annotated Bibliography* (Chicago: University of Chicago Press, 1984), 3-4; 30-34.

29. W. I. Thomas, "Race Psychology: Standpoint and Questionnaire, with Particular Reference to the Immigrant and the Negro," *American Journal of Sociology* 17 (May 1912): 725-775; William I. Thomas and Florian Znaniecki, *The Polish Peasant in Europe and America*, 5 vols. (Boston: Badger, 1918-1919; reprint, 2 vols., New York: Alfred A. Knopf, 1927).

30. On *The Polish Peasant* and its influence in Chicago sociology, see John Madge, *The Origins of Scientific Sociology* (New York: Free Press, 1962), 52-87; Morris Janowitz, introduction to *W. I. Thomas on Social Organization and Social Personality*, ed. Morris Janowitz (Chicago: University of Chicago Press, 1966); Martin Bulmer, *The Chicago School of Sociology*, 45-63; and Eli Zaretsky, introduction to William I. Thomas and Florian Znaniecki, *The Polish Peasant in Europe and America*, ed. and abr. Eli Zaretsky (Urbana: University of Illinois Press, 1984).

31. Robert E. Park, "The City: Suggestions for the Investigation of Human Behavior in the Urban Environment," *American Journal of Sociology* 20 (March 1915): 577-612; Robert E. Park and Ernest W. Burgess, *Introduction to the Science of Sociology* (Chicago: University of Chicago Press, 1921); the indispensable source for understanding the work of Robert E. Park and his contribution to Chicago sociology is Fred H. Matthews's *Quest for an American Sociology: Robert E. Park and the Chicago School* (Montreal: McGill-Queen's University Press, 1977).

32. Thomas and Znaniecki, *The Polish Peasant*, 1: 3.

33. Park and Burgess, *Introduction to the Science of Sociology*, 47.

34. Berenice Fisher and Anselm Strauss offer an insightful discussion of the Chicago sociologists' applied concerns in "The Chicago Tradition and Social Change: Thomas, Park, and Their Successors," *Symbolic Interaction* 1 (Spring 1978): 5-23.

35. On the connections between Chicago Sociology and John Dewey, see Matthews, *Quest for an American Sociology*, 20-29, 96-97, 143-147; Dennis Smith, *The Chicago School: A Liberal Critique of Capitalism* (New York: St. Martin's Press, 1988), 57-74; Barbara Ballis Lal, *The Romance of Culture in an Urban Civilization: Robert E. Park on Race and Ethnic Relations in Cities* (London: Routledge, 1990), 69-91; and Donald N. Levine, *Visions of the Sociological Tradition* (Chicago: University of Chicago Press), 251-268. David A. Hollinger provides an especially useful discussion of Dewey's pragmatism in "The Problem of Pragmatism in American History," chap. in *In the American Province: Studies in the History and Historiography of Ideas* (Bloomington: Indiana University Press, 1985; reprint, Baltimore: Johns Hopkins University Press, 1989).

36. For an excellent, albeit controversial, account of the efforts of American social scientists during the 1910s and 1920s to study and control the process of social change, see Dorothy Ross, *The Origins of American Social Science* (Cambridge: Cambridge University Press, 1991), 303-389; Paul F. Kress also offers a useful discussion of development of the processual view in American social science in *Social Science and the Idea of Process: The Ambiguous Legacy of Arthur F. Bentley* (Urbana: University of Illinois Press, 1970).

37. Park, "The City," 612; Park, "The City as Social Laboratory," in *Chicago: An Experiment in Social Science Research*, ed. T. V. Smith and Leonard D. White (Chicago: University of Chicago Press, 1929), 19, 12; Park, "Human Migration and the Marginal Man," *American Journal of Sociology* 33 (May 1928): 890.

38. Ernest W. Burgess, "The Growth of the City: An Introduction to a Research Project," chap. in Robert E. Park, Ernest W. Burgess, and Roderick D. McKenzie, *The City* (Chicago: University of Chicago Press, 1925), 50-52.

39. Park, "The City as Social Laboratory," 2.

40. Park, "The City as Social Laboratory," 3.

41. Park, "The City as Social Laboratory," 3.

42. On Ross's view of the relationship between the Chicago sociologists and history, see *Origins of American Social Science*, 312-326, 346-367. Ross views the effort of Chicago sociologists to develop a theory of social change as "scientistic." Although an element of scientism can be recognized in their work, the efforts of the Chicago sociologists to use empirical knowledge to confront a rapidly changing world can be seen as a modernist strategy. The Chicago sociologists viewed the new urban order as a tangible manifestation of the grand epistemological shift of the late nineteenth century. In the absence of traditional moral constraints—or moral knowledge—these theorists viewed it as their role to construct the intellectual basis for a new contingent notion of social morality. In discussing the modernist sensibility displayed by certain intellectuals and artists during the first decades of the twentieth century, David A. Hollinger has suggested that we distinguish between two very distinct orientations: that of the "artificer" and that of the "cognitivist." Through their ethnographic studies, the Chicago sociologists of the 1910s and 1920s attempted to develop a knowledge of the new urban order that embraced both the objective and subjective aspects of human experience. I suggest the efforts of the Chicago sociologists are better seen as manifestations of "cognitive modernism" than as mere reductionism or scientism. See David A. Hollinger, "The Knower and the Artificer, *with* Postscript 1993," in *Modernist Impulses in the Human Sciences, 1870-1930*, Dorothy Ross, ed. (Baltimore: Johns Hopkins University Press, 1994), 26-53.

43. On the Laura Spelman Rockefeller Memorial and the Chicago sociology department, see Bulmer, *The Chicago School of Sociology*, 129-150.

44. Faris had come to the sociology program in 1919, replacing W. I. Thomas, after studying philosophy and psychology at Chicago under Dewey, Mead, and Robert C. Angell. Faris has often been overlooked in discussions of Chicago sociology. He played a critical role in the department, nevertheless, by acting as a bridge between the Chicago philosophy department—the stronghold of pragmatism—and the Chicago sociology department. On Faris's role at Chicago, see Anselm Strauss's introduction to *George Herbert Mead on Social Psychology: Selected Papers*, ed. Anselm Strauss (Chicago: University of Chicago Press, 1964), vii-xxv.

45. Robert Redfield, official transcript, Registrar's Office, University of Chicago.

46. *Social Forces* 4 (June 1926): 715-721.

47. Frederick. J. Teggart, *The Process of History* (New Haven, Conn.: Yale University Press, 1918).

48. Clark Wissler, *Man and Culture* (New York: Thomas Y. Crowell, 1923; reprint, New York: Johnson Reprint Corporation, 1965).

49. Redfield, "Anthropology, A Natural Science?" 720.

50. Redfield, "Anthropology, A Natural Science?" 721.

51. Park and Burgess, *Introduction to the Science of Sociology*, 42-43.

52. Park clearly anticipated the development of urban anthropology by several decades. "Anthropology, the science of man, has been mainly concerned up to the present," he observed, "with the study of primitive peoples. But civilized man is quite as interesting an object of investigation, and at the same time his life is more open to observation and study. Urban life and culture are more varied, subtle, and complicated, but the fundamental motives are in both instances the same. The same patient methods of observa-

tion which anthropologists like Boas and Lowie have expended on the study of the life and manners of the North American Indian might be even more fruitfully employed in the investigation of the customs, beliefs, social practices, and general conceptions of life prevalent in Little Italy on the lower North Side in Chicago, or in recording the more sophisticated folkways of the inhabitants of Greenwich Village and the neighborhoods of Washington Square, New York." Robert E. Park, "The City: Suggestions for the Investigation of Human Behavior in the Urban Environment," chap. in *The City* by Robert E. Park, Ernest W. Burgess, and Roderick D. McKenzie (Chicago: University of Chicago Press, 1925), 3.

53. Bob and Greta were both aware that Park held this expectation for Bob, and they occasionally spoke of the unique demands it placed upon Bob. See Robert Redfield to Margaret Park Redfield, August 1933, box 3, folder 1, RR-UC and Margaret Park Redfield to Robert Redfield, August 1933, RRA-UC.

54. On student life in the social sciences at Chicago during the 1920s, see Faris, *Chicago Sociology,* 33-34; James T. Carey, *Sociology and Public Affairs: The Chicago School* (Beverly Hills, Calif.: Sage Publications, 1975), 154-159; Bulmer, *The Chicago School of Sociology,* 112-118.

55. See Harold Lasswell to Fred H. Matthews, 9 December 1965, box 1, folder 1, Fred H. Matthews Papers, Special Collections, Joseph Regenstein Library, University of Chicago, Chicago.

56. Everett C. Hughes wrote several unpublished accounts of his and Redfield's experiences as graduate students at Chicago during the 1920s. These documents provide an invaluable source of information not only on Hughes and Redfield, but also on the general character of the department during the 1920s. See "Redfield Lecture," 16 January 1959, transcript (delivered in Milton Singer's "Social and Cultural Change" course, Anthropology 241, a few months after Redfield died), box 45, folder 5, Everett C. Hughes Papers, Special Collections, Joseph Regenstein Library, University of Chicago, Chicago (hereafter cited as ECH-UC); and two transcripts of Hughes's autobiographical reflections: (1) "Dictated January 23, 1976, Everett C. Hughes," 26 January 1976 and (2) an untitled autobiographical dictation, 29 January 1976, box 1, folder 11, ECH-UC.

57. Lawrence A. Cardoso, *Mexican Emigration to the United States, 1897-1931* (Tucson: University of Arizona Press, 1980); John A. Higham, *Strangers in the Land: Patterns of American Nativism, 1860-1925,* 2d ed. (New Brunswick, N.J.: Rutgers University Press, 1963; reprint, New York: Atheneum, 1963), 316-330.

58. On the ameliorative aspects of Chicago sociology, see Smith, *The Chicago School,* 21-28.

59. Redfield's research notebook on his Mexicans in Chicago project is located in box 59, folder 2, RR-UC; his interim report, "The Mexicans in Chicago," is in *A Copy of Reports Made to the Executive Committee of the Local Community Research Committee on Progress of Local Community Research Projects during the Winter Quarter 1925,* series 3, box 71, folder 755, Laura Spelman Rockefeller Memorial Archives, Rockefeller Archive Center, Sleepy Hollow, New York (hereafter LSRM-RAC).

60. Stenographers recorded the entire proceedings of the Hanover Conference; the transcript of Cole's discussion provides an excellent summary of the results of Redfield's Mexican immigrant survey. Fay-Cooper Cole, "Investigation of Mexican Immigration," in *Report of Joint Conference of the Committee on Problems and Policy of the Social Science Research Council Meeting with Other Representatives of the Social Sciences in*

Attendance upon the Dartmouth Conference of Social Scientists and Allied Groups, 31 August to 3 September 1925, series 3, box 53, folder 569, LSRM-RAC.

61. On Redfield's application to the John Simon Guggenheim Foundation and need to find a teaching position for the fall of 1925, see Robert Redfield to Norman F. Coleman, 7 May 1925 (erroneously dated 1935), box 4, folder 10, RRA-UC; on Redfield's position and teaching duties at Colorado, see E. J. Fjeld to Robert Redfield, 27 June 1925, box 4, folder 11, RRA-UC.

62. Cole, "Investigation of Mexican Immigration"; Cole, "Project 4 B. A Study of Mexican Peasant Communities," Supplement to Appendix 4 of *The Report of the Committee on the Scientific Aspects of Human Migration to the Chairman of the Social Science Research Council*, by Edith Abbott (entire report attached to letter by Charles E. Merriam to Beardsley Ruml, 11 January 1926), series 3, box 68, folder 711, LSRM-RAC.

63. Charles E. Merriam to Beardsley Ruml, 12 June 1926, series 3, box 67, folder 707, LSRM-RAC.

64. Redfield described the circumstances surrounding his choice of Tepoztlán as a site for study and the experiences he and his family had in the village in his article "Among the Middle Americans," *University of Chicago Magazine* 20 (March 1928): 242-247. In their 1958 *American Anthropologist* essay on Redfield, Fred Eggan and Milton Singer erroneously listed this article as "My Adventures as a Mexican"; several authors have subsequently perpetuated this error by referring to Redfield's article by the title attributed to it by Eggan and Singer. See also Robert Redfield to Robert and Clara Park, 28 February 1927, box 1, folder 2, RR-UC.

65. Robert Redfield, "Statement of the Nature of the Field Work Proposed," [summer 1925], box 1, folder 4, RR-UC; Cole, "Investigation of Mexican Immigration."

66. Redfield, "Statement of the Nature of the Field Work Proposed"; Robert E. Park, "Magic, Mentality, and City Life," *Publications of the American Sociological Society* 18 (September 1924): 102-115.

67. See, especially, Robert Redfield to Robert E. Park, 2 December 1926, box 1, folder 2, RR-UC; Park to Redfield, 8 December 1926, box 2, folder 5, RPA-UC; Redfield to Park, 16 December 1926, box 1, folder 6, RRA-UC; Redfield to Park, 11 January 1927, box 1, folder 6, RRA-UC; Redfield to Park, 2 February 1927, box 1, folder 2, RR-UC; Redfield to Park, 23 May 1927, box 1, folder 4, RR-UC.

68. Fay-Cooper Cole to Robert Redfield, 2 November 1926; Cole to Redfield, 17 March 1917; Redfield to Cole, 22 March 1927, box 1, folder 4, RR-UC.

69. During this year, Redfield's teaching load included these courses: Ethnology, Present-Day Mexico, Anthropological Literature, History of Anthropology, and Ethnography of Middle America. Some authors, in particular Ricardo Godoy and Joan Vincent, have suggested that Redfield approached his study of Tepoztlán with little formal training in theoretical anthropology. Godoy based his claim upon a comment Redfield made to Cole regarding the teaching of the history of anthropology course during the same year he was teaching five other courses (six courses total, five separate preparations). Redfield's protests over teaching the course seem related, however, more to fear of overwork than an admission of ignorance of anthropology (as Godoy suggests). A comparison of Redfield's graduate transcript along with that of his colleague Leslie White indicates that both White and Redfield took the same number of formal course units in anthropology and sociology in the Chicago Ph.D. program (each student was required to complete 27 "major" units). Moreover, Redfield had taught anthropology and sociology full-time at

Colorado for a year before he went to Tepoztlán and for an additional year at Chicago and Cornell while he was writing his Tepoztlán manuscript. The claim that Redfield was a neophyte in anthropology when he wrote his Tepoztlán dissertation thus seems unpersuasive. Godoy's remarks are in his "The Background and Context of Redfield's *Tepoztlán*," 52; Vincent's comments are in her *Anthropology and Politics*, 206; Redfield's graduate transcript is available at the University of Chicago Registrar's office; Leslie White's transcript is in box 1, folder 2, Leslie A. White Papers, Bentley Historical Library, University of Michigan, Ann Arbor, Michigan; on Redfield's teaching duties, see Cole to Redfield, 17 March 1927, box 1, folder 4, RR-UC; Redfield's response to this proposed schedule is in Redfield to Cole, 22 March 1927, box 1, folder 4, RR-UC.

Chapter 2

A Science of Social Change: Constructing the Folk-Urban Continuum

Redfield's research in Tepoztlán marked the beginning of a fifteen-year project aimed at elucidating the general nature of social change. Tepoztlán provided Redfield his first opportunity to conduct an anthropological investigation organized along the sociological lines in which he had been trained at Chicago. Redfield gained wide attention through his Tepoztlán work, and his growing reputation secured for him the support necessary to launch an extensive study of social change in the Yucatan peninsula that was to occupy him throughout the 1930s. Through a series of ethnographic community studies, Redfield explored the dynamics of urbanization in Yucatan, and he constructed a generalizing terminology to describe this transformation. Redfield's "folk-urban" terminology gained wide currency during the 1940s through the 1960s, and it is for this conceptualization that he is best remembered today.

Tepoztlán: A Laboratory of Change

Redfield's dissertation, "A Plan for a Study of Tepoztlán, Morelos," was largely an ethnographic account of the village of Tepoztlán. It differed from a strict ethnographic account, however, because it did not offer a full description of the "round of life" in the village. Instead, Redfield presented only a selective portrayal of life in Tepoztlán. This account reflects Redfield's attempt to satisfy the divergent expectations of his two advisers, Fay-Cooper Cole and Robert E. Park. Cole expected Redfield to conduct a full ethnographic study of a Mexican peasant village to provide social workers in Chicago and other American cities with background information on Mexican immigrants. Park expected Redfield to conduct an ethnological study of the process of social change in a peasant village situated on the frontier of North American civilization. Redfield attempted to satisfy both expectations with a single monograph. The resultant text is a hybrid. It is neither a full ethnographic account nor a strict ethnological or socio-

41

logical study. Redfield acknowledged the impressionistic nature of his work and suggested, presciently, that virtually all ethnographic accounts displayed similar limitations of personal selection as those in his work. He defended the approach he took in his dissertation:

> The following pages are, generally speaking, ethnography. But ethnography is not photography; any ethnographic description is more than depiction and involves a selection of elements which will vary with the interests, temperament and experience of the ethnographer. And the selection that has been made here was determined by the interest of the present ethnographer in the possibility of studying, in the field, the social changes following upon contact of modern industrial civilization with the marginal peoples.

Redfield thus understood from the outset that his work on Tepoztlán was not a well-rounded report. Instead, it was a study that intentionally sought out the "frontier of social change" in a particular Mexican village and attempted "to set down some of the respects in which the older culture [was] changing." As such, Redfield regarded his dissertation as a plan to be used later in a more thorough "study of contemporary change" in Tepoztlán.[1]

After completing his dissertation, Redfield realized that teaching obligations and financial limitations were going to prevent him from returning soon for additional study in Tepoztlán. Consequently, he arranged for the University of Chicago Press to publish his dissertation with slight modifications as *Tepoztlán, A Mexican Village: A Study of Folk Life*. Redfield's title change indicated that he considered his manuscript more than simply a plan for further study. Significantly, he introduced in this new title a specialized term, "folk," that was to serve as a constant theme in his work throughout his career. In the introduction to his dissertation, Redfield had devoted most of his attention to justifying social anthropologists' concern with the study of social change. But in the published version of *Tepoztlán*, Redfield devoted his introduction primarily to defining the cultural identity of the Tepoztecans. He proposed that the word "folk" be applied in a specialized sense to describe the culture of the Tepoztecans and the majority of other Mexicans who lived in small rural villages and who derived from mixed Indian and Spanish heritage. By suggesting the term "folk," Redfield was attempting to distinguish an intermediate type of culture characteristic of peoples who occupied a place between tribal or "primitive" peoples and urban or "civilized" peoples. Other than the difference between the title and the introduction, no substantive changes existed between Redfield's published version of *Tepoztlán* and his dissertation. The published version still presented itself as a hybrid study, part ethnographic account and part theoretical study of social change.[2]

Of the two juxtaposed accounts in *Tepoztlán*, the ethnographic report is the one most readily perceived; indeed, it is the primary narrative of the book. Redfield began his text in this mode describing first the physical setting of the village. He portrayed Tepoztlán as a remote village nestled high in the mountains above Mexico City. Even though by sheer distance "Mexico City is no more than fifty miles from Tepoztlán," Redfield presented the village as wholly removed from the city and given to a profoundly different way of life. Tepoztecans had no need for clocks or machines. The "great clocks of the sky" were sufficient for keeping time and, since "no wheel ever moves" in the streets of Tepoztlán, the only form of transportation was walking or riding on the back of a burro.[3]

Work in the village was also different from that in the city. "Not only [did] Tepoztlán maintain itself almost entirely by farming, but nearly every Tepoztecan [was] a farmer." Tepoztlán was not, however, without specialists; the village was filled with craftsmen such as carpenters, ironworkers, silversmiths, masons, and herb doctors. But for virtually all these specialists, devotion to their craft was only part-time. They also tended at least a small field or milpa in which they planted the traditional maize. Economic specialization had thus not sundered their shared way of life. Economic forces, moreover, made but small claim on the villagers. While work was part of life, so also was play. "The Mexican folk," Redfield observed, "enjoy[ed] a great number of festivals which are in part worship but in greater part play." On close to a third of all days in the year, some festival or calendrical ritual was observed in the valley of Tepoztlán. The Mexican peasant, in Redfield's depiction, lived his life in harmony—his work as a craftsman-farmer was fully balanced with symbolic and joyful festivals. He lived, in short, a life that made sense.[4]

The primary narrative of *Tepoztlán* thus focused on social stability. The image it presented was of a timeless, tradition-bound village. This timeless view— a perspective referred to as the "ethnographic present"—was the typical approach then used by anthropologists to describe tribes and villages. But in *Tepoztlán*, Redfield departed from ethnographic genre conventions by focusing his secondary narrative upon social instability. Specifically, he described here the contemporary changes that were transforming Tepoztlán from a traditional village to a modern town.

Redfield constructed his secondary narrative through a series of contrasts. In a conventional ethnographic account, each major aspect of village or tribal life, such as family, marriage, recreation, property, and religion, receives treatment in an individual chapter. Redfield generally adhered to this convention in his division of chapters, but he deviated from the standards of the genre within individual chapters. Rather than presenting straight descriptions of individual aspects of village culture in his chapters, Redfield presented split descriptions. In almost every chapter of *Tepoztlán*, he first presented a description of the prevailing (seemingly timeless) state of affairs in the village and then opposed it with a sketch of how the dominant culture was starting to change, of how city ways were starting to penetrate and disrupt the organized pattern of village ways.

The first contrast between village and city ways that Redfield explored arose from the different style of clothing that Tepoztecans wore in the village versus that which they wore when going to the city. He devoted several pages of his second chapter to describing the traditional dress for men and women in the village. This dress consisted of loose white cotton trousers and blouses for men and loose cotton blouses, skirts, and rebozos or shawls for women. Men either went barefoot or wore sandals; women wore sandals when traveling but otherwise always went barefoot. Redfield noted in closing this chapter, though, that many Tepoztecan men have "a separate costume for city wear: dark trousers, a dark hat, and shoes, worn only on visits to the city." The choice made by Tepoztecans to adopt the clothing of the city when they ventured beyond their village reflected, in Redfield's view, an emerging self-consciousness among Tepoztecans, an awareness that their culture was not all-inclusive and that a larger world with its own cultural symbols existed beyond the borders of their village. The self-consciousness the villager felt in relationship to the city, Redfield argued, "express[ed] the nature of the community of Tepoztlán: no longer a primitive tribal society nor yet an urbanized community, it must nevertheless be defined, as it tends to define itself, with reference to the world-wide city culture within which it is now included."[5]

In subsequent chapters, Redfield examined several additional contrasts between village and city ways. He discussed changing patterns in the following areas: (1) observance of holy days and religious festivals; (2) adherence to traditional rituals of birth, marriage, and death; (3) division of labor; (4) attitudes toward magic and folk medicine; and (5) literacy. In each of these areas, Redfield found a cluster of villagers who represented a vanguard of change. These villagers, for example, were rejecting magical remedies for disease and seeking instead medicines from the city, or they participated in the celebration of holy days but paid little heed to the religious meaning of the ceremonies.

Redfield referred to the few villagers on the leading edge of change as *los correctos*, the "correct"; he called the many other villagers who adhered to traditional ways *los tontos*, the "ignorant." These labels are constructions Redfield used to portray the social and cultural diversity he perceived in Tepoztlán. He commented in a footnote upon introducing these labels that "these two terms" are used "not in their original Spanish meanings but merely to designate two groups in Tepoztlán that are *sometimes* so designated by themselves."[6] He acknowledged that these terms took on added meaning in his usage. They became ideal types, one designating the traditional, village-directed Tepoztecan, the other the cosmopolitan, city-directed Tepoztecan. As such, they provided Redfield a way to structure his dual portrait of Tepoztlán. His primary narrative depicted the core culture of *los tontos*, while his secondary narrative explored the processes by which *los tontos* were being transformed into *los correctos*. Redfield wove these two distinct narratives together in *Tepoztlán* to produce a complex text that attempted to portray a traditional village in the process of becoming modern.

Underlying Redfield's analysis of the transformation of Tepoztlán was a sophisticated theory of social and cultural change. Redfield's theory rested upon two distinct bodies of thought. The first of these influences was the general tradition of nineteenth-century European social theory, especially as mediated by Robert E. Park. The American anthropologist Clark Wissler provided the second major influence, particularly through his theoretical and empirical work on the diffusion of cultural traits.

While Park's social evolutionary notions provided Redfield a grand conceptual scheme with which to interpret the sociocultural transformation occurring in Tepoztlán, Clark Wissler supplied Redfield with a practical methodology for studying cultural change "as it happens." Redfield drew, in particular, upon Wissler's "age-area" hypothesis. By mapping the distribution of American Indian cultural traits, Wissler had concluded that culture complexes could be seen as diffusing outward from cultural centers in uniform concentric patterns. These cultural areas, Wissler argued, displayed internal chronology: those culture complexes found at the periphery of an area, or those having the widest distribution, were the oldest; correspondingly, those complexes found at the center of an area, or at the zone of innovation, were the newest.[7] Redfield admired Wissler's systematic and comparative approach to the study of cultural processes, and he followed Wissler's lead in attempting to determine empirically the nature of culture transmission. Yet he rejected Wissler's emphasis on the geographical distribution of culture traits. He suggested that Wissler's model of cultural transmission applied only to the most "primitive" peoples who communicated solely through face-to-face exchange and for whom "closeness of contact is largely proportionate to geographical distance." For "civilized" peoples, however, communication operated primarily by means that transcended the limitations of space. "In understanding culture process," Redfield argued, "the mode and character of communication should be the center of attention, not the geographic distribution of the culture traits."[8]

Not surprisingly, Redfield derived his ideas about communication directly from Robert Park. In his conceptualization of human ecology, Park had depicted communication as one of the most important of all social processes. Indeed, communication represented the central engine of change in Park's social interaction cycle. In one of his most influential articles, "Human Migration and the Marginal Man" (1928), Park had argued that social process—or the contact and interaction between distinct cultures—arose predominantly through the agency of those persons who for various reasons stood at the margins of their own culture and thus represented convenient points of contact between neighboring cultures. Park referred to these figures as "marginal men," and he suggested that such persons were best typified by the "Mulatto in the United States and the Eurasian in Asia." Park concluded this article by suggesting that it was "in the mind of the marginal man—where the changes and fusions of culture are going on—that we can best study the processes of civilization."[9]

In his field study of Tepoztlán, Redfield applied both Park's notion of studying the culturally marginal figures in the village and Wissler's method of analyzing the geography of trait distribution. Redfield found these two techniques to be complementary. By mapping the distribution of *correctos* and *tontos*, he found that the social structure of Tepoztlán had a geographic order that reflected a distinct social and cultural order. The *correctos*, intellectuals, artisans, and tradespeople "who practice[d] European techniques and mostly acquired their specialties through economic competition," lived almost exclusively in the center of the town near the plaza; on the other hand, the tontos, midwives, herb doctors, and fireworks makers "who practice[d] more ancient, traditional techniques and who in more cases came into their roles by birth," lived toward the periphery of the village. In Redfield's view, the *correctos*, represented the "marginal men" in Tepoztlán, and it was this small group who served as conduits of communication with the larger world and interjected novel ideas and cultural practices into the village. Redfield attempted to go beyond Wissler, moreover, and to not merely map the distribution of cultural traits associated with the *correctos*, but also to determine the effects those traits exercised on the villagers. Rather than looking at the cultural trait being transferred as a mere artifact, he regarded it as a live agent. As this new cultural trait was adopted, he observed, "it may be said that the whole mentality correspondingly changes, if by 'mentality' is understood a complex of habits employed in meeting unfamiliar problems." Becoming modern, therefore, was more than simply adopting new tools or techniques; it was adopting a new way of looking at the world, of solving problems. It was this psychological change that resulted from the diffusion of culture complexes that most interested Redfield.[10]

Redfield published *Tepoztlán* in the summer of 1930, just as the United States was sliding into the Great Depression. The reviewers' response would have gratified a mature author who had spent years laboring on the text, much less a fledgling professor who had simply turned his dissertation over to the in-house press for publication. Not only did social scientists receive *Tepoztlán* positively, but also reviewers beyond the specialized world of academia responded enthusiastically to the book. Indeed, Redfield's text created a minor sensation among reviewers for the literary weeklies. The *Saturday Review of Literature*, the *Nation*, the *New Republic*, and the *Times Literary Supplement* all provided *Tepoztlán* with prominent reviews.[11] Carleton Beals asserted in the *Saturday Review of Literature* that *Tepoztlán* was "of far greater importance for a proper understanding of Mexico than nearly all the books on political and institutional life which have appeared in English." Beals also remarked that Redfield's *Tepoztlán* immediately suggested comparison with the Lynds' *Middletown*. A few months later, Stuart Chase offered the same observation in his *New Republic* review of

Tepoztlán. By the end of the year, Chase had begun to publish in the *New Republic* serial installments of *Mexico: A Study of Two Americas* (1931), his best-selling comparison of Tepoztlán and Middletown.[12]

Redfield's *Tepoztlán* spoke directly to those intellectuals and artists of the 1920s and thirties who believed that Mexico, especially village Mexico, represented a superior way of life to contemporary Western civilization. Specifically, *Tepoztlán* represented a key contribution to the culture-civilization discourse of the 1920s. Redfield's worldview had been greatly influenced by this discourse, and it was fitting that his first major work should address this conversation. *Tepoztlán* held special meaning for the culture-civilization debate, moreover, because having been written by an anthropologist, it seemed to bring *scientific* verification that village life in Mexico was indeed superior to life in industrialized, urbanized America. Redfield had not overdramatized this comparison—not the way his populizers would; but the implication lurked nevertheless within his text.[13]

Scholarly readers of *Tepoztlán* paid less attention to the metaphysical pathos of Redfield's work than to his methodology and observations about social process. Robert Lynd, in his review for the *American Journal of Sociology*, praised it as a "beautiful example of sensitive observation and reporting" and judged it to be "full of acute analytical suggestion about the dynamics of cultural processes."[14] A. L. Kroeber reviewed it for the *American Anthropologist* and was even more enthusiastic. *Tepoztlán*, he asserted, was "a work which pioneers its field." Kroeber called particular attention to the processual emphasis in the book. Redfield's "interest is not in how things came to be in Tepoztlán," Kroeber observed, "but in how they interact now. . . . Social change is his theme." Kroeber concluded by predicting:

> Partly because of the leaning toward sociology and partly because of the relative unfamiliarity of the subject matter, it may be anticipated that some anthropologists will perhaps appreciate Redfield's volume less than students in other circles. It is likely however to influence them more than they realize. Its originality, saturation, and skilled scholarship, expressed through the medium of a style both restrained and felicitous, render it a landmark and should make it a model.[15]

Kroeber proved correct in his expectation that *Tepoztlán* would exercise a powerful influence within the discipline of anthropology. When Redfield commenced work in the village of Tepoztlán, he was one of the first anthropologists to study a "semicivilized" rather than a nonliterate village. At the same time as Redfield was moving in this direction, though, several other anthropologists in both the United States and Britain were becoming interested in similar studies. Interest in such studies stemmed from a variety of sources, such as growing concerns over colonial peoples and immigration as well as the simple fact that anthropologists were running out of so-called primitive tribes to study. A common thread linked together these new studies of complex societies: the concern with the dynamics of social and cultural change, specifically the change that ensued from the impact of the urbanized, industrialized West upon less developed cultures. During the early 1930s, anthropologists began to use the term "acculturation" to refer to the process by which cultures interacted and modified each other, with one culture, especially, exerting a disproportionate influence upon the other. Redfield's *Tepoztlán* represented one of the first acculturation studies, and with its publication he emerged as one of the leaders of this new movement within anthropology.[16]

Tepoztlán proved particularly influential, moreover, in helping to establish the community study as the primary method used in analysis of acculturation. The community study differs from the typical round-of-life study that anthropologists were used to conducting when analyzing an isolated, nonliterate village. In a conventional ethnographic study, the village can be portrayed as an entity unto itself. Yet in a community study, the investigator needs to view the village or town as an integral component of a larger social and cultural system. Most important, the community study investigator must not only describe the social and cultural system of the individual village, but also the network of connections, communications, and interactions that integrate the village into the larger sociocultural system. Viewed in such a way, the village or town represents a sample or microcosm of the larger system. Study of a community is thus seen as providing information not merely on the individual town or village but on the entire sociocultural system. Redfield attempted to depict Tepoztlán as a village suspended within a wider sociocultural web through his description of the intricate communication system that linked the village to the nearby cities of Cuernavaca and Mexico City, a network formed largely through the social and commercial activities of *los correctos*. Following publication of *Tepoztlán*, moreover, Redfield continued to base his field research on community studies, and over the course of his career he became one of the most articulate expositors and defenders of this methodology.[17]

Despite the success *Tepoztlán* achieved in helping to establish and define the analysis of acculturation and the methodology of community studies, Redfield's text failed to achieve some of its more ambitious theoretical goals. Redfield's attempt to introduce into anthropological practice the notion of social organization, which he had derived from Chicago sociology, and his effort to use Robert Park's "marginal man" concept as an analytical device through which to explore social change both failed to deliver meaningful results. Redfield proposed that the "influence of the city" had thrown Tepoztlán into a state of "disorganization and perhaps . . . reorganization," and he attempted to use these notions of social process to add interpretative depth to the diffusionist ideas he had borrowed from Clark Wissler.[18] But Redfield provided no standards by which to evaluate the dynamics and direction of these processes. Furthermore, his notion that *los correctos* represented the "marginal men" of the village failed to offer any analytical leverage; instead, the marginal man idea operated purely on the descriptive metaphorical level and added little more to the discussion of change than offered by older concepts, such as Simmel's notion of the stranger. Nevertheless, while *Tepoztlán* did not fulfill the grand theoretical agenda that Redfield had advanced in his provocative introduction, his book delivered on much that it promised. Redfield's success in influencing with his first book the general direction of anthropology as well as helping to define a promising new methodology proved sufficient, moreover, to garner Redfield wide recognition among social scientists and to mark him as an anthropologist headed for success.

Culture and Civilization in Yucatan

In the fall of 1928, but a few weeks after he had defended his dissertation, the University of Chicago hired Redfield as an assistant professor of anthropology. Redfield planned to return soon to Tepoztlán to continue his research, but he was preoccupied by his teaching duties and he had no immediate source of funds to support his field studies. In late 1929, however, Redfield received an invitation from the Carnegie Institution of Washington to conduct an ethnological survey of the Yucatan peninsula. This invitation proved to be an extraordinary boon to Redfield as he was able to secure ample funding for his research for the next fifteen years.[19]

While the CIW devoted itself largely to the support of research in the natural sciences, it also supported archaeological research. The principal archaeological program was devoted to the exploration of ancient Maya civilization in Yucatan. This program had been initiated in 1914 with the cooperation of the Mexican government, and for the first ten years of existence had been devoted to little more than restoration of ancient Maya ruins. The leadership of the CIW changed in 1924, however, and under its new president, John C. Merriam, the CIW elected to expand its Yucatan work beyond mere excavation. Merriam hired Harvard archaeologist Alfred V. Kidder to transform the Institution's Yucatan effort into a wide-ranging, interdisciplinary research project. Kidder, who went on to direct the project for the next twenty-one years, moved quickly to broaden the project to complement ongoing archaeological work with historical, biological, sociological, ethnological, and linguistic research. Kidder chose Redfield, whom he viewed as an up-and-coming authority in Mexican ethnology, to conduct the sociological and ethnological research.[20]

Kidder expected Redfield to conduct a standard ethnographic survey of contemporary Yucatan; in particular, he wanted Redfield to prepare a catalog of indigenous versus Spanish elements in contemporary Yucatecan culture. Redfield had much larger designs, however, for his Yucatan studies; he intended to continue the study of social change processes that he had started in Tepoztlán. Although Kidder initially resisted Redfield's efforts to conduct his studies along such sociological lines, he eventually agreed to Redfield's directions and largely provided him a free hand to conduct the Yucatan work according to his own intentions.

Redfield announced the basic scheme for his study in a survey proposal he prepared at the request of the CIW during the winter of 1930. Redfield began his proposal stating that his plan was "designed to result in a well-rounded description of contemporary society in the Yucatan peninsula." Just as in Tepoztlán, though, he stated that the central aim of his work would be to study social change "as it happens." Yucatan, he observed, offered an ideal setting in which to study such a process. Within a very small geographic region, there existed a wide range of cultural types extending from the "primitive tribesman to the *Méridano* educated in Paris or New York." Yucatecan society was undergoing rapid social change, moreover, as "modern industrial civilization" impinged upon the "primitive or largely primitive" inhabitants of the peninsula. Redfield proposed that he could best study the "process of change from folk society to urban society" by conducting a series of comparative community studies in Yucatan. The sample communities for this investigation needed to be selected, he continued, "so as to represent different aspects of this change." In short, these communities needed to represent the full range of sociocultural "sophistication" or "modernization" found on the Yucatan peninsula. Redfield cautioned, however, that these communities could only be studied by taking into account the larger society in which they were situated. "The student living in a [Yucatecan] village and describing its culture," he observed, "will soon find that the answer to many of his problems lie outside of that community, in the contemporary social, economic, and political organization of the State."[21]

When he submitted his proposal for an ethnographic survey of Yucatan in March of 1930, Redfield only had a preliminary conception of which communities to include in his study. He had identified four types of communities that "represent[ed] the points of the scale of modernization and two intermediate points": (1) the city; (2) the "mestizo" community, in which "European ways have largely displaced Indian custom"; (3) the Indian village, in which "Indian customs largely prevail over European ways"; and (4), the tribal community, in which "Indian customs and local institutions overwhelmingly predominate." In selecting actual locations for study, the choice for a city study was obvious; only one city, Mérida, existed in Yucatan. Selection of the other sites required more effort. In his 1930 proposal, Redfield identified only one additional site for study, the Indian village of Chan Kom. He did not select a mestizo town or tribal village for study until well into the third year of his investigation.[22]

Redfield chose to study Chan Kom for two reasons. First, it was close to Chichén Itzá, the great Maya pyramid; this was the site of the CIW's most concentrated excavation effort and served as a central base of operations for CIW personnel in Yucatan. Second, the village schoolteacher in Chan Kom, Alphonso Villa Rojas, indicated a great willingness to assist with anthropological work. Redfield enlisted his help immediately and placed him upon the CIW payroll to help in study of the village. Villa Rojas proved to be an adept student and learned rapidly as he and Redfield collaborated during the early 1930s in their study of Chan Kom. Villa Rojas then complemented his field training with formal study at the University of Chicago during the mid-1930s and went on to be recognized as one of Mexico's leading ethnographers.[23]

Redfield spent the first few years of his Yucatan study performing ethnographic surveys of the village of Chan Kom and the city of Mérida. He was assisted in these studies by his wife Greta, Villa Rojas, and an ethnographically inclined sociologist, Asael Hansen, who had taken his doctorate under Ralph Linton at Wisconsin and had come to work for Redfield immediately upon graduation. The CIW paid half of Redfield's salary at Chicago and thus provided him the means to spend extended periods in the field.[24] In 1930 he was only able to stay in Yucatan from January through March, but he was able to return with Greta in January 1931 for a five-month stay and again for the first six months of 1933. During these years, Redfield and Villa Rojas wrote the first community study to come out of the project, *Chan Kom: A Maya Village* (1934). This was a much more comprehensive round-of-life ethnography than what Redfield had produced on Tepoztlán, and the anthropological community received it with strongly positive reviews.[25] With the assistance of Greta and Asael Hansen, Redfield also completed during this period most of the field study of Mérida. Finally, in 1933 he selected and began studying the third town in his series of comparative community studies, a mestizo town called Dzitas.

After he completed the first draft of his *Chan Kom* manuscript, Redfield's project entered a second phase. During the first few years of his study, Redfield had devoted his time primarily to data collection and had paid little attention to developing a theoretical explanation of the cultural change occurring in contemporary Yucatan. In his 1930 proposal, he had informally suggested that Yucatecan society was undergoing a "process of re-organization" as a result of its contact with "modern industrial civilization." Here he was referring to the notion of social disorganization that lay at the heart of social change theory as developed by the Chicago sociologists, especially, W. I. Thomas, Robert E. Park, and Ernest Burgess. But Redfield did not expand upon this idea and discuss how the process of disorganization and reorganization was set in motion or how he intended to analyze it in his field studies. In short, while Redfield claimed that the results of his comparative community studies would have a "dynamic character" that would "sketch out . . . the process of becoming civilized," his study operated during its first few years almost exclusively on the descriptive level.[26]

Yet beginning in 1932, Redfield had begun to struggle with the need to develop a more sophisticated theoretical basis for his study. Robert E. Park played a crucial role in helping Redfield to reorient his empirical studies of Yucatan along more theoretical lines. In early 1932, Redfield had sent Park a copy of his annual CIW status report in which he had published for the first time the nature and scope of his Yucatan work.[27] Park, having read the report with "very great interest," responded by suggesting to Redfield a way that he might refine his thinking about the general process of social change in Yucatan:

> In order to make knowledge in this field more precise and in order to make studies in this field more systematic it seems to me important to define our working concepts, i.e. the tribe and the state, with logical precision. Thus conceived, whatever the tribe and the state are now or have been, historically, they become ideal concepts, to which perhaps nothing real actually conforms, but to which every type of society tends to conform. Such a procedure will probably be abhorrent to most social anthropologists but I believe it will be useful to any one who wants to think clearly in this field. Furthermore I conceive these terms not as doctrines but as working hypotheses and as such they might be accepted with a certain amount of tolerance even by the historical schools of anthropology and sociology.
>
> To you and others who are seeking to study and make intelligible the processes by which a society makes a transition from one fundamental type of social organization to another they seem to me almost indispensable.

Park concluded by urging Redfield to use his Yucatan research to enrich his introductory ethnology course. Specifically, Park suggested that Redfield expand his course so that it treated human societies ranging in complexity from small tribal groups to modern "political society." Redfield used both of Park's suggestions. Park's idea of using polar ideal types to explore change in Yucatan became not only the theoretical basis for the Yucatan study, but also for Redfield's much-discussed notion of the folk-urban continuum. Furthermore, Park's idea of teaching a class on the transition from folk to urban society provided the impetus for Redfield to develop his course "The Folk Society," which became Redfield's most popular course at Chicago.[28]

Redfield first announced the new directions for his Yucatan work in his 1932 annual CIW status report.[29] But he offered a much more comprehensive discussion of his experimental design and theoretical framework in his 1934 *American Anthropologist* article, "Culture Changes in Yucatan." Here he first defined the rationale that linked together his comparative community studies. The overall goal of his project, he stated, was to examine the processes that transpired in Yucatecan villages and towns "under the influences of increasing mobility and communications." Ideally, he commented, a study of this process would be conducted through observation of a single village over an extended period of time. Because transformation of a village into a town or city requires decades or centuries, this experiment realistically defied completion. Redfield attempted to get around this time limitation, however, by manipulating experimental variables to simulate the effect of passing time. He had made the simple observation that as one traveled southward out of Mérida toward the rain forest, each town or village appeared progressively more primitive. Traveling from the modern city of Mérida down to the primitive tribal villages of Quintana Roo produced the effect, therefore, of passing through discrete cultural zones, of traveling backwards into time. By allowing space, or distance from Mérida, to substitute for the passage of time, Redfield attempted to devise an experimental scheme that would allow him to create the illusion that he was actually observing the transformation of a single village into a town and then city. His comparative community studies would represent, in short, a series of still sociological photographs that when taken together could be seen as offering a dynamic depiction of the intermediate stages in the process of a single transformation.[30]

The logic for Redfield's notion that space could substitute for time rested upon the peculiar geography of Yucatan. Although Yucatan is a peninsula, in the 1930s it existed as a virtual island. Surrounded on all sides by either sea or dense rain forests, Yucatan could only be entered through a single point, the port city of Mérida. Since Mérida was not only the sole city in Yucatan, but also served as the sole connection point for Yucatan with the rest of the world, Redfield reasoned that Mérida represented the primary source of modernizing influences for the entire peninsula. With modernizing influences radiating from only a single source, distance from that source thus became, Redfield proposed, the critical variable controlling sociocultural change in a town or village.

Redfield also offered in "Culture Changes in Yucatan" a theoretical framework in which to interpret the sociocultural transformation taking place in Yucatan. He proposed that the comparison of his sample communities could be expressed "in terms of a process of transition . . . from one type of society, which the most isolated village represent[ed] towards another type illustrated by the Yucatecan capital city but even better by our mobile northern cities." Five distinct developments, he argued, characterized this general transition: (1) moving from town to village, one found the communities "increasingly mobile and heterogeneous; (2) the division of labor within the towns became more complex; (3) a gradual breakdown of familial organization occurred; (4) religious belief and ritual diminished in importance; (5) a change took place "in the ideas as to the causes of diseases." Sickness in the village is "proof of a lapse from piety," but in the town, "sickness . . . becomes secularized."

Redfield concluded his article by defining the two poles of his dichotomy. The ideal type of society "approached in the village," he proposed, was relatively immobile, local, personal, sacred in nature, and governed largely through familial controls and morally enforced customs. Most important, this was a "culturally homogeneous" society, in which "the ways of life form[ed] a single web of interrelated meanings." As one moved from the village toward the town and then city, Redfield suggested, one approached an opposite type of society. This society was "much more mobile and culturally heterogeneous." Relationships here were "increasingly impersonal" and family organization was weakened; life here was secularized, and the actions of individuals were governed by "constraint or convenience rather than deep moral convictions." Finally, in this society, "the ways of life [were] less closely interrelated; group-habits exist more in terms each of itself and do not to the same degree evoke a body of closely associated and definatory acts and meanings." Redfield referred to the first type of society as "Culture" and the second as "Civilization." He suggested, further-more, that the transformation in Yucatan represented not a process of accultura-tion but rather of "deculturation." He acknowledged, however, that "as there are objections to denying the term 'culture' to the life-ways of the city man, it may be more acceptable to describe this study as that of the change from folk culture to city culture."[31]

The publication of "Culture Changes in Yucatan" marked a high point in the Yucatan project. Redfield exuded great confidence here as he asserted that his methodology would lead to "scientific generalizations" about social and cul-tural change. Redfield maintained this confidence for the next two years, more-over, and in early 1936, he began to work on a manuscript to sum up the entire project. Calling his proposed book *Culture and Civilization in Yucatan*, Redfield wrote a forty-page prospectus in which he provided narrative descriptions of each chapter. He described in these chapters the progressive secularization, loss of cultural unity, growth of a money economy, and rise of individualism as one moved in Yucatan from "folk culture" toward "city culture." All the data seemed to fit his model, and by the mid-1930s, Redfield appeared to be well on his way to completing the Yucatan project.[32]

Yet at the same time Redfield published "Culture Changes in Yucatan" and began working to bring his Yucatan project to completion, doubts began to set in among his own research team as to the generality of the Yucatan data. Specifi-cally, Redfield's junior colleague, Sol Tax, began to discover that the patterns of cultural dynamics Redfield was reporting for the Maya of Yucatan did not seem to hold for the Maya living but a few hundred miles to the south in Guatemala. A. V. Kidder had encouraged Redfield to expand his ethnological investigation of the Maya in Yucatan to include the Maya in Guatemala. In the fall of 1934, Redfield hired Sol Tax, who had just completed his doctoral work at Chicago under Radcliffe-Brown, to undertake the anthropological survey of the Maya in Guatemala. After working in the Guatemalan town Chichicastenango for only five months, though, Tax wrote Redfield and told him that his findings differed markedly from what Redfield had reported for Yucatan. Most important, the culture of the Maya Indians in the Guatemalan highlands did not seem to be as "integrated" as that of the Maya in Chan Kom. In Chichicastenango, Tax ob-served, "there seem to be as many conflicts as in Chicago; the culture is not that simple little one we like to think a Folk has—in fact, I should be willing to gam-ble right now that it has all the complexities of a rural community of ten thou-sand in Illinois." Despite the "primitive" nature of culture in Chichicastenango, Tax expressed doubts that the notion of "Folk culture" could be applied to Gua-temalan culture.[33]

Redfield responded with great interest to Tax's comments about folk culture in Guatemala. Redfield was working in Chan Kom when he received Tax's let-ter, and he wrote immediately telling him that he would soon visit Guatemala and that he was "look[ing] forward . . . to talking about 'folk.'" Redfield cautioned Tax, however, not to equate the notion of folk culture with simplicity or a necessarily peaceful existence:

> I am not sure what you mean by "complexity." Complexity, in the sense of "a great number of parts and interrelated beliefs and institutions," is of course consistent with folkness. In this sense Zuni is a very complex culture. Also I am interested in learning what kinds of conflicts are characteristic of Chichicaste-nango and the cantones. Certain kinds of conflicts—interpersonal rivalries, suspicions, etc. (Dobu, NW Coast), are certainly characteristic of many folk cultures.[34]

Yet Tax's initial perceptions about cultural differences between the Maya in Guatemala and Yucatan proved to be borne out by subsequent research. Over the next two years, Tax conducted an extensive field survey of several Maya *municipios* in the Guatemalan highlands. He determined that Maya culture in Guatemala was not sacred in character but was, in fact, decidedly secular; familial bonds were weak, moreover, and relationships quite impersonal. While Guatemalan Maya villages demonstrated many of the qualities Redfield had associated with "folkness," such as cultural homogeneity, strong sense of in-group identity, and highly conventionalized behavior, these villages did not display many other traits that Redfield had identified as characteristic of folk culture. Tax's findings thus did not accord well with Redfield's data on culture in Yucatan.

Redfield also initiated work in Guatemala in April 1937, and he and Tax worked together closely for the next two years trying to come to terms with the unique cultural situation in Guatemala.[35] Redfield was loathe to abandon his culture-to-civilization notion, though, and he and Tax argued at length over how the observed differences in Guatemala could be made to fit within Redfield's theoretical framework. Redfield and Tax carried their dispute far beyond themselves, moreover, by presenting in the fall of 1937 the results of their Guatemalan work to their Chicago colleagues in the Seminar on Race and Cultural Contacts. This was an interdisciplinary graduate student and faculty seminar that drew members from both sociology and anthropology. Redfield had joined with Robert E. Park, Louis Wirth, and Herbert Blumer in initiating this seminar at Chicago in 1934. This seminar met weekly throughout the academic year from 1934 to 1949 to discuss ongoing research concerning cultural and racial contact, and it proved to be a nexus of interdisciplinary exchange at Chicago.[36] During the fall of 1937, the seminar participants—including Ernest Manheim (leader), Horace Cayton, Fred Eggan, Herbert Goldhamer, Donald Pierson, Robert Redfield, Edward Spicer, Leo Srole, Sol Tax, and Louis Wirth—spent several weeks discussing Redfield's and Tax's work. Wirth and Goldhamer, especially, pushed Redfield to clarify and sharpen the theoretical scheme he had advanced to explain the trend of social change among the Maya in Yucatan and Guatemala.[37]

Redfield found it difficult, however, to refashion his interpretation to accommodate the data from both Yucatan and Guatemala. One of the primary axes of transition in Redfield's model of the folk to urban transition was sacred to secular. But while the folk culture in Yucatan could be described as sacred, the folk culture in Guatemala could only be described as secular. In an unpublished manuscript that he wrote in the summer of 1938, "The Sacred and the Secular in Yucatan and Guatemala," Redfield attempted to explain the secular nature of folk society in Guatemala. He proposed that the local cultures of the Guatemalan Maya had once had a sacred character but that this sacred order had been progressively modified by the political structure and trade patterns that had emerged in the Guatemalan highlands. He asserted that secularization could arise, moreover, from more than a single cause. The nature of Redfield's argument indicates, however, that he was struggling to explain the disjuncture between the Guatemalan and Yucatan data. His argument is labored and overly abstract; indeed, it borders upon being almost too clever.[38]

During the summer of 1938, moreover, Redfield acknowledged that his theoretical scheme had run into difficulties. Tax and Redfield exchanged a series of written arguments over the "Sacred and Secular" manuscript, and Redfield acknowledged that he needed to modify some aspects of his social change model. In particular, he stated the need to clarify the terminology he had used in his description of ideal societal types. Redfield had proposed in 1934 that the grand process of social change involved a shift from "culture" to "civilization." Yet in writing to Tax in 1938, he stated "this terminology seems confusing and undesirable." The word "culture" seemed especially inappropriate and Redfield proposed changing it to the "ideal type of folk society." These exchanges between Redfield and Tax suggest that by mid- to late 1938, Redfield had come to regard his earlier conception of the Yucatan work as too ambitious and was working to construct a new way to frame his project.[39]

Redfield spent the next two years writing his summary volume on the Yucatan study. Instead of calling it *Culture and Civilization in Yucatan*, as he had originally intended, he changed its title to the more cautious *The Folk Culture of Yucatan*. Redfield focused in this book almost solely on sociocultural change in Yucatan. Using a series of comparative indicators—family structure and cohesion, medical practice and attitudes toward illness, division of labor, and forms of religious observance—he explored how social and cultural customs and patterns changed as one moved from Tusik, the tribal village located in the rain forest of Quintana Roo, to the peasant village of Chan Kom, to the railroad nexus of Dzitas, to the capital city of Mérida.

Over the course of eleven chapters, Redfield depicted the rise of complexity that accompanied this progression toward the city. The logic of his analysis of this rise in complexity depended upon his analysis of culture. He offered here a more rigorous definition of culture than was then used by most other anthropologists, a definition that strongly emphasized the symbolic nature of culture.[40]

Culture, he proposed, was "an organization of conventional understandings manifest in act and artifact" that characterizes a human group.[41] Redfield was most interested in exploring the transformation involved when a single unified "organization of conventional understandings" that characterized life in the ideal type of folk society gave way to a plural world of overlapping subcultures. In the most eloquent chapter of the book, "The Villager's View of Life," Redfield presented a description of the nature of this "organization of conventional understandings," this single "web" of meanings—or culture—that bound together the folk village. In such a village:

> Men and women go about as they do elsewhere, attending to immediate concerns. They solve the present difficulty. They do the day's work; they plan to sow or to harvest; they laugh at something that amuses them, or they worry over illness or misfortune. Yet the scheme of ideas is there, nevertheless. It is forever implicit in their conduct. It provides the goals of their action. It gives a reason, a moral worth, to the choices they make. It says: "Yes, this is right" and "This is why." With such a charter they may be unhappy because unfortunate, but they cannot feel themselves lost.[42]

In short, meaning in the ideal folk society was a *given*. Modernity connoted for Redfield the moment of transition from the community in which meaning was given to the community in which the "web" of meaning began to lose its organizational totality, in which meaning had to be constructed rather than simply being given.

Redfield invested much effort in trying to determine the mechanism or process that occurred when the culture of the village came in contact with the influence of the city. By charting the change in indicator variables from the tribal village to the city, he concluded that the loss of isolation and the increase in heterogeneity caused by increasing proximity to the city resulted in a rise in disorganization, secularization, and individualization. Culture, the single unified web of meaning, thus declined with increasing urbanization and was replaced by a collection of less organized, coexisting subcultures.

Redfield devoted almost the entire length of *The Folk Culture of Yucatan* to describing social transformation within the Yucatan peninsula. As he discussed the materials derived form the various Yucatecan communities, his discussion reflected confidence. He drew upon a copious body of data—produced by almost a decade of fieldwork by a team of investigators—and his data seemed to fit together neatly. But when he moved into his final chapter, the tone of his writing changed. Here he introduced Tax's Guatemalan data and ventured to discuss the process of civilization in general terms. For the Guatemalan data, he offered the same explanation he had developed in his earlier "Sacred and Secular" manuscript. He proposed that the transition from sacred to secular society need not necessarily stem from the same cause—loss of isolation and introduction of heterogeneity—as in Yucatan. It could also arise, he suggested, through alternative mechanisms, such as the introduction of a money economy, as seemed to have occurred in Guatemala. Yet in this final chapter, Redfield's prose lost its fluidity; it became somewhat awkward and labored. Rather than supporting or complementing the argument drawn from the Yucatan materials, the Guatemalan data seemed to be contradictory. The more Redfield labored to account for this divergent data, the weaker his overall argument seemed. *The Folk Culture of Yucatan* thus ended on a somewhat equivocal note. Redfield had provided an impressive array of data to support a general theory of change in Yucatan. But he had not convincingly demonstrated that this pattern of change was empirically verifiable beyond Yucatan, nor if it was even verifiable for all villages and towns within Yucatan.[43]

Redfield's *Folk Culture of Yucatan* appeared in print in the summer of 1941. Like *Tepoztlán*, it was reviewed by both the popular and scholarly press. Unlike *Tepoztlán*, though, *Folk Culture* did not meet with overwhelming reception. Of the popular press, the *New York Times Book Review* and New York *Herald Tribune* paid most attention to it. Yet the *New York Times Book Review* focused solely on how well the book depicted contemporary life in Yucatan and virtually ignored Redfield's larger theoretical agenda. The New York *Herald Tribune* offered a more judicious assessment, but observed critically that while Redfield promised to explore the processes of civilization in general, his data and conclusions seemed largely limited to sociocultural processes within Yucatan. The little magazines, moreover, which had devoted much attention to *Tepoztlán*, paid little heed to *Folk Culture*. Only the *Nation* mentioned it, and their reviewer spoke solely of how well Redfield had charted the long-term effects of the Mexican Revolution within Yucatan.[44]

Scholarly reviewers read *The Folk Culture of Yucatan* with a greater sense of appreciation. Nevertheless, the academic community offered Redfield's work a mixed reception. Sociologists responded, in general, much more positively than anthropologists. In the *American Journal of Sociology*, Charles S. Johnson praised the book as "one of the most significant contributions yet made by social anthropology." Redfield's success at reducing into general principles a wealth of ethnographic data about Yucatecan society produced, Johnson observed, a volume "exceedingly rich in suggestions and in its contribution generally to the understanding of the cultural process in modern as well as primitive or preliterate societies." Harry Alpert, writing in the *American Sociological Review*, echoed Johnson's assessment. Alpert especially praised Redfield's success at infusing empirical ethnographic work with theory. Reflecting a view of anthropologists then commonly held by sociologists, Alpert observed that Redfield's volume undermined the "widespread stereotype" that "ethnographic field workers are incapable of conceptual organization of their field materials." Alpert also noted that while Redfield's Yucatan evidence served simply to confirm and reinforce "propositions of long standing in sociological theory," his "original contribution [lay] in the recognition of sub-types and compromise or combination types which serve to correct some of the overstatements and exaggerations inhering in the traditional dichotomous schemes." Despite the generally positive reception that Johnson and Alpert provided, both criticized Redfield for his failure to take psychological considerations into account in his assessment of the phenomena and experience of the social change process. Overall, though, sociologists who reviewed *The Folk Culture of Yucatan* rendered extremely positive judgments.[45]

Most anthropologists, on the other hand, greeted the book with substantially less enthusiasm.[46] In his review for the *Journal of American Folklore*, Julian Steward sharply criticized Redfield for the ahistorical approach he took to comparative study. Steward argued that Redfield's sociological approach ignored important local differences among various towns in Yucatan and produced an oversimplified picture of cultural dynamics on the peninsula. He questioned, moreover, the logic of assuming that distance from Mérida was the sole variable affecting cultural development in Yucatecan towns and villages. Did it not matter, he asked, if a town was in the henequen or chicle zone? And did not the unique experience of a town during the Mexican Revolution affect future change in that town? Steward also questioned Redfield's attempt to draw generalizations from his Yucatan evidence about social and cultural processes in other societies. He argued that the reach of such generalizations was limited by flaws in Redfield's assumptions. Most important, he challenged Redfield's assumption that the sacred society of Tusik represented a model "primitive" society. "We know," he argued, "that all primitive societies were not like Tusik. Most marginal tribes—e.g. Shoshoneans, Bushmen, Fuegians, Athapascans—were individualized, comparatively secularized, and organized differently in kind and degree from Yucatan." He suggested, furthermore, that Redfield's conclusions about the correlation of disorganization, secularization, and individualization may be peculiar to European urbanization, which Mérida represented, and not urbanization everywhere.[47]

George Peter Murdock, in his *American Anthropologist* review, rendered an even harsher judgment of *The Folk Culture of Yucatan* than did Julian Steward. Murdock praised Redfield's mastery and presentation of the ethnography of Yucatan, but he suggested that Redfield's book should not be judged on such criteria. It was clearly a theoretical work, and it was on this basis that it should be judged. As a work of anthropological theory, though, Murdock found *The Folk Culture of Yucatan* to be a grave disappointment. "The two most powerful movements in twentieth century anthropological theory," he proposed, "are the historical and functional," two approaches that were once distinct but by the early 1940s had come to be "widely recognized as complementary." These two theoretical traditions, Murdock observed, had resulted in contemporary acculturation studies, "which have clarified the universal processes of culture change" and by "culture and personality" investigations that had made evident the relevance of psychology to anthropology. In evaluating Redfield's text, therefore,

Murdock sought to situate it against what he perceived as the mainstream of anthropological theory. He found, though, that Redfield's work fit into none of the major theoretical movements within anthropology. It could not be viewed as historical, functional, or psychological. Indeed, Murdock observed, Redfield seemed to stand "aloof from the problems that engage most of his contemporaries." Given such disengagement, Murdock asked, "is [Redfield], then, to be regarded as the prophet of a new movement in anthropological theory or as the defender of an approach which his colleagues have discarded? The reviewer, in all humility, inclines toward the latter interpretation."

Murdock further dismissed Redfield by suggesting that he was a nineteenth-century evolutionist, a charge in 1940s anthropology tantamount to heresy. "Like the evolutionists," Murdock claimed, Redfield "tends to conceive of cultural change, not in terms of a dynamics of process, but as an apparently inevitable transition from one conceptual pole to its opposite." Murdock concluded his review by predicting "*The Folk Culture of Yucatan* will ultimately be remembered rather for its ethnographical synthesis and its interpretation of Yucatecan folk life than for its broader theoretical generalizations."[48]

Folk Society and the Folk-Urban Continuum

By most measures, *The Folk Culture of Yucatan* met with a poor reception upon its publication in 1941. Yet over the course of the forties, Redfield's text found slow but progressive acceptance, especially among younger social scientists. Furthermore, Redfield succeeded in introducing the central ideas from this text into the mainstream of anthropological and sociological discourse through two alternative channels: (1) his teaching and direction of research at Chicago and (2) a single highly influential article he published in the *American Journal of Sociology* in 1947.

In 1932 at the urging of Park, Redfield began to develop his "Folk Society" course while pursuing his research in Yucatan. This course became a conceptual workshop for Redfield, and he used it to explore the empirical findings and theoretical implications of his Yucatan work. Redfield used this class, in particular, as a forum in which to develop his ideal-type concept of folk society, which served as the foundational idea for his Yucatan project.

In constructing his ideal-type concept of folk society, Redfield drew upon the work of the major nineteenth-century theorists who had first proposed use of abstract typologies for conceptualization of so-called primitive and civilized societies. These theorists included Henry Sumner Maine, Lewis Henry Morgan, Émile Durkheim, and Ferdinand Tönnies. Redfield's goal was to construct an ideal-type definition of "primitive" society that incorporated the principal attributes each of these theorists had proposed as characteristic of such societies. Rather than merely formulating a composite definition, though, Redfield set himself the task of trying to determine the functional relationships that existed among these attributes. In short, Redfield was trying to push his typology beyond the descriptive level. By trying to determine which characteristics were correlated with one another, he was attempting to understand the causal connection among variables. He wanted to know, for example, if the overall characteristics of folk society depended more upon one variable than another. Furthermore, he wanted to understand if the individual characteristics associated with folk society displayed covariance or, in other words, changed in response to each other. In doing so Redfield was attempting to advance a conceptualization of folk society that was not simply a listing of attributes but constituted instead of a hypothesis about the nature and interaction of variables associated with tribal and peasant societies conceived in the abstract.

Most important, Redfield wanted to incorporate the anthropological concept of culture into his typology of folk society. For the first few decades of the twentieth century, anthropologists had regarded culture primarily as an inventory of traits. Culture was seen as the sum of a people's beliefs, customs, activities, and art, and different cultures were distinguished from one another largely by comparing and contrasting elements that made up each culture. During the mid-1920s, however, several British and American anthropologists, including Malinowski, Radcliffe-Brown, Benedict, and Linton, began to criticize this trait-list conception of culture. In general, these anthropologists argued that the most important aspect of culture was not the *content*—or inventory of cultural elements—but rather the *organization* of those elements.[49]

Redfield grounded his definition of the folk society upon the critique of the inventory conception of culture. Indeed, the folk society model served as a way for Redfield to extend this critique and to contribute to the vigorous discourse that emerged in the late 1930s over the conceptualization of culture. He depicted folk society as a form of social existence that represented the ultimate expression of systematization and conventionalized behavior and belief. The folk society, he proposed, was small, isolated, nonliterate, and homogeneous. Such a society had a strong sense of collective identity and group solidarity. Kinship formed the primary bond among group members, and the family rather than the individual was the unit of action. Behavior was traditional and uncritical. Most important, the folk society was bound together through a system of shared meanings or conventional understandings. Acts and objects carried virtually the same connotations for all members of the folk society. This body of conventional understandings—this shared construction of meaning—thus formed a describable whole, a single and consistent "design for living."[50]

Redfield aimed to provide through his folk society construct a distinctly tangible representation of culture. Although folk society was clearly an abstraction—no actual society conformed in all respects to Redfield's definition of the folk society—it had greater specificity and was more apprehensible than conventional definitions of culture. Redfield was striving, in short, to describe what culture looked like on the ground.

The folk society, in Redfield's conception, represented the polar opposite of urban society. Whereas he characterized folk society as isolated, homogeneous, and sacred, he described urban society as mobile, heterogeneous, and secular. In his 1934 article "Culture Changes in Yucatan" and more fully in *The Folk Culture of Yucatan*, Redfield proposed that ideal constructions of folk and urban society would provide a conceptual terminology useful for considering the process of social change or "civilization." All real towns, villages, and cities, he proposed, could be seen as lying on a continuum from predominantly folk to predominantly urban, a distribution he referred to as the "folk-urban continuum." Although Redfield advanced the full conception of his folk-urban notion in *The Folk Culture of Yucatan*, most who came to use his idea did not encounter it through this work. *Folk Culture* is a rather difficult abstract text, and it never found a wide audience. But Redfield presented a summary of his folk-urban idea in a 1947 *American Journal of Sociology* article called "The Folk Society," and it was this article that introduced Redfield's ideas to a wide audience of students and professional social scientists during the 1940s through the 1960s.[51]

Commentators have frequently noted that Redfield invested little effort in formulating a definition of urban society. He devoted much attention to describing folk society, but he defined urban society as merely the opposite of folk society. This claim is true. Yet to consider it as a shortcoming is to miss one of the most important reasons that Redfield attempted to construct such a typology. He intentionally defined folk and urban societies in terms that could be inverted, because he wanted to maintain congruency between his two polar types. Thus, he defined the characteristics of folk and urban societies so that they could be conceived as variables, as qualities that varied along a linear "more or less" scale.

Redfield expected use of the folk-urban construct to facilitate a more profound understanding of the nature of urban society and, more important, of the nature of modernity. Nowhere was this more apparent than in Redfield's Folk Society class. Here he presented the folk society notion as a defamiliarizing device to stimulate students to recognize and come to terms with the unique character of modern urban society. Redfield designed his course so that students spent time considering the nature of folk society as both an abstract idealized definition of tribal and peasant society and also as approximated by several actual societies. Yet students spent an equal amount of time considering the nature of modern society and exploring the "institutional developments" that "brought about the transition to civilization." Much of the reading Redfield assigned on modern urban society derived from conventional social science sources. However, Redfield also assigned numerous readings that would have been more typical of a humanities course, including Walter Lippmann's *A Preface to Morals*, T. S. Eliot's *The Waste Land*, John Dewey's *The Public and Its Problems*, and Sigmund Freud's *Civilization and Its Discontents*. Redfield first offered his Folk

Society course in the winter of 1935, and he continued to teach it until 1955. More than anything else he taught, it became his trademark course. It not only served as an arena for him to discuss and extend his theoretical notions about social process, but also it provided him a formal setting in which he could communicate his most central concerns to his students.[52]

Influence and Critique of Redfield's Folk-Urban Notion

During the mid-1930s, Redfield developed a devoted body of followers, especially among his Chicago students and colleagues. Several of his graduate students undertook studies of social change based upon his folk-urban notion. Two students in particular, Horace Miner and Edward Spicer, distinguished themselves through such studies. Miner studied social change within a small peasant village in Quebec. His *St. Denis: A French-Canadian Parish* (1939) closely resembled Redfield's *Tepoztlán*. And in *Pascua: A Yaqui Village in Arizona* (1940), Edward Spicer analyzed a community of Yaqui Indians who lived outside Tucson, Arizona. He devoted his attention especially to examining the changes in Yaqui society and culture that were set in motion by economic contacts Yaquis had with people in Tucson. Spicer's and Miner's studies also reflected the functionalist influence of Radcliffe-Brown. Nevertheless, in their discussions of social change, Miner and Spicer both depicted change as operating—in Redfieldian terms—along a folk-urban axis. *Pascua* and *St. Denis* were widely reviewed, and both have come to be regarded as minor classics in the literature of American anthropology.[53]

Redfield's colleague Everett Hughes also pursued work under Redfield's influence during the thirties. After graduating from Chicago in 1928, Hughes accepted a position at McGill University. He began to study French Canadians almost as soon as he arrived in Montreal. He spent the early thirties working with his McGill colleague Carl Dawson on problems and patterns of unemployment in Quebec. After a few years of working with Dawson, though, Hughes shifted his attention toward studying French-Canadian society with a focus on more theoretical sociological issues. Hughes believed Quebec offered similar opportunities as Yucatan for study of the processes of urbanization and industrialization, and during the mid-thirties he began to formulate a comprehensive plan to investigate such issues. He consulted frequently with Redfield about his ideas and projected a series of community studies in Quebec similar to what Redfield was then conducting in Yucatan.

Hughes recognized that the study Miner had initiated in 1936 of the rural traditional village of St. Denis de Kamouraska could be the baseline study in the series, and he assisted Redfield by serving as Miner's field adviser. Hughes then undertook study of a middle-sized community that he called Cantonville, a French-Canadian town undergoing rapid industrialization. Hughes was especially interested in exploring the effect that new industry had upon French-Canadian institutions. Hughes published the results of this study as *French Can-*

ada in Transition (1943). Here Hughes demonstrated that introduction of industry into a traditional village established a division of labor along distinct ethnic lines. Rank-and-file workers invariably were French; managers were English. An "industrial hierarchy" based upon ethnic distinction was thus imposed upon the village. Ethnic distinctions spread, furthermore, into other social institutions, such as schools and voluntary organizations. Hughes intended to complete his examination of industrialization and urbanization in Quebec with a study of Montreal, but in 1938 he received an offer to return to the University of Chicago, and he subsequently discontinued his Canadian studies.[54]

In the studies they conducted during the mid- to late thirties, Miner, Spicer, and Hughes worked closely within the model Redfield had established for studying social change. Most important, they used his notion of the folk-urban transformation as the central organizing idea for their studies. In 1938, following completion of his manuscript for *St. Denis*, though, Miner attempted to go beyond the conventional usage of Redfield's folk-urban notion by exploring its application in a non-Western setting. Miner wanted to see if the characteristics that Redfield and Wirth had identified with city life, specifically secularization, disorganization, and individualization, were characteristic of all cities or merely Western cities. Miner chose to study the West African city of Timbuktu, a city he determined to be virtually free of Western influence. The ancient city of Timbuktu, Miner noted, was not only free of Western cultural influence, it was also untouched by technological or industrial influence—it was, in short, a "primitive" city. Miner found that life in Timbuktu was "a surprising mixture of traditional folkways with secular and impersonal behavior of an urban sort." Most of the round of life in the city was sacred and folklike. Yet the economy showed a "non-folk level of specialization and [was] marked by conflict, dishonesty, and theft." Miner concluded his account by calling the inhabitants of Timbuktu, and other similar preindustrial cities, "city-folk." He did not accomplish the sweeping assessment of the Wirth-Redfield definition of urbanism that he had projected. Nevertheless, he did provide persuasive evidence that certain cultural and social phenomena Chicago theorists had associated with the urban milieu did indeed appear to be independent of Western civilization.[55]

Most of the research based directly upon the folk-urban notion emerged directly from Redfield's circle of students and colleagues at Chicago. Yet his folk-urban concept exercised an influence that far transcended its Chicago origins. This influence operated primarily on the heuristic level. Redfield's folk-urban continuum implied a theory of social change, but it was not expressed in terms sufficiently formal to constitute a model. It offered a description of change that could be easily explained, and it found its greatest usage as a pedagogical device. During the 1940s and 1950s, authors of numerous anthropological and sociological textbooks used the folk-urban construct as a means to explain urbanization. Many of these textbooks reprinted part or all of Redfield's "Folk Society" article, often pairing it with Wirth's "Urbanism as a Way of Life."

Redfield's notion of folk culture thus gained wide currency because it played an integral role in the Chicago construction of urbanism. Wirth expressed his conception of urbanism as a polar type that was best understood when viewed in contrast to its opposite ideal-type concept of folk society.[56]

Redfield's folk-urban notion influenced not only those who accepted its premises and worked within its general framework, but also many who rejected some or all of its assumptions. Indeed, the folk-urban continuum frequently served as a stimulus for research designed specifically to test or disprove its claims. The first and most dramatic challenge to Redfield's construct came during the early fifties from a young Columbia-trained anthropologist, Oscar Lewis. In the early 1940s, shortly after receiving his doctorate, Lewis had gone to Mexico to direct a study designed "to provide government agencies working in rural areas" of Latin American "with a better understanding of the psychology and needs of the people." This study was jointly sponsored by an American agency, the National Indian Institute, headed by John Collier, and a Mexican agency, the Inter-American Indian Institute, headed by Manuel Gamio. Collier and Gamio were pioneers in the development of applied anthropology, the use of anthropological study to alleviate contemporary social, political, and economic problems.

Lewis chose to conduct a restudy of the village of Tepoztlán. He assumed Redfield's study would provide a baseline from which he could measure change. He wanted to know especially if material conditions in the village had improved since 1926 when Redfield conducted his study. Lewis shared a similar scientific aim as Redfield. "The changes which had occurred in Tepoztlán," he argued, "were taking place over wide areas of Mexico and the world." Intensive study of a single village offered an opportunity, he proposed, "to get at some of the fundamental processes and principles of culture change." Lewis also intended his work to have value as applied anthropology, and he hoped his study would "be useful to administrators concerned the with task of carrying out welfare programs in the so-called backward areas of the world."

After working only briefly in Tepoztlán, Lewis found that Redfield's study would not suffice as a baseline survey against which he could measure cultural change. Redfield's *Tepoztlán* did not provide a comprehensive description of the social, economic, and political characteristics of the village. Moreover, Lewis found that many of the changes that had occurred from the late 1920s through the early 1940s stemmed from processes set in motion from 1910 to 1920, the years of the Mexican Revolution. Lewis thus found that understanding of contemporary problems in Tepoztlán could only be gained through in-depth historical study coupled with ethnographic and psychometric examination. Since one of Lewis's major goals was to produce a study that could be used to inform government officials of the needs of Indians living in undeveloped rural areas, Lewis focused on material needs of the people. In his interviews with villagers, Lewis asked specifically about problems faced in everyday life. The villagers complained at length about ill-health, agricultural shortages, and poor schools.

Lewis also surveyed the psychological status of the Tepoztecans. Assisted by his wife, Ruth Maslow Lewis, a psychologist, they administered Rorschach tests to 106 villagers to assess emotional and psychological outlook.

Lewis found Tepoztlán to be strikingly different from the way that Redfield had portrayed it. Whereas Redfield had seen Tepoztlán as a harmonious and contented village, Lewis discovered it to be riven with strife. Not only were villagers discontent because they were ill fed and disease ridden, but also they were filled with jealousy for and mistrust of their fellow villagers. Tepoztlán, in short, did not resemble the intimate folk society Redfield had described. Lewis published his view of the town in a comprehensive monograph, *Life in a Mexican Village: Tepoztlán Restudied* (1951). He devoted most of this book to a detailed exploration of contemporary conditions and problems in Tepoztlán. He concluded, however, by advancing a sharp critique of Redfield's study of Tepoztlán and his notion of the folk-urban continuum. Redfield erred in his study, Lewis charged, because he went to Tepoztlán with a preconceived notion of folk society. Believing Tepoztlán resembled his image of a folk society, Redfield thus glossed over elements of discord and focused solely on harmonious aspects of the village. Lewis proposed, furthermore, that Redfield placed undue emphasis on the city as the source of social change. Understanding change in a village, such as Tepoztlán, required a broader field of vision—one that operated on a grander scale in both space and time than that allowed by Redfield's urban focus. The gravest failing of Redfield's folk-urban notion lay, however, in its value connotations. "Underlying the folk-urban dichotomy," Lewis asserted, "is a system of value judgments which contains the old Rousseauan notion of primitive peoples as noble savages, and the corollary that with civilization has come the fall of man."[57]

Life in a Mexican Village constituted a major event in American anthropology. It was the first time in which an anthropologist attempted to reassess an ethnographic account of a certain people or village. Moreover, Lewis, but a young anthropologist only a few years out of graduate school, had launched an attack against one of the major figures in mid-century American anthropology. Lewis attempted to soften the blow of his critique by dedicating *Life in a Mexican Village* to Redfield; he also asked Redfield to write a promotional blurb for the book jacket. Redfield did not respond directly to the frontal attack Lewis had launched on his theoretical system, but he did use the blurb he wrote for Lewis's book as an opportunity to offer an underhanded response to Lewis's critique. "Dr. Lewis has written an account of a Mexican people that is rich in fact and in provocative ideas," he remarked. He commended Lewis for taking the "sketch of this same people" that he had written several years earlier and "greatly deepening that sketch." Redfield concluded, however, on an equivocal note by observing that "in putting before other students my errors *and his own*," Lewis had "once more shown the power of social science to revise its conclusions and move toward the truth."[58]

At the same time Oscar Lewis was reassessing Redfield's work in Tepoztlán, other American anthropologists were launching studies designed to revise or rebut Redfield's notions about social change. One especially important project that derived much from Redfield's work was the comprehensive survey of Puerto Rico that Julian Steward directed. Steward certainly rejected Redfield's antihistorical and idealistic approach; nevertheless, he borrowed much of Redfield's theoretical framework in conceptualizing his grand study of Puerto Rico. During the late 1940s to early 1950s, Steward led a team of investigators, composed primarily of his graduate students, in conducting a series of comparative community studies designed to investigate the cultural dynamics and political economy of Puerto Rico. Graduate students, including Eric R. Wolf, Sidney W. Mintz, Robert A. Manners, and Raymond Scheele, each selected a different type of community in Puerto Rico to study. While each used the results of his study as the basis for a dissertation, Steward wove all the studies together into *The People of Puerto Rico*, a sweeping comparative analysis of the island society.[59]

Sidney Mintz, in particular, conceived his community study within the Redfieldian framework. Mintz conducted as a test case an investigation of a plantation community, a type not included in Redfield's set of studies. Specifically, Mintz studied a plantation community of sugar laborers in Puerto Rico. On the basis of his study of this community, Mintz challenged the methodology and conclusions of Redfield's Yucatan study. Mintz charged that Redfield erred gravely by not including a plantation community in his sample of Yucatan towns and villages. Had he included one, Mintz asserted, Redfield would have been forced to conclude that Mérida was not the source of all social change in Yucatan. The international economic system, represented by plantation agriculture, transcended the metropolis in importance. Mintz suggested that Redfield's typological scheme may still have value, but it needed to be expanded to include types shaped by additional factors than those Redfield had acknowledged. The plantation was more, Mintz argued, than an economic system; it operated on a cultural level and produced, in short, a distinct culture.[60]

Mintz's use of Redfield's *Folk Culture of Yucatan* as a point of departure was not an isolated incident. During the mid-1950s and especially the 1960s, numerous anthropologists reexamined different elements of Redfield's Yucatan study and offered, invariably, dramatically different interpretations than those Redfield had advanced. The most important of these studies were those conducted during the mid-1960s by Victor Goldkind, D. E. Dumond, and Arnold Strickon. Goldkind and Dumond followed Oscar Lewis in reexamining communities that Redfield had first studied. Goldkind studied Chan Kom and Dumond examined Tusik. Both found that Redfield had overemphasized the degree of harmony that existed in these communities. Conflict and material inequity appeared, they reported, to be larger issues in the lives of villagers than Redfield and Villa Rojas had described. Moreover, Goldkind and Dumond demonstrated—as Lewis, Steward, and Mintz had already shown—that ethnographic study gained much when combined with historical analysis. At the same time

Goldkind and Dumond were conducting their restudies of Chan Kom and Tusik, Arnold Strickon challenged Redfield's general interpretation of social change in Yucatan. Basing his work upon Steward's historical-ecological approach, Strickon claimed that contemporary social change in Yucatan could only be understood by taking into account the long-term effects of such major historical events as the Caste War of the mid-nineteenth century and the subsequent development of the monoculture of henequen in Yucatan. Strickon concluded by charging that Redfield's folk-urban continuum, based as it was on a synchronic approach that largely ignored discrete historic events, rendered a distorted and incomplete view of change in Yucatan.[61]

Although anthropologists were first to subject Redfield's notions about social and cultural change to critical review, sociologists during the mid-1950s also added their voices to the growing critical chorus. Gideon Sjoberg was one of the first sociologists to criticize the folk-urban notion. He called attention to the failure of Redfield and his fellow Chicago urban theorists to recognize the distinction between contemporary and ancient cities. Sjoberg argued that ancient cities differed drastically from modern cities and the Chicago definition of urbanism needed a historical dimension. During the early 1960s, numerous sociologists joined Sjoberg in his critique of Redfield's folk-urban notion. Sociological critics largely echoed the anthropological critics of Redfield. The sociologists most interested in Redfield's work during the late 1950s and early 1960s were those involved in formulating a new approach to urban sociology. They represented a new academic generation, and they were anxious to revise the urban theory developed by Redfield, Wirth, and their Chicago colleagues during the 1930s and 1940s. These sociologists, including Philip Hauser, William Kolb, Albert Reiss, and Leonard Reissman, were more favorably disposed to the use of ideal-type concepts as guides for research than were anthropological critics of Redfield's work. Thus, instead of simply denouncing Redfield's use of the folk-urban notion, as Oscar Lewis had done, the new urban sociologists focused on the shortcomings of Redfield's folk-urban notion. The most frequently discussed shortcomings were: (1) the cultural limitations of Redfield's construct—it was based on a Western conception of urbanism; (2) the vagueness of the terms in which Redfield had expressed his folk society definition; (3) the difficulties associated with trying to convert Redfield's folk society characteristics into operational variables; and (4) the antiurban bias of Redfield's ideas.[62]

Each of these shortcomings was viewed as a serious limitation. Yet sociological critics generally regarded the first three as issues that could be addressed through more informed use of ideal-type concepts in research and reformulation of the folk-urban notion in terms less ambiguous and more suitable for operational research. The final issue of antiurban bias, however, constituted a more intractable problem. Oscar Lewis had first claimed that Redfield's folk-urban continuum reflected a distinct antiurban bias, and this charge followed Redfield for his entire career. The new urban sociologists brought a decidedly positive view of the city to their work, and they were anxious to rid urban theory of the antiurban bias they associated with Redfield and Wirth. Leonard Reissman, in his *The Urban Process: Cities in Industrial Societies* (1964), offered an extended consideration and critique of Redfield's contribution to urban theory, and he devoted special attention to the antiurban bias he perceived in Redfield's work. "There is no doubt," Reissman observed, "that Redfield was neither sanguine nor pleased about the changes" that occurred when a small village gave way to "the larger, urban, secular society." Redfield, he asserted, "preferred the small, primitive, isolated community."[63]

Whereas criticisms of Redfield's folk-urban notion for the vagueness of its terms and for its failings as an operational hypothesis were largely justified, criticisms of Redfield's antiurban bias demonstrated a grave misunderstanding of his ideas. Redfield indeed discussed societies that displayed much folk character, like Tepoztlán and Chan Kom, in sympathetic terms. His abstract conception of folk society highlighted, furthermore, the intimacy, warmth, and sense of shared meaning that characterized folk life. Yet Redfield was aware of the multiple limitations of the folk society, such as the lack of individual expression and the nonexistence of imaginative reflection, and he constantly affirmed that he did not "prefer" the folk society.

The confusions over Redfield's feelings about urbanism stemmed primarily from his use of the term disorganization to describe the shift from folk to urban society. Redfield proposed that this shift involved the necessary disorganization of the cultural whole, the integrated "design for living," of the folk society and the concomitant formation of a less-integrated world of overlapping subcultures. But it was not the pluralities of modern life that troubled Redfield. Rather, Redfield struggled to come to terms with the seeming loss of design that accompanied modern life. From the world of the folk society where design (or meaning) was a given, modern society demanded its members to construct their own design and coherency out of the multiple cultural alternatives available. Yet in Redfield's view, few in modern society rose to this existential challenge. Most simply immersed themselves in the pressing but insubstantial concerns of popular culture.

In addition to the theory of change implicit in Redfield's folk-urban notion, therefore, was a moral vision. Redfield structured his Folk Society class around this moral conception, and he placed it at the center of the numerous lectures on the "Folk Society" and the "Good Life" that he delivered during his career at Chicago. This moral vision spoke to the duties modern men and women had to construct a meaningful cultural order, an intentionally established organization of social "truths" to replace the "automatic" or given design of the lost world of folk society.

Redfield's Folk Society lecture presented a synopsis of his Folk Society class. He began by describing the nature of the folk society, focusing especially on how the integrated culture provided an "automatic" design for living.

Through urbanization, though, the integrated culture of folk society gave way to the fragmented plural overlapping subcultures characteristic of modern societies. Redfield did not conclude, however, merely by describing the cultural disorganization of modern society. Rather, he urged his students to go beyond "designless living." Asserting that modern humanity could never return to the ready-made certainties of the folk society, and indeed would not want to exchange their intellectual freedom for such a world, Redfield urged his students to realize that it was their responsibility to construct a sense of cultural order. Society depended upon them to apply their intelligence to the formation of a design for modern living. Redfield was thus not antiurban; he was anti–mass culture. Mass culture represented to him the ultimate in disorganization and emptiness. Yet through the Deweyan application of human intelligence, he suggested, members of modern societies could construct a cultural order that had power to satisfy their craving for a meaningful existence.[64]

Redfield's critics erred in viewing Redfield as antiurban; they were justified, however, in recognizing that his folk-urban continuum had a serious conceptual weakness. In viewing urbanization as a process consisting solely of increasing disorganization, secularization, and individualization, Redfield's construct failed to account for the order that did seem to prevail in modern societies. During the 1950s, Redfield shifted his attention away from folk societies and toward consideration of the dynamics of civilizations. This new focus allowed him to reconceptualize the theory of change implicit in his folk-urban notion. Redfield's folk-urban notion provided, nevertheless, one of the central ideas in mid-century American social science. That anthropologists and sociologists continued to conduct studies designed to extend or refute Redfield's notion for a full twenty-five years after his publication of *The Folk Culture of Yucatan* offers some indication of the level of his influence.

Notes

1. Robert Redfield, "A Plan for a Study of Tepoztlán, Morelos" (Ph.D. diss., University of Chicago, 1928), 9, 10.

2. Robert Redfield, *Tepoztlán, A Mexican Village: A Study of Folk Life* (Chicago: University of Chicago Press, 1930).

3. Redfield, *Tepoztlán*, 30, 23, 83.

4. Redfield, *Tepoztlán*, 91.

5. Redfield, *Tepoztlán*, 51.

6. Redfield, *Tepoztlán*, 68, italics mine.

7. See Clark Wissler, *Man and Culture* (New York: Thomas Y. Crowell, 1923; reprint, New York: Johnson Reprint Corporation, 1965).

8. Redfield provided this description of his Tepoztlán methodology in "The Regional Aspect of Culture," *Publications of the American Sociological Association* 24, no. 2 (1930): 145-151.

9. Robert E. Park, "Human Migration and the Marginal Man," *American Journal of Sociology* 33 (May 1928): 881-893.

10. Redfield, *Tepoztlán*, 220, 222.

11. Carleton Beals, "Mexico's Middletown," *Saturday Review of Literature* 6 (19 July 1930): 1201-1202; C. G. Poore, "From Sun-Up to Bedtime in a Village of Old Mexico," *New York Times Book Review* (27 July 1930): 10; Stuart Chase, "Corn and Fiestas," *New Republic* 64 (24 September 1930): 160; Ernest Gruening, "The Mexican," *Nation* 131 (15 October 1940): 417-418; and anonymous review of *Tepoztlán* in the *Times Literary Supplement* (24 July 1930): 613.

12. Stuart Chase in collaboration with Marian Tyler, *Mexico: A Study of Two Americas* (New York: Macmillan, 1931); on Chase's cultural and political role during the 1930s, see Robert B. Westbrook, "Tribune of the Technostructure: The Popular Economics of Stuart Chase," *American Quarterly* 32 (Fall 1980): 387-408.

13. For more on the culture-civilization discourse of the 1920s, see pages 26-37. Richard Pells and Frederick Pike provide valuable insight into the symbolic position Mexico held within the culture-civilization discourse. Richard H. Pells, *Radical Visions and American Dreams: Culture and Social Thought in the Depression Years* (New York: Harper and Row, 1973; reprint, Middletown, Conn.: Wesleyan University Press, 1984), 96-103; Frederick B. Pike, *The United States and Latin America: Myths and Stereotypes of Civilization and Nature* (Austin: University of Texas Press, 1992), 235-257; finally, George Stocking's "The Ethnographic Sensibility of the 1920s and the Dualism of the Anthropological Tradition" is indispensable for situating Redfield's *Tepoztlán* within the larger intellectual discourse of the twenties and thirties. In George W. Stocking, Jr., *The Ethnographer's Magic and Other Essays in the History of Anthropology* (Madison: University of Wisconsin Press, 1992), 276-341.

14. Robert S. Lynd, review of *Tepoztlán, A Mexican Village: A Study of Folk Life*, *American Journal of Sociology* 36 (March 1931): 823-824.

15. A. L. Kroeber, review of *Tepoztlán, A Mexican Village: A Study of Folk Life*, *American Anthropologist* 33 (April-June 1931): 236-238.

16. Many established figures within American anthropology resisted the growth of acculturation studies and pressured the editor of the *American Anthropologist* not to accept such studies for publication. In the mid-1930s, Redfield joined with Melville J.

Herskovits and Ralph Linton to produce what became known as a "manifesto" of accul-turation studies. Robert Redfield, Ralph Linton, and Melville J. Herskovits, "Memoran-dum for the Study of Acculturation," *American Anthropologist* 28 (January-March 1938): 149-151. On the role of Redfield in the development of acculturation studies, see Ralph Beals, "Acculturation," in *Anthropology Today: An Encyclopedic Inventory*, ed. A. L. Kroeber (Chicago: University of Chicago Press, 1953), 621-641, and Edward H. Spicer, "Acculturation," in *International Encyclopedia of the Social Sciences*, ed. David L. Sills (New York: Macmillan and Free Press, 1968).

17. On the relationship between community studies and acculturation, see Anne-marie De Waal Malefijt, *Images of Man: A History of Anthropological Thought* (New York: Alfred A. Knopf, 1974), 247-253.

18. Redfield, *Tepoztlán*, 13-14.

19. Andrew Carnegie had founded the Carnegie Institution of Washington in 1901 to stimulate and support original scientific research in the United States. In the late nine-teenth century, the United States lagged far behind western European nations in support for basic research. The research university was only beginning to emerge in the United States, and no American government agencies existed to coordinate and support research. Carnegie, motivated by strong ideals of cultural and economic nationalism, believed that America could only take its place among the great nations of the world if it asserted itself as a power in the development of new knowledge. He envisioned the CIW as a national super agency dedicated to finding and supporting "the best men" who could establish the basic research program necessary to drive such an effort. Rather than founding a separate research university, Carnegie chose to create an agency that would work with existing universities and promote and support the pursuit of pure research within these institu-tions. Nathan Reingold, "National Science Policy in a Private Foundation: The Carnegie Institution of Washington," in *The Organization of Knowledge in Modern America, 1860-1920*, ed. Alexandra Oleson and John Voss (Baltimore: Johns Hopkins University Press, 1979), 313-341.

20. Kidder saw in Yucatan a situation in which he could investigate the rise and fall of the once-great Maya civilization and the dynamics of the historic clash between the Old and New Worlds, issues that had tremendous resonance in the years immediately following World War I. He never articulated a workable plan to guide exploration of these momentous issues, but he generated great interest in the possibilities for study in Yucatan and brought together a large number of capable scholars who were able to use the largesse of the CIW to pursue their own research agendas in Yucatan. Despite failing to deliver on his larger promises, Kidder did succeed in elevating the CIW-sponsored studies far beyond mere excavation. A. V. Kidder, "Annual Report of the Chairman," Division of Historical Research, *Carnegie Institution of Washington Year Book 29* (Washington, D.C.: Carnegie Institution of Washington, 1930), 91-118; on A. V. Kidder, see Douglas R. Givens, *Alfred Vincent Kidder and the Development of Americanist Ar-chaeology* (Albuquerque: University of New Mexico Press, 1992); Helen Delpar provides a good overview of the entire CIW program in Yucatan in *The Enormous Vogue of Things Mexican: Cultural Relations between the United States and Mexico, 1920-1935* (Tuscaloosa: University of Alabama Press, 1992), 91-124; for a critique of the general accomplishments of the CIW's Yucatan program, see Clyde Kluckhohn, "The Concep-tual Nature of Middle American Studies," in *The Maya and Their Neighbors* (*Essays on*

Middle American Anthropology and Archaeology), ed. Clarence L. Hay et al. (New York: Dover, 1940), 41-51.

21. Robert Redfield, "A Plan for the Study of the People of Present-Day Yucatan," 19 March 1930, box 6, folder 17, Robert Redfield Papers, Special Collections, Joseph Regenstein Library, University of Chicago, Chicago (hereafter cited as RR-UC).

22. Despite the emphasis Redfield placed upon degree of modernization in selection of communities, he noted that the sample of communities chosen for study should also "take into account local differences other than differences of sophistication." The most important of these local differences, he observed, were "the hacienda [henequen plantation] versus the independent village" and the "regions of old settlement versus the frontier." He added, however, that practical as well as theoretical considerations would dictate selection of towns and villages for study. Redfield, "A Plan for the Study of the People of Present-Day Yucatan."

23. See Villa Rojas's autobiographical essay, "Fieldwork in the Maya Region of Mexico," in *Long-Term Field Research in Social Anthropology*, ed. George M. Foster, Thayer Scudder, Elizabeth Colson, and Robert V. Kemper (New York: Academic Press, 1979), 45-64.

24. On Hansen's background and participation in the Yucatan project, see Asael T. Hansen, "Robert Redfield, The Yucatan Project, and I," in *American Anthropology: The Early Years, 1974 Proceedings of the American Ethnological Society*, ed. John V. Murra (St. Paul, Minn.: West Publishing, 1976), 167-186.

25. Robert Redfield and Alfonso Villa Rojas, *Chan Kom: A Maya Village* (Washington, D.C.: Carnegie Institution of Washington, 1934; reprint, Chicago: University of Chicago Press, 1962). For reviews, see Ruth Benedict, *American Anthropologist* 39 (April-June 1937): 340-342; Stuart Chase, *New Republic* 82 (20 February 1935): 51; Clark Wissler, *American Journal of Sociology* 41 (September 1935): 266.

26. Redfield, "A Plan for the Study of the People of Present-Day Yucatan."

27. Robert Redfield, "Sociological Investigation in Yucatan," *CIW Year Book 30* (Washington, D.C.: Carnegie Institution of Washington, 1931), 122-124.

28. Robert E. Park to Robert Redfield, 23 January 1932, box 1, folder 8, RR-UC.

29. Robert Redfield, "Ethnological Research," *CIW Year Book 31* (Washington, D.C.: Carnegie Institution of Washington, 1932), 111-114.

30. Robert Redfield, "Culture Changes in Yucatan," *American Anthropologist* 36 (January-March 1934): 57-69.

31. Redfield, "Culture Changes in Yucatan," 68-69. Redfield also described his Yucatan work in two other mid-1930s articles; both are less formal than the *Anthropologist* article and offer useful views of Redfield's conception of his study. See "The Long Road Back," *University of Chicago Magazine* 27 (February 1935): 131-134, and "The Second Epilogue to Maya History," *Hispanic American Historical Review* 17 (May 1937): 170-181.

32. Robert Redfield, "Culture and Civilization in Yucatan," (1936), box 51, folder 1, RR-UC.

33. Sol Tax to Robert Redfield, 19 March 1935, box 34, folder 4, RR-UC.

34. Robert Redfield to Sol Tax, 4 April 1935, box 34, folder 4, RR-UC.

35. The cooperative work that Tax and Redfield pursued in Guatemala is well portrayed in the many letters the two exchanged from 1934 to 1941, most of which have

been reprinted with commentary in *Fieldwork: The Correspondence of Robert Redfield and Sol Tax*, ed. Robert A. Rubinstein (Boulder, Col.: Westview Press, 1991).

36. The first announcement for this seminar appeared in December 1933 in the *Bulletin of the Society for Social Research*. "The analysis," this announcement read, "of the contrast between the two types of social organization—the folk society, based on kinship and personal relationship; and the typical modern industrial society, based on territory, trade, and formal political control—will offer the central problem of the seminar. The impact of these two orders, the transition from one to the other, and the problems of social readjustment arising out of this meeting and the reverberation of this upon the contemporary world will be subjected to study by reference to local studies and investigations in the field." *Bulletin of the Society for Social Research* 13 (December 1933): 2; box 94, folder 1, Everett C. Hughes Papers, Special Collections, Joseph Regenstein Library, University of Chicago, Chicago. The winter 1935 seminar brought together a particularly distinguished group of scholars including Herbert Blumer, Bronislaw Malinowski, Robert Park, A. R. Radcliffe-Brown, Robert Redfield, and Louis Wirth. "Minutes of the Meetings of the Divisional Seminar in Race and Culture Contacts," 1935, box 49, folder 1, Fred Eggan Papers, Special Collections, Joseph Regenstein Library, University of Chicago, Chicago (hereafter FE-UC).

37. Much of this discourse has been preserved since many of the participants submitted their arguments in written form. See Fred Eggan, "Introduction"; Herbert Goldhamer, "Guatemala"; Louis Wirth, "Comments on Dr. Redfield's Reply"; Robert Redfield, "Replies to Dr. Wirth's Comments"; Sol Tax, "Reply to Dr. Wirth's Comments on Dr. Redfield's Reply to Dr. Wirth"; Louis Wirth, "Comments on Dr. Redfield and Dr. Tax's Papers on Guatemala and Agua Escondida"; and Herbert Goldhamer, "Yucatan," box 48, folder 19, FE-UC.

38. Robert Redfield, "The Sacred and the Secular in Yucatan and Guatemala" (summer 1938), box 51, folder 2, RR-UC.

39. During the summer of 1938, Tax and Redfield exchanged an extensive series of written arguments over Redfield's "Sacred and Secular in Yucatan and Guatemala" manuscript; these arguments are filed with identifying cover pages (e.g., "Sol Tax's initial comments on Redfield's 'The Sacred and the Secular in Yucatan and Guatemala'") in box 51, folder 2, RR-UC; Sol Tax, "Culture and Civilization in Guatemalan Societies," *Scientific Monthly* 48 (May 1939): 463-467; Robert Redfield, "The Relations between Indians and Ladinos in Agua Escondida, Guatemala," *America Indigena* 16 (October 1956): 253-276.

40. For a critical consideration of Redfield's definition of culture, see A. L. Kroeber and Clyde Kluckhohn, *Culture: A Critical Review of Concepts and Definitions* (Cambridge, Mass.: Papers of the Peabody Museum of American Archaeology and Ethnology, Harvard University, vol. 47, no. 1, 1952; reprint, New York: Vintage, 1963), 118-120.

41. Robert Redfield, *The Folk Culture of Yucatan* (Chicago: University of Chicago Press, 1941), 133.

42. Redfield, *Folk Culture of Yucatan*, 130-131.

43. Sol Tax and Leo Srole each provided Redfield detailed and insightful critiques on his *Folk Culture of Yucatan* manuscript. See Tax to Redfield, "Comments on ms of *Folk Culture of Yucatan*" (June 1940), box 56, folder 10, Sol Tax Papers, Special Collections, Joseph Regenstein Library, University of Chicago; Leo Srole to Robert Redfield, 15 June 1940, box 32, folder 13, RR-UC.

44. Philip Ainsworth Means, *New York Times Book Review*, 28 September 1941, 11, 29; Bertram D. Wolfe, New York *Herald Tribune*, 5 October 1941, 29; Ralph Bates, *Nation* 153 (20 September 1941): 258-260.

45. Charles S. Johnson, *American Journal of Sociology* 48 (November 1942): 430-431; Harry Alpert, *American Sociological Review* 6 (December 1941): 896-898.

46. Redfield's students and close followers stood as exceptions, of course, to this generalization. Redfield student Edward H. Spicer, for example, reviewed *The Folk Culture of Yucatan* and roundly praised it as "a landmark, a point of reference in social anthropology." *Annals of the American Academy of Political and Social Science* 219 (January 1942): 201-202.

47. Julian Steward, *Journal of American Folklore* 57 (April-June 1944): 146-148.

48. George Peter Murdock, *American Anthropologist* 45 (January-March 1943): 133-136.

49. On the shift in American anthropology from a concern with "elements" to "processes" and "patterns," see George W. Stocking, Jr., "Ideas and Institutions in American Anthropology: Thoughts toward a History of the Interwar Years," in *Ethnographer's Magic*, 136-138.

50. Redfield articulated his ideas about the folk society first in a detailed syllabus, "Synopsis of the Course on *The Folk Society*"; this item bears no date (Redfield rarely dated his papers or letters); however, internal dating indicates this to have been written around 1937-1938 (box 72, folder 21, RR-UC).

51. "The Folk Society," *American Journal of Sociology* 52 (January 1947): 293-308. Redfield's "The Folk Society" has been widely anthologized and is currently available in the Irvington Reprint Series in Sociology (New York: Irvington Publishers, Inc., 1991).

52. Robert Redfield, "Outline of Lectures for a Course on *The Folk Society*, with Collateral Readings," box 41, folder 7, Fred Eggan Papers, Special Collections, Joseph Regenstein Library, University of Chicago, Chicago (hereafter cited as FE-UC).

53. Horace Miner, *St. Denis: A French-Canadian Parish* (Chicago: University of Chicago Press, 1939; Phoenix Books, 1963); Edward H. Spicer, *Pascua: A Yaqui Village in Arizona* (Chicago: University of Chicago Press, 1940; reprint, Tucson: University of Arizona, 1967). Reviews for Miner's *St. Denis* include, George Peter Murdock, *American Anthropologist* 42 (April-June 1940): 323-324; W. C. Lehmann, *American Sociological Review* 4 (December 1939): 866-868; reviews for Spicer's *Pascua* include, Ralph L. Beals, *American Anthropologist* 43 (July-September 1941): 440-442; W. C. Bennett, *American Sociological Review* 5 (October 1940): 795; Florence Kluckhohn, *American Journal of Sociology* 47 (November 1941): 517.

54. Everett Cherrington Hughes, *French Canada in Transition* (Chicago: University of Chicago Press, 1943); Hughes described the genesis and development of his study of French Canada in "French Canada: The Natural History of a Research Project," in *Reflections on Community Studies*, ed. Arthur J. Vidich, Joseph Bensman, and Maurice R. Stein (New York: John Wiley and Sons, 1964), 71-83.

55. Horace Miner, *The Primitive City of Timbuctoo* (Princeton, N.J.: Princeton University Press, 1953). Miner discussed the design of his Timbuctoo study at length with Redfield. His SSRC proposal and several letters he and Redfield exchanged are in box 22, folder 7 of the Redfield Papers (RR-UC).

56. For treatments of the folk-urban notion in popular anthropology and sociology texts of the 1940s and 1950s, see A. L. Kroeber, *Anthropology* (New York: Harcourt,

Brace and Company, 1948), 280-288; Ronald Freedman et al., *Principles of Sociology: A Text with Readings*, rev. ed. (New York: Henry Holt and Co., 1956), 261-355; Arthur Naftalin et al., ed., *An Introduction to Social Science* (Chicago: J. B. Lippincott, 1953), 3: 81-94.

57. Oscar Lewis, *Life in a Mexican Village: Tepoztlán Restudied* (Urbana: University of Illinois Press, 1951), ix-xxvii, 311, 427-440.

58. Italics mine. Although Redfield did not respond immediately to Lewis's critique, Horace Miner published an insightful defense of Redfield's ideas shortly after Lewis's book appeared. Horace Miner, "The Folk-Urban Continuum," *American Sociological Review* 17 (October 1952): 529-537. On the Lewis-Redfield dispute, see Susan Rigdon, *The Culture Facade: Art, Science, and Politics in the Work of Oscar Lewis* (Urbana: University of Illinois Press, 1988), 40-47, 185-215, and George W. Stocking, Jr., "Ethnographic Sensibility of the 1920s," in *Ethnographer's Magic*, 319-341.

59. Julian H. Steward, Robert A. Manners, Eric R. Wolf, Elena Padilla Seda, Sidney W. Mintz, and Raymond L. Scheele, *The People of Puerto Rico: A Study in Social Anthropology* (Urbana: University of Illinois Press, 1956). A sense of Steward's appreciation of Redfield's work can be gained from reading his review of the first volume of Redfield's papers, *Human Nature and the Study of Society* in *Science*, 141 (2 August 1963): 419. Joan Vincent provides an excellent description of the general conception of Steward's Puerto Rico project in *Anthropology and Politics: Visions, Traditions, and Trends* (Tucson: University of Arizona Press, 1990), 296-302.

60. Eric R. Wolf, interview by author (Tarrytown, New York, 26 April 1995); Sidney W. Mintz, interview by author (Baltimore, 29 June 1995); Sidney W. Mintz, "Cañamelar: The Culture of a Rural Puerto Rican Proletariat," Ph.D. diss., Columbia University, 1951; Mintz also advanced his notion of the proletarian culture type in "The Folk-Urban Continuum and the Rural Proletarian Community," *American Journal of Sociology* 59 (July 1953): 136-143.

61. Victor Goldkind, "Social Stratification in the Peasant Community: Redfield's Chan Kom Reinterpreted," *American Anthropologist* 67 (August 1965): 863-884; Goldkind, "Class Conflict and Cacique in Chan Kom." *Southwestern Journal of Anthropology* 22 (Winter 1966): 325-345; D. E. Dumond, "Competition, Cooperation, and the Folk Society," *Southwestern Journal of Anthropology* 26 (Autumn 1970): 261-286; Arnold Strickon, "Hacienda and Plantation in Yucatan: An Historical-Ecological Consideration of the Folk-Urban Continuum in Yucatan," *America Indigena* 25 (January 1965): 35-63.

62. Philip Hauser provided a succinct summary of these shortcomings in his "Observations on the Urban-Folk and Urban-Rural Dichotomies as Forms of Western Ethnocentrism," in *The Study of Urbanization*, Philip M. Hauser and Leo F. Schnore, eds. (New York: John Wiley & Sons, 1965), 503-517.

63. Leonard Reissman, *The Urban Process: Cities in Industrial Societies* (New York: Free Press, 1964), 131.

64. A representative version of this lecture given in 1935 has appeared in print as "Designs for Living," in *The Social Uses of Social Science: The Papers of Robert Redfield*, vol. 2, ed. Margaret Park Redfield (Chicago: University of Chicago Press, 1962), 255-261; Kurt Vonnegut, Jr. (a Redfield student) describes the impression Redfield's folk society notion made upon him in his "Address to the National Institute of Arts and Letters, 1971," in *Wampeters, Foma, and Granfalloons* (New York: Delacorte Press, 1974), 173-181.

Chapter 3

A Broadening of Perspective: Beyond Anthropology as a Natural Science

After publishing steadily throughout the 1930s—three books plus scores of articles—Redfield virtually stopped publishing for most of the 1940s.[1] When he began to publish again in the late 1940s, his work differed dramatically from that produced in the first half of his career. The most important difference lies in his changed conceptualization of social science. Throughout the late 1920s and the 1930s, his work was characterized by a pronounced nomothetic generalizing approach. This theme is most obvious in his articles "Anthropology, A Natural Science?" (1926) and "Culture Changes in Yucatan" (1934).[2] By the late 1940s, though, this natural science approach to anthropology all but disappeared in Redfield's work. Instead, he began to emphasize the power of anthropology and its sister social sciences to assist in the determination of transcendent social and moral values. In short, he moved during this period from conceptualizing the social sciences, particularly anthropology and sociology, in a narrow instrumentalist sense to viewing these fields in a broader manner, essentially as moral disciplines.

The new directions in Redfield's work do not derive from a sudden shift in his thinking. Rather these changes reflect an extended process of personal and intellectual development. During the late 1930s through the 1940s, Redfield was strongly influenced by his participation as both an academic in the tumultuous atmosphere of the University of Chicago and as a public intellectual in several national-level social and political causes. These experiences impressed themselves upon him with particular force and contributed powerfully to the changes he began to display in his work.

Hutchins and Chicago

Chicago during the thirties and forties was probably the most intellectually charged environment within American higher education. The arrival of Robert Maynard Hutchins in 1929 as president of Chicago set in motion a series of con-

77

troversies that did not cease until his departure in 1951. Most of these controversies centered on curricular issues. These were not, however, mere political squabbles. They involved important issues over academic governance, faculty independence, and educational philosophy. At the most serious level, the president and faculty members of the University of Chicago can be said to have carried on an almost two-decade-long argument over the meaning of liberal education.

When Hutchins accepted the presidency at the University of Chicago in 1929, he was but thirty years old, the youngest man ever to be appointed to this position. He came into the presidency with the reputation of being a "boy wonder," having previously been dean of the Yale Law School, a position he had achieved after having been a member of the Yale law faculty for only two years. The board of trustees had considered older, more established men for the Chicago presidency. They selected Hutchins, however, because of all those considered, he appeared to be the most intelligent, original, and innovative. The Chicago prestige had eroded somewhat in the two decades following the Harper years, and the trustees, particularly Harold Swift, were anxious to see the university return to its erstwhile position. Hutchins appeared to be just the man who could restore Chicago to the eminence it had enjoyed under its founding president, William Rainey Harper. Harold Swift captured the air of expectancy surrounding the Hutchins appointment when he remarked that in selecting the young but promising Hutchins, he and his fellow trustees had taken "a gamble on youth and brilliance."[3]

Faculty members and students also greeted Hutchins enthusiastically. He was tall, strikingly handsome, and he exercised through power of personality and obvious intelligence a great effect upon the entire Chicago academic community. Hutchins enjoyed a "honeymoon" of less than two years, however, before he lost much of his support among the faculty. He was intent upon implementing numerous academic reforms at Chicago, and he often adopted a high-handed manner in dealing with professors that turned many against him. He suffered greatly, moreover, from his association with the abrasive Mortimer Adler, a professor he had brought to Chicago with him when he accepted the position as president. Yet, despite the conflicts that Hutchins frequently provoked, he retained the support of a strong core of loyal faculty members who responded to his charisma and ideas, and who stood by him through the entire two decades of his administration.[4]

Redfield was one of the many who was deeply stirred by the Hutchins charisma. He and Hutchins not only became close personal friends, but Redfield also played a key role in the Hutchins administration, serving as dean of social sciences from 1934 to 1946.[5] The relationship between Hutchins and Redfield went beyond mere friendship. In many ways, Hutchins was a philosophical mentor for Redfield. Hutchins was a man who was driven, almost haunted, by a peculiar sense of mission, and he communicated this sense to those in his inner circle. He was essentially a secular moralist, and he inspired his close associates with his moral vision—his notion of a moral community with a university rather than a church at its center.[6]

While Redfield acknowledged the philosophical impact that Hutchins had exercised upon him, he also realized that Hutchins's vision was not without limitations. Immediately after Hutchins published his essay "University Education" in the *Yale Review*, which appeared shortly thereafter as chapter 4 of *The Higher Learning in America*, Redfield wrote Hutchins and expressed his strong disagreement with the conception of higher education, especially Hutchins's elevation of "metaphysics" over empirical social science.[7] "It was you who made educational matters a concern of mine," he told Hutchins, "and it is your leadership that keeps me concerned with them." However, he added, "when I cannot follow your leadership, I feel that I must tell you so."[8] Redfield continued to clearly separate himself, moreover, from the overt hostility that Hutchins displayed toward the social sciences from the mid-1930s onward. Yet he managed to keep this dispute on an intellectual level and never allowed it to interfere with the friendship that he and Hutchins maintained up to the time of his death.[9]

Almost as soon as he assumed the Chicago presidency, Hutchins began to initiate changes in the undergraduate curriculum. Although he introduced curricular reforms throughout the 1930s and 1940s, the most drastic modifications to the undergraduate curriculum appeared in two separate initiatives, one launched in 1931, the other in 1942. In the 1931 action, Hutchins implemented the "New Plan."[10] This plan was aimed at changing the course of study for first and second year, or "Junior College," students. The primary result of the New Plan was to change the curriculum from a diversified, elective-based system to a predominantly standardized curriculum. The 1942 reforms resembled those of 1931 but applied to the entire College rather than to only the Junior College. In 1942, successful completion of the entire undergraduate curriculum at Chicago became contingent upon examination performance instead of credit accumulation. Moreover, a series of mandatory survey courses in the humanities, natural sciences, and social sciences was established as the primary focus of the College curriculum.

Although Hutchins easily won approval for his 1931 curricular initiatives, he faced fierce opposition from many faculty members when he proposed his 1942 reforms.[11] Only by taking the unusual (and unpopular) move of casting his own vote in the Senate was Hutchins able to break a tie vote and obtain approval for his comprehensive restructuring of the College curriculum. Once this approval was achieved, the College faculty proceeded to design and implement the core courses of what had become a largely prescribed curriculum in undergraduate education at Chicago. Controversy among students, professors, and trustees raged for the entire decade of the forties, however, over not only the content of these core courses, but also over the larger issues implicit in the drastic curricular modifications. This curricular controversy served as a focal point, furthermore, for a charged debate over the aims of education and the purpose of a university which gripped the Chicago academic community for virtually all the years of Hutchins's long tenure as president at Chicago.[12]

Much of the controversy that developed over the college curriculum at Chicago stemmed from the effort by Hutchins and his supporters to establish liberal arts as the central focus of study for undergraduates. Hutchins, assisted largely by Dean of Humanities Richard McKeon and Chairman of English Richard Crane, pushed to define a curriculum that elevated study of classic literary and philosophical texts above all other pursuits. This liberal arts emphasis marginalized studies in mathematics, foreign languages, and the social and natural sciences and engendered great resentment among faculty members in these fields.

The College social science faculty responded with a particular vigor, however, to attempts by liberal arts zealots to minimize their place in the academy. From the very initiation of the social science survey courses, designed first by Harry Gideonse and Louis Wirth in 1932, the social science faculty refused to see their disciplines subordinated to Mortimer Adler's metaphysics or to the pervasive liberal arts chauvinism. Instead, professors who designed and taught the Social Science 1, 2, and 3 courses presented social science as the intellectual equal of literary and philosophical studies. By defining their courses in opposition to traditional liberal arts courses, College social science faculty were challenged to expand not only the scope of their courses, but also the manner in which they conceptualized their scholarly disciplines. The resulting courses are still taught today and have become probably the most celebrated undergraduate social science courses in America.

These courses have become famous both for the roster of instructors who have taught them as well as for their innovative organization around central themes and problems in American society. Chicago recruited a brilliant faculty to teach these courses, particularly in the decade following World War II, and the competition that arose among this cluster of scholars created an environment which proved remarkably stimulating for both instructors and students.[13] Several "alumni instructors" have written memoirs describing their experiences in teaching in "Soc" 2 and 3, especially during the 1940s and 1950s. Almost all these memoirs emphasize the intense competition coupled with a sense of an elite esprit de corps that existed among fellow instructors.[14]

Redfield spent almost two decades in this charged milieu. He was a frequent guest lecturer in Soc 2 during the 1930s, served for numerous terms during the 1940s as a regular staff instructor for both Soc 2 and 3, and chaired the Soc 3 course during the 1947-1948 academic year. Like most other instructors in Soc 2 and 3, moreover, he often assumed the role of student and attended lectures of his colleagues. The opportunity to teach in such an environment proved intensely stimulating to Redfield, and much of his development as a thinker can be traced to his participation in these courses.[15]

Becoming a Public Intellectual

During the 1930s through the mid-1940s, Redfield focused almost all his energies on his teaching and administrative duties at Chicago and his research in Yucatan and Guatemala. From the mid-1940s through the early 1950s, however, he began to participate in a wide range of activities whose scope extended far beyond his formal research and university duties. These activities offered Redfield the opportunity to contribute as a public intellectual to a number of different issues of national import. Three concerns commanded his attention most powerfully during this period: (1) the challenge that mass communications posed to the American democratic process; (2) the effort to establish some form of world government following World War II; (3) the efforts of blacks to eliminate discrimination in housing and education.[16]

Redfield became involved in the consideration of issues surrounding mass communications at the urging of Robert M. Hutchins. During the 1930s and early 1940s, the relationship between the American press and the federal government had grown increasingly strained. The Roosevelt administration implemented several policies that mandated changes in the way in which the press functioned, and a number of powerful publishers considered these actions a major threat to American press freedom.[17] In December 1942, Henry Luce, publisher of *Time*, *Life*, and *Fortune*, in an effort to halt what he perceived as the encroachment of government upon the press, asked his Yale classmate Robert Hutchins if he would chair a blue-ribbon commission to clarify publicly the scope of American press freedom. Hutchins, intrigued with the problem, accepted Luce's request and after securing a commitment of $200,000 from Luce to support the inquiry, appointed a commission of a dozen intellectuals to join him in considering the issue.[18]

Hutchins announced the formation of the Commission on the Freedom of the Press in 1944. Among the members he selected were Robert Redfield, Harold D. Lasswell, Charles E. Merriam, Reinhold Niebuhr, Zechariah Chafee, Arthur M. Schlesinger, Sr., Archibald MacLeish, and William E. Hocking. The members of this commission met over a three-year period holding in the process seventeen two-day or three-day meetings and interviewing fifty-eight leading members of the press and 224 individuals in government and industries concerned with the press. On March 26, 1947, they published their report, *A Free and Responsible Press, a General Report on Mass Communication: Newspapers, Radio, Motion Pictures, Magazines, and Books*.

This report was not, however, what Luce had expected. Indeed, he was so displeased with the draft he saw in 1946 that he refused to supply the additional funds necessary to publish the report. Hutchins had to obtain funding from Bill Benton, publisher of the *Encyclopedia Britannica*, to underwrite the University of Chicago Press's publication of the 137-page report. Luce reacted most negatively to the report's extensive criticism of the press. While strongly asserting the need for the United States to preserve a press free from government censorship, the authors of the report stressed that this freedom carried with it enormous responsibility to the American public. This responsibility consisted not only of the need to maintain professional standards of truth and objectivity within the journalism community, but also the obligation to educate the American public. And in this role as educator, the commission charged, the press had failed miserably. Another point that Luce rejected, and that most newspaper publishers and editors bristled at as well, was the commission's decision to include all current forms of mass communications, particularly the emerging electronic variety, within their definition of the "press." This inclusion was instrumental, however, in extending First Amendment protection to the burgeoning radio and television news industry.

Luce had wanted a tract to beat against government officials who attempted to meddle with press freedoms. What he received instead was a measured philosophical-sociological consideration of the role of the press in the modern world. The authors of this report addressed their comments to an emerging public debate over mass society and mass communications rather than to a cabal of vindictive editors and publishers. As such, this report created little sensation upon publication. Most newspapers buried their coverage of it on back pages. Nevertheless, a few young editors read it with enthusiasm and used it as a guide for instilling a sense of press responsibility during the 1950s and 1960s. And in a twenty-year retrospective assessment, the *Columbia Journalism Review* found it to be a document well ahead of its times.[19]

While *A Free and Responsible Press* did exercise some measure of influence at its time of publication and certainly has achieved retrospective acclaim, it must be seen as a project that fell short of expectations. Yet failure to create a public stir should not be the only standard by which this project is measured. Most important is the evidence this report provides of the effort that Hutchins and his associates invested in attempting to create a public that transcended the walls of the university. This project was but one of many similar efforts to which Hutchins committed himself during his life in his attempt to create a "national community of thinking people."[20] But it was a representative project, and the report produced reflects that Hutchins's fellow commission members were equally committed to the goals that Hutchins espoused. Redfield joined Hutchins on a number of such projects throughout the 1940s and 1950s, despite maintaining a schedule crowded with academic and administrative commitments. His willingness to contribute to these projects reflects the belief he shared with Hutchins that the good society could be realized only by conscious striving to extend reason and to further public dialogue.

Another cause Redfield participated in during the late 1940s stemmed from America's actions in World War II. Redfield, like many intellectuals in his generation, was deeply troubled by America's use of atomic weapons in the war. Following the bombing of Japan, academics, policy-makers, and journalists engaged each other in a protracted national debate over the social and political consequences associated with atomic energy. Two distinct movements can be discerned within the postwar nuclear discourse, those associated with the atomic scientists and those associated with the world government advocates. Several senior members of the Manhattan Project, such as Leo Szilard and James Franck, had expressed grave concerns as early as 1943 over moral consequences associated with use of atomic weapons, and in the spring of 1945, they had desperately attempted to dissuade Truman from using them against Japanese citizens. Upon having their requests ignored, indeed almost spurned by the government and military leaders, a number of scientists in Los Alamos, Oak Ridge, Tennessee, and Chicago banded together to form a cluster of local organizations committed to wresting control of atomic weapons and energy away from the military and placing them under civilian control. Scientists at the University of Chicago formed the Atomic Scientists of Chicago, an organization that not only catalyzed much activism on the Chicago campus, but also came to exercise a powerful national voice within the postwar debate over nuclear policy. Robert Hutchins stood firmly behind the Chicago scientists and provided them with $10,000 in university funds, an amount sufficient for them to launch a monthly journal, the *Bulletin of the Atomic Scientists*, and to open a Washington office from which to direct lobbying activities. Redfield participated only peripherally in the atomic scientists' movement, but he involved himself deeply in the world government effort.[21]

The world government movement emerged simultaneously with the atomic scientists' movement. Driven by a number of small organizations, the most prominent of which was the United World Federalists, the world government advocates lobbied for the formation of a powerful international body to assert political and military control beyond national lines. Since atomic weapons appeared to represent the primary destabilizing force in the postwar world, international control of nuclear energy emerged as the leading concern of the world government movement and provided a powerful bridge to the postwar scientists' movement.

World government activists joined with the atomic scientists at Chicago in exercising a powerful influence on campus discourse. The best organized world government initiative at Chicago was represented by the formation of the Committee to Frame a World Constitution. Led by Chicago professors Richard McKeon and G. A. Borgese, this committee included a dozen other academics drawn from the faculties of Chicago, Columbia, Harvard, and Stanford; among those included were Robert Redfield, the deans of the Harvard and Chicago law schools, James Landis and Wilbur Katz, the prototypical member of the New Deal brains trust, Rexford Tugwell, and Mortimer Adler.

Like the Atomic Scientists of Chicago, the Committee to Frame a World Constitution enjoyed the direct support of Robert Hutchins. Not only did Hutchins provide financial and administrative support for the organization, but also he agreed to serve as president of the committee. While their primary goal was to produce a model world constitution, a task they viewed as the first step necessary in the establishment of a world government, they also published a monthly journal, *Common Cause*, through which they examined and reported on numerous issues related to the world government movement. They published their constitution in March 1948, a product of two-and-a-half years of effort. The initial publication appeared in *Common Cause*, and it was reprinted in full shortly thereafter in the *Bulletin of the Atomic Scientists* and *Saturday Review of Literature*. Although over 200,000 copies of this constitution were distributed in its first year in publication and the document was translated into several different languages, this constitution exercised little direct political influence. It appeared just as the world government movement was starting to lose momentum. At the time of publication, however, this model constitution represented one of the major accomplishments for this important but short-lived social-political movement.[22]

Of the three public issues that he participated in most heavily during the 1940s, Redfield devoted his greatest efforts to assisting the National Association for the Advancement of Colored People in their legal battles against racial discrimination in housing and education. The NAACP launched in the 1930s a legal assault on discrimination against blacks. NAACP attorneys—led first by Charles Houston and, beginning in 1938, by Thurgood Marshall—initiated litigation throughout the 1930s on behalf of numerous plaintiffs. As the nation entered war in the 1940s, though, NAACP attorneys slowed their actions, because they believed that pressing their requests during wartime would seem unpatriotic and prove counterproductive. But as soon as the war came to an end, they redoubled their efforts to assist blacks in achieving their rights in American society.

Beginning in the mid-1940s and continuing for the next decade, Thurgood Marshall focused the energies of the NAACP Legal Defense Fund attorneys on eliminating discrimination blacks faced when attempting to purchase houses or to obtain access to educational institutions. The hundreds of thousands of blacks, who moved to northern cities in search of work during the 1930s and 1940s, routinely found themselves blocked from purchasing homes by restrictive covenants. And the tens of thousands of black veterans found themselves unable to take advantage of benefits offered by the GI Bill because too few existing institutions of higher education would admit black students. Following the war, blacks began to demand with increasing frequency and intensity equal access to housing and education. Marshall mobilized his staff of lawyers to assist blacks in these demands, and through a decade of litigation, which culminated in the 1954 *Brown v. Board of Education* decision, they achieved some of the most important Supreme Court decisions in American legal history.[23]

One of the most distinctive aspects of the NAACP's attorneys' strategy for litigating the postwar housing and education cases was their choice to rely heavily upon social scientific evidence to support their arguments against segregation. Following World War I, American social scientists, particularly at such northern institutions as Columbia, Harvard, Chicago, and Northwestern, had devoted much attention to study of racial issues and over the course of two decades had been systematically dismantling the intellectual justifications advanced to support racial discrimination in the United States.[24] The 1944 publication of Gunnar Myrdal's *An American Dilemma*, moreover, greatly helped to push consideration of America's race problem into national discussion and demonstrated the power of social science to clarify moral and social issues surrounding race problems in America.[25] The NAACP lawyers recognized the value of these intellectual developments and moved aggressively to incorporate these scientific arguments against discrimination into their litigation.[26] By bringing social scientists as expert witnesses into the courts and by submitting briefs either written by social scientists or with their assistance, the NAACP attorneys introduced a strikingly new strategy in American legal practice.

Robert Redfield exercised a leading role in working with Thurgood Marshall and his staff to prepare and execute what has come to be called the sociological argument.[27] Not only was Redfield the first social scientist to serve as a courtroom expert witness for the NAACP, but also he persuaded other social scientists to testify, helped write briefs, and advised in formation of strategy and litigation proceedings from the 1940s restrictive covenants and Texas and Oklahoma law school cases through the 1954 *Brown v. Board of Education* decision.[28]

While *Brown* is certainly the most renowned of the NAACP desegregation cases, the decision in *Brown* rested upon precedents set in several cases the NAACP fought during the previous decade. The most important of these is *Sweatt v. Painter*, a case challenging the University of Texas Law School's refusal of admission to a black mail carrier named Heman Sweatt. The *Sweatt* case was one of a cluster of lawsuits Thurgood Marshall initiated during the mid-1940s in order to attack the notion that separate could ever be equal. *Sweatt v. Painter* became in the process of litigation a key case which forced the Supreme Court to move beyond mere comparison of physical facilities to also include intangible factors, such as quality of student body, alumni connections, extracurricular activities, and professorial contact, in assessing equality of institutions.

By pushing the Court to consider such intangible institutional factors, Marshall also opened the door for consideration of intangible sociological and psychological factors associated with segregated education. In making his argument for the importance of sociological factors associated with segregated education, Marshall relied most heavily upon the testimony of Redfield, whom he introduced into the district court in Travis County, Texas, as an expert witness in race relations. While the Texas courts were not persuaded by the NAACP's case, the Supreme Court sided with the NAACP and not only reversed the Texas decision barring Heman Sweatt entrance to the University of Texas Law School,[29] but also delivered the NAACP attorneys a clear signal that the Court was now willing to consider additional sociological factors associated with segregated education.[30]

Redfield's participation in the NAACP's legal battle against segregation coupled with his involvement in other public causes, such as the world government movement and the responsible press commission, demanded much of his time during the mid- to late 1940s. These activities allowed him to explore, however, a role that he had previously avoided—as a social scientist actively engaged in the public sphere. And this new role well fit changes emerging in his conception of the purpose of social science in society.

A suggestion of the change in Redfield's thinking can be seen in his correspondence from this period. Shortly after the United States bombed Hiroshima, Redfield and his wife drove out to New Mexico, to Alamagordo and Las Cruces, the land in which the bomb was developed. Redfield found that the people in New Mexico had little interest in talking about the wider implications of the bomb. In a letter to his daughter Lisa, he described how surprised he was at their detachment. He also expressed a conviction that social science needed to speak more directly to such people.

> One feels that the importance of special knowledge about men and society is more important than it ever was, but is also, relatively, less effective. There is this great gap between what the specialist understands and what is understood by the people of Las Cruces. So, to my mind, a social scientist, if he cares about human problems, has to turn to education. Years ago I thought of science as something that ought just to go ahead finding out. Now it seems to me that the specialists already know so much, so much which, if understood generally, would go far to meet the human crisis. So it seems to me that education, in the broad sense, is what one has to be concerned with, if one wants to help to get us out of this mess. Research must go on; but its chief function is to refresh the spirit of investigation at its source; the main effort now should go to the dissemination of the results and the spirit of investigation and of rational discussion to the people.[31]

Redfield was thus following his own advice in committing himself to these various public causes during the late 1940s. He was also putting into action the message Robert M. Hutchins had preached since arriving at Chicago, namely, that intellectuals bore an obligation to reach beyond the walls of the university to create a moral dialogue within the community at large.

Social Science as Morality

After the bombing of Hiroshima, a number of American social scientists called upon their colleagues to assert a more forceful intellectual leadership in society. Chicago social scientists, stirred possibly by the activism of the atomic scientists on campus, were probably the most vigorous champions for this cause. William F. Ogburn, chairman of the Chicago sociology department, Louis Wirth, and Redfield all advocated through public lectures and articles an increased activism for social scientists. The initial responses of these three sounded very much alike. They invoked the well-worn cultural lag theme that social scientists had been using to justify their role for the past generation. According to this theme, technological developments had so far outstripped existing norms of social control that only conscious effort by expert social technicians could bring threatening new technology under control. The development of atomic energy, moreover, represented the ultimate threat to humanity and, consequently, the supervising capabilities of social scientists had never been more necessary.

Yet the Chicago social scientists influenced few people in their efforts to secure greater political power for sociologists. The notion of the expert-controlled society was neither novel nor easily realized in practical terms. After publishing a few articles dealing with atomic energy issues, Ogburn and Wirth moved on to other concerns. Redfield chose, however, to push beyond the considerations that he raised in his first article dealing with the social consequences of nuclear energy. Indeed, this article, "Consequences of Atomic Energy" (1946), proved to be but his opening move in an extended exploration not only of the relationship of social science to nuclear technology, but also of the larger relationship of social science to modern society.[32]

In January 1947, he published a second article on nuclear issues, "Social Science in the Atomic Age." He advanced here a much broader conception of the nature and obligations of social science in the post-Hiroshima world than he had offered in his earlier article. He minimized the social engineering solution to the nuclear crisis and emphasized instead the role social science needed to play in general education and in the development and clarification of ethical standards for society. "Social Science in the Atomic Age" marks a turning point in Redfield's thinking—it clearly reflects his progressive movement away from his earlier nomothetic orientation—and points the direction for the conception he was to hold of social science for the rest of his career.[33]

In "Social Science in the Atomic Age," Redfield challenged the claim—commonly made in the mid-1940s—that the social and natural sciences closely resembled each other in being able to benefit society through both pure and applied research. Redfield argued that while the natural sciences benefited the public almost exclusively through applied research (only a tiny sector of specialists could appreciate the results of pure research), social science benefited society through both pure and applied research. Indeed, the pure research—or better, the theoretical, generalizing approach in social science—clearly represented the most significant aspect of social science. "Social science," he stated, "is not in its most important aspect, information, or invention, or technical skill." Because the social sciences had so striven to imitate the natural sciences, however, it was "that aspect of social science that results in inventions" that had been emphasized. Redfield dismissed this conception, stating, "I think it is a distortion and a disservice to define or to justify social science as primarily a series of inventions. Social science is rather a series of understandings."[34]

By challenging the value of social science's technical contributions, Redfield was actually staging an indirect attack against the national social science establishment. Since World War I, American social scientists had been making inroads into government service jobs and had been increasingly successful in demonstrating the practical aspects of social science. This trend accelerated greatly during the World War II years when social scientists left their posts at colleges and universities in droves to lend their services to governmental agencies. Access to government positions not only provided social scientists greater opportunities to implement their ideas, but also helped elevate their collective status within American society. Following the war, numerous social scientists proudly described the contributions they and their colleagues had made to the war effort; they stressed, furthermore, the power that applied social science held for the postwar era.[35] Redfield was one of the few who dissented from this view and attempted to chart a different course for postwar social science.

Through a series of lectures and articles written during the late 1940s to the early 1950s, Redfield advanced a comprehensive exposition of his alternative conception of social science. The heart of this exposition consisted of a group of lectures that he delivered at the University of Frankfurt[36] in April 1949. A year earlier, Robert Hutchins had initiated a program to send several senior University of Chicago professors to teach for a term at the University of Frankfurt. Dubbed "Chicago-at-Frankfurt," this program represented one of the many efforts in cultural politics that the United States implemented in Occupied Germany following the war.[37] Redfield's close friend Everett C. Hughes had been a member of the first group of Chicago professors to participate in the Frankfurt program, and upon his return to the United States, he urged Redfield to take part. In the fall of 1948, Redfield had gone to China on a sabbatical leave to study Chinese peasant villages, but he had been forced to leave in January 1949 by the Chinese Revolution. Hughes persuaded Redfield to devote some of his remaining sabbatical time to teaching during the spring of 1949 at the University of Frankfurt and assisted him in making the necessary arrangements to do so.

When Hughes first encouraged Redfield to go to Frankfurt, Redfield responded that he was unsure that any of his work might be of interest to German students. He asked Hughes, however, if he thought they might be interested in the ideas he had been developing about the role of social science in society. Redfield had just published another article on this theme, "The Art of Social Science" in the *American Journal of Sociology*,[38] and he suggested to Hughes that he might use this as the starting point for a series of lectures at Frankfurt. Hughes strongly encouraged Redfield to pursue this idea, and he arranged to have the lectures that Redfield prepared translated into German for his delivery at Frankfurt.[39]

In his previous writings, Redfield had dealt only with selected aspects of social science. The Frankfurt lectures challenged him, however, to develop a more comprehensive view of his ideas on these issues. And although he did not publish them as a unit, these lectures represent an integrated, tightly argued thesis on the philosophy and methods of social science. He presented five lectures at Frankfurt, and in these lectures he advanced a methodically constructed argument based upon four points. First, he established his basic definition of social science; second, he analyzed the methods by which social science proceeds; third, he examined the relationships between social science and other academic disciplines; and fourth, he explored the role or purpose of social science in society.[40]

"An anthropologist," Redfield proposed, "may study social science just as he would study anything else in a society." In "present-day society it is an institution, just as the market, the family, and the church," and it is subject to study, therefore, in the same fashion as these other institutions. Social science, he emphasized, is not merely a set of methods, interpretations, and results, but also a community of practitioners. These practitioners "are engaged in making order of experience, an order that is objective, systematic, and comprehensive." The "structured body of knowledge" that is produced, moreover, belongs "to no one thinker" but "is accessible to all who will study it." This body of knowledge, Redfield acknowledged, is not as "systematic or as comprehensive as physics or biology," but he suggested that generalization possibly played a different role in social science than in physical and biological science. "Perhaps it is not so much a final or nearly final summing up of accepted understanding as it is a provider of a more tentative and yet illuminating point of view." Finally, he commented, "in much of social science the generalizations tend to be constructions some considerable way from acceptable 'truth,'" yet these constructions "guide us among real cases that always escape the generalization," and we can "grasp and deal with the case better for looking at it with the generalization."[41]

The definition that Redfield presented in his first Frankfurt lecture emphasized the processual aspects of social science. Rather than focusing on formal characteristics, he advanced a definition that stressed the functional role of social science within human society. Social science in his view was thus a cultural activity undertaken by a community of practitioners for the purpose of constructing contingent truths—truths that while tentative could serve as guides for human action in the face of modern uncertainty.

Once he had established a definition of the structure and function of social science within society, Redfield proceeded to explore the methods of social science. He suggested that this methodology included elements common to both the natural sciences and humanities. Similar to the natural scientists, he argued, social scientists regarded the "scientific method" as their fundamental guide for action. He characterized this method as the effort to (1) impose logic upon the process of inquiry through use of a hypothesis, and (2) to reduce the wide range of objectively made observations obtained through this inquiry to a comprehensive and hierarchical "architecture of description."[42]

In describing the methods by which scientists gathered and organized knowledge, Redfield intentionally minimized the role of quantitative analysis. Here he was clearly sounding a different note from the majority of those discussing scientific method, particularly most social scientists, during the mid-twentieth century. This was not a new theme with Redfield; he had been asserting the independence of scientific method from quantification since the 1930s.[43] But the trend toward quantification had increased so dramatically in the 1940s and 1950s, that social scientists who chose not to follow this path risked being read out of the profession. Redfield refused to yield any ground to the quantifiers, however, and insisted that science was distinguished through the power of its conceptual ordering of knowledge and not through its use of one or another data manipulation techniques.

Yet Redfield spent little time in discussing similarities between the methods of the natural and social scientists—he suggested that this ground had been well covered by others—and focused his remarks instead upon the less-discussed similarities in method between the humanities and social science.[44] Most obvious in this comparison, he suggested, was the common interest humanists and social scientists share in the study of "expressive documents." These documents or texts exist in a multiplicity of forms. Tools, works of art, letters, spoken words, folktales, liturgies, life histories, interviews, and novels—all represent expressive texts that reflect the inner worlds of their authors. Humanists and social scientists both approach these texts with the same purpose: the desire to determine the ways "in which other men have expressed their states of mind, their schemes of values."[45] Humanists and social scientists both brought, moreover, similar thoughts and feelings to bear upon these texts in the effort to understand their various meanings. Interpretation of these texts required, however, a facility beyond that which could be taught; it required, in short, the insights of a creative artist. "Like the novelist, the scientific student of society must project the sympathetic understanding which he has of people with motives, desires, and moral judgments into the subject he is treating."[46]

By emphasizing the element of "art" in social science, Redfield was attempting to establish a new conceptualization of the social scientific enterprise. For the last century, social scientists had been predicting the imminent emergence of a set of methods for social science equally rigorous to those used in natural science. Redfield broke with this tradition and argued that what had been perceived as social science's weakness—its failure to match natural science in rigor—was actually its strength. For the social scientific enterprise was inherently split between two tasks, the need to conduct systematic observations of social phenomena and the subsequent need to derive far-reaching generalizations from these observations. The same sort of methods, however, could not be used for these two separate tasks. The systematic scientific approach served well for the collection of observations, for study of real humans in discrete social situations. But the construction of generalizations required an entirely different methodology. What was needed here was artistic intuition sufficient to discern human motivations and attitudes that lay beneath overt actions. "In the reaching of a significant generalization as to man in society," Redfield proposed, "there is an exercise of a gift of apprehension so personal and so subtly creative that it cannot be expected to result merely from application of some formal method of research."[47] Social science thus needed to accept its dual nature and learn to nurture both its scientific and artistic aptitudes.

While the methods of the social sciences, Redfield argued, drew equally upon those of the humanities and natural sciences, the subject matter of social science aligned much more closely with that of the humanities. Simply put, the link between the social sciences and the humanities is their common concern with humanity. "Humanity is the common subject matter of those who look at men as they are represented in books or in works of art and of those who look at men as they appear in institutions and directly visible actions." It is only an accident of modern scholarship, he further asserted, that separated social science from the humanities. "In Montaigne's day there was no separation," and if the academic disciplines were grouped today with emphasis given "to subject matter rather than to method, the social sciences and humanities would be one group, distinct from the other sciences."[48]

Given the essential similarity in the concerns of humanists and social scientists, moreover, Redfield encouraged the two groups to seek actively to cooperate in scholarly endeavor. He suggested that their mutual interest in "culture" might provide a fruitful field of common exploration. Too much had been made, he argued, of the difference between the social scientists' concern with universal culture, particularly as defined by anthropologists, and the humanists' focus upon normative, hierarchical culture. These two constructs were truly just "different phases of the same thing." While the student of the humanities looks at the "thoughtful, deliberate, original, and creative aspects of a people's life," essentially viewing "culture" as "cultivation," the social scientist "looks usually at the spontaneous, common, average, and less original aspects," regarding "culture" primarily as "folkways" or "customs."

Yet these two conceptual poles are not absolutely distinct. Anthropological "primitive" culture does not represent an unchanging entity held completely separate from the cultivated, normative culture of the "civilized" world. Rather, "primitive" culture is subject to change, to transformation into "cultivated" culture. In short, Redfield argued that culture is not a fixed entity but is instead a process. While two distinct theoretical vantage points can be adopted for viewing this process—that of the humanists who viewed culture from the "top" down and that of the anthropologists who viewed culture from the "bottom" up— neither of these perspectives is adequate for studying the phenomena of culture. For actual human groups do not align themselves simply at one theoretical pole or the other. Instead, human groups can be seen to lie on a continuum between these two theoretical poles—cultivated or "civilized" versus custom-bound or "primitive"—with no group fitting exactly the ideal characteristics for either theoretical pole. Humanists and social scientists, Redfield argued, needed to collaborate, to combine the views from the top with those from the bottom. The results of such an effort, he proposed, would be a richer and more dynamic view of the "culture-civilization" process than that yet achieved by conventional scholarly approaches.[49]

By merely suggesting that social science shared a close affinity with the humanities, Redfield provided sufficient cause for mainstream social scientists of the 1940s to consider him a heretic. He pushed his conception of social science even farther from the center, though, in his last two lectures at Frankfurt. In these, "Social Science and Values" and "Social Science as Morality," he attacked the common conception that held social science to be value-free inquiry. He argued that not only did social scientists routinely project values onto their work, but also this action represented proper and not aberrant procedure in social science. Because the issues they concerned themselves with were inherently value laden, to expect social scientists to approach these issues from a value-free perspective made no sense. Values, instead, lay at the heart of social scientific practice. On the larger level, the entire community of social science functioned through commitment to the values of truth and accuracy; and on an individual level, a social scientist needed to draw upon his or her own constellation of values in order to enter imaginatively and empathically into another person's scheme of values.[50]

Social science also provided modern society with an invaluable tool for the construction of values. Because values derived through tradition had been "rendered broken and helpless in a changing world," society needed such a mechanism for constructing new values through the application of reason. "There is no return," he warned, "to the relative ease of a traditional mental and moral life, for all such local traditions are now broken." Modern society must either "choose reason, with all its pains," or "submit to the coercion of opinion by tyranny." Social science offered society a means of negotiating the conflicting claims of tradition and reason, for mediating value conflicts, and it deserved consequently to be recognized as more than a "mere machine for grinding out facts or turning out social formulas." It stood, Redfield concluded, as an expression of one of modern society's deepest values—its commitment to reason—and represented, ultimately, "a fundamental part of our morality."

Social science thus offered humanity not merely a batch of techniques or inventions, but a means for self-understanding, for the further cultivation of human nature and human society. The social sciences, Redfield argued, constituted "one of the principal parts of humanism," and stood with philosophy and literature as tools for the "cultivation of humanity." By suggesting that the role of social science was the "cultivation of humanity," Redfield was proposing that social science needed to judge and criticize society. This role implied an activist stance for the social scientist, one far different from the value-neutral role advocated by many during the 1940s and 1950s. Redfield devoted his final lecture in Frankfurt to examining how social science should fulfill this function; he offered in this lecture one of the first explorations of the sociology of social science.[51]

Redfield was one of the first American social scientists in the 1940s to raise doubts about the social science orthodoxy of value neutrality and the increasing drive among social scientists toward positivism. He was soon joined, however, by a number of other social scientists who sounded similar notes. Most prominent among these fellow critics were Alfred Kroeber, Clyde Kluckhohn, Ruth Benedict, Gunnar Myrdal, and later, C. Wright Mills. In voicing opposition, especially against the notion of value neutrality, Redfield and his colleagues were rekindling a debate that had greatly energized American social science in the late 1920s and the 1930s. In his superb analysis of American social science during this same period, Mark C. Smith offers an extended analysis of the conflict that emerged among social scientists who saw it as their job to provide technical expertise to government and corporate bureaucracies versus those who saw it as their role as social scientists to question the basic institutions within American society and the purposes to which social scientific knowledge was being applied. Smith refers to the technical experts as "service intellectuals" and those intent upon challenging the aims of social science as "purposivists." Fueled by the economic and institutional destruction of the Great Depression, the purposivists, led primarily by economist Wesley Mitchell, political scientist Charles Merriam, historian Charles Beard, sociologist Robert Lynd, and political scientist Harold Lasswell, challenged the reserved neutral approach of the service intellectuals and aggressively sought to connect their conceptions and practice of social science with their activist stance within social and political affairs.[52] In a very real sense then, Redfield and his fellow critics were simply re-energizing a forgotten theme in American social science. Redfield spoke from the margins of the profession in the late 1940s, but within a decade many of the ideas he had advanced came to be espoused by numerous other social scientists. The most obvious reflection of Redfield's intellectual influence was Robert Bierstedt's 1959 presidential address to the American Sociological Association, "Sociology and Humane Learning." In this address, Bierstedt not only paid direct tribute to Redfield's effort to orient sociology toward the humanities, but also he quoted extensively from Redfield's 1948 "The Art of Social Science" to support his contention that sociology "owns a rightful place in the domain of humane letters and belongs, with literature, history, and philosophy, among the arts that liberate the human mind."[53]

Social Change in Yucatan: An Existential View

Redfield did almost no fieldwork during the 1940s. When he did return to the field, he approached research with a different objective from that which had guided his earlier studies. This shift in his approach to research stemmed largely from the changes he had undergone during the previous decade in his thinking about the meaning and purpose of social science. The conception he had come to hold of social science as a moral discipline provided him, in short, with a new way of seeing that transformed his approach to fieldwork.

In 1948, Redfield returned to Chan Kom for a restudy. He designed this investigation in a much different manner, however, from his 1931 study.[54] Then he examined Chan Kom not out of interest in the village itself but rather as part of a larger project directed toward elucidating general principles involved in the process of social change. While the field techniques he employed for his 1931 study were anthropological, the overarching framework was sociological. His concerns were with general, processual trends and not with historical, particularistic aspects of village life. But in 1948, his concern was historical. This time he came to assess how the ethos or values of the villagers had changed over the last generation, during the period in which they had initiated rapid social change by consciously committing themselves to modernizing their way of life.

The leaders of Chan Kom had been particularly receptive to the program of progressive reform offered by the leaders of the Mexican Revolution and from the late 1910s had pushed to bring progress, as defined by revolutionary activists, to their village. In the early 1920s, Chan Kom was but a rude settlement peopled by a few dozen Maya families. Yet in 1923, the people of Chan Kom sought to improve the status of their village by having it officially recognized as a pueblo by the Mexican revolutionary government. The government had promised that it would grant land in the form of ejidos to any Indian village that chose to be recognized as a pueblo. As further incentive, the government promised also to grant tools, schools, furniture, drums, and flags to villages that became pueblos. Chan Kom was distinguished among Maya villages in Yucatan in being one of the few villages to accept the government's offer. Most Indian peasant villages were not receptive to the offer and chose to remain aloof, apart from the modernization program espoused by the Mexican government. The people of Chan Kom, however, aligned themselves eagerly with progressive Mexican reform. In 1935, they advanced their official standing from that of a pueblo to that of an independent municipality, the highest political status possible for a rural village.[55]

From the time he first visited Chan Kom in 1931, Redfield was aware that Chan Kom was unusual in its drive to become modern. He returned in 1948 to assess the results of the villagers' single-minded dedication to the pursuit of progress. He wanted, essentially, to determine what the consequences of modernity were for this little village.[56]

Redfield and his wife spent six weeks during the winter of 1948 studying the changes which had occurred in Chan Kom over the previous two decades. He described these changes and explored the meanings they held for the citizens of Chan Kom in *A Village That Chose Progress: Chan Kom Revisited* (1950). The most important changes experienced by the villagers during this period, he argued, were political and economic. In 1931, Chan Kom had been strictly an agricultural village; all men in the village had made their living through cultivation of maize. By 1948, while each man still maintained at least a small milpa, several had taken up the more lucrative pursuit of raising cattle and hogs. Economic change also resulted from the introduction into the village of new technology, such as automatic gristmills and mechanically drilled wells.

Yet, aside from these practical and commercial changes, Redfield argued that the village had changed little during the seventeen years from when he had first studied it. Chan Kom was still "a community of one kind of people: rural Maya toilers in the milpa." The transformation of the pueblo into an independent municipality and the introduction of hog and cattle raising had brought complexity in government and a new spirit of commercialism to Chan Kom. But commercialism had not permeated all aspects of the village. Most significantly, it had not penetrated into the family nor into religious practice. Close relatives did not do business with each other, women were almost untouched by commercial practices, and religious festivals had not begun to attract vendors—as in larger towns and cities—and taken on a carnivalesque atmosphere.[57]

Redfield dwelt, in particular, on the many aspects of modernity that the people of Chan Kom rejected. Foremost among these was Protestantism. American evangelical missionaries had come to Chan Kom in 1931 and were initially well received. The villagers were inspired by the moral exhortation the missionaries preached and were attracted to Protestantism because the missionaries linked it with the idea of progress. "They told the villagers that the people of the towns and the city were Protestants and that the Americans—a people then coming into importance among the villagers as powerful and admirable—were Protestants too." The leaders of Chan Kom, sensing the missionaries to be valuable allies in the cause of progress to which they had committed the village, led the villagers in 1932 in mass conversion to Protestantism.[58]

This conversion, however, proved to be short-lived. The villagers had found Protestantism easy to accept because the emphasis placed by the missionaries on sobriety and hard work simply reinforced values that were already central to their way of life. But the missionaries wished to change more than mere work habits and pushed the townspeople also to give up numerous traditional practices, such as praying to the saints, lighting prayer candles, chanting during times of stress, and finally, dancing—the most loved recreational outlet in the village. After a year of tension between the missionaries and the villagers, village head Eustaquio Ceme led a mass exodus away from Protestantism and back to traditional ways, which the people had learned to call Catholicism.[59]

The villagers also rejected several other aspects of modernity that had been introduced into the village during the early 1930s, the years of greatest zeal for progress. For a few brief years, girls in Chan Kom had begun wearing dresses in place of traditional huipils and cut their hair short. Parents supported coeducation and accepted dancing in which boys and girls embraced. Some villagers even entertained skeptical and rational thought, and Villa, the schoolteacher and Redfield's assistant, offered a class on sex physiology and birth control. But upon his return in 1948, Redfield found that enthusiasm had disappeared for nearly all these new practices. Of all the changes introduced during the 1930s and 1940s, only technological and commercial innovations had persisted. While the villagers had eagerly accepted new tools to expand their control over the environment and to enable them to attain what they perceived as the good life, they had rejected virtually all social, religious, and moral reforms. In 1948, village leaders judged Chan Kom to be at a plateau. They had achieved the political and material improvements they set out to obtain in the early 1930s and had no further aspirations for progress.

Combined with this sense of achievement, moreover, was a growing recognition among Chan Kom's leaders that material improvements and growth in the village had exacted a heavy cost. Village population had nearly doubled between 1931 and 1948, and signs of land overuse were glaringly apparent. Crop yields for corn, the villagers' primary food and cash crop, had dropped during this pe-

riod by one-third to one-half. The thick trees which once surrounded Chan Kom
had been cleared too frequently, in the slash-and-burn field development technique, and been replaced only by small, sparse bush. Soil depletion also discouraged the once-popular practice of planting and cultivating fruit trees. A few of
the village leaders, upon witnessing these changes, had even begun to withdraw
from Chan Kom and were starting to develop fields and dwellings in small rural
settlements outside the village.[60]

Although Redfield, in keeping with standard ethnographic practice, con-
cealed the identities of all his informants in *A Village That Chose Progress*, he
did allow the identity of one man to emerge in his text. This man, Sr. Eustaquio
Ceme, was the one who had mobilized Chan Kom to embrace progressive ways
in the early 1930s and who had presided paternally over the village throughout
the thirties and forties, maintaining control with a benevolent but sometimes iron
rule. Eustaquio Ceme, or Don Eus, had combined his exercise of authority with
articulation of a vision of progress for the village for an entire generation. It was
Don Eus, however, who had grown most skeptical about the course of future
events. Not only was he discouraged because of the declining yields in the
fields, but also he sensed imminent moral decline in the younger people. Vices,
such as drunkenness and idleness, he predicted, were soon going to come to the
village. And where he once advocated building a road to the city so that material
goods could be more easily transported to the village, he now voiced disap-
proval of the plan to connect the village's little road with the major highway to
the city. "Wherever roads come," he warned, "villages grow poor." While the
road may bring useful material goods, it also brought vices, commercial pleas-
ures, and poverty. Gravely, he predicted in a memorandum to Redfield, that
when the village road joined the highway to the city, there would then be a tav-
ern in Chan Kom.[61]

While Redfield reported that he saw no demonstrative signs among the villagers of the moral decline Don Eus so ominously envisioned, he concluded that
"the prediction of Don Eus is probably right." But Redfield suggested that the
mechanism of change is much subtler than that envisioned by Don Eus. Indeed,
not only is the mechanism subtle, but also it is cloaked in irony. This change is
not a matter of behavior—drunkenness or idleness—but rather a matter of ideas,
of meanings. Culture, in Redfield's definition, is a "web of meanings," and it is
subtle shifts within this web that Redfield found so profound. The meaning shift
for the villagers, he predicted, was rooted in their acceptance of new technology
and commercial practices. Using the new pursuit of cattle raising as his example,
he argued that the conflict raised over traditional methods of healing versus scientific veterinary techniques provided a site of contention at which the traditional web of meaning begins to come apart. Some of the villagers, especially
the younger ones, Redfield claimed, were quietly rejecting the traditional Maya
rituals as effective means for maintaining the health of their herds—herds which
represented a new level of concentrated wealth and, hence, concern for villagers—and placing their faith instead in vaccination. This rift, introduced solely

within the technological and commercial sphere, introduced division in what was once an integrated web of meaning.[62]

Redfield explored this example because it illustrated a most troubling aspect about the nature of progress, namely, the problem of unintended consequences. While the villagers had labored to select only the aspects of modernity that they wanted, merely some tools to make their lives easier, to bring more of the good life to themselves, they actually had introduced into their lives agents of change that had the potential to transform their entire system of meaning. And as Western technology is inevitably linked to science, which is embedded within a rational framework, the villagers had unwittingly admitted corrosive seeds of rationalism into their once-complete circle of traditional religious belief. The future of the village, in Redfield's view, was thus tied inexorably to rationalistic, mechanistic Western civilization. He concluded *A Village Chose That Chose Progress* on an ironic, poignant note:

> The people of Chan Kom are, then, a people who have no choice but to go forward with technology, with a declining religious faith and moral conviction, into a dangerous world. They are a people who must and will come to identify their interests with those of people far away, outside the traditional circle of their loyalties and political responsibilities. As such, they should have the sympathy of the readers of these pages.[63]

The major strength of *A Village That Chose Progress* is Redfield's analysis of the relationship between values held by the villagers and social change in Chan Kom during the 1930s and 1940s. Several reviewers praised Redfield's approach to the study of values in *A Village That Chose Progress*. Indeed, most critics responded positively overall to this book. Howard Cline, who had been particularly harsh in his criticism of Redfield in his earlier Mexican community studies for his inattention to the contribution of historical factors in social change, strongly praised the new sensitivity Redfield displayed toward historical data. Two anthropologists, Ralph Beals and Edward Spicer, both deeply interested in problems of acculturation and social change, commended the subtlety of Redfield's argument and praised him for calling attention to the many potential problems associated with Point Four-style modernization. Finally, Spicer especially praised Redfield for bringing focus to the discussion of values within a community and of the power these values had to shape the future of the community.[64]

Modernization, in Redfield's account, was not a nondescript process that encroached upon the village and mysteriously transformed it from "traditional" to "modern." Rather, Redfield argued, social change in the village stemmed primarily from choices made by villagers to incorporate new tools and techniques into their way of life. Such a view perceived the villagers as active agents engaged in choosing their future; they were not merely passive victims of a bloodless, impersonal social force.

However, as Redfield warned repeatedly, change carried multiple unintended consequences. In the same way that a subtle shift toward rational modes
of thought accompanied the introduction of new technologies into the village, so
also, Redfield suggested, did new social attitudes enter the village. The villagers' "tastes and manners, norms of the enjoyable and good" changed and became "more varied" and "less exclusively fixed by village tradition." While
these changes were not pronounced, he stated pointedly, "the general direction is
significant." Continuing his understated but astringent commentary on the direction of change in the village, Redfield concluded, "'the road to the light,' starts
out toward Chicago rather than toward Mexico City. The changes in Chan Kom
are in the direction of North American or cosmopolitan urbanized life rather
than in the direction of Latin culture."[65]

Some have interpreted this statement to represent Redfield's preference for
modern American over Latin culture. Furthermore, several readers have understood Redfield's primary intention in *A Village That Chose Progress* to be that
of praising the village of Chan Kom for having undergone successful modernization.[66] I think this view is profoundly at odds with Redfield's published and
unpublished writings. In stating that the villagers were changing in the direction
of Chicago rather than Mexico City, Redfield was actually offering subtle criticism and not praise regarding the overall pattern of change in Chan Kom. He
followed his comment about North American and Latin culture with two para-
graphs in which he examined the aspects of Latin culture that the Maya villagers
had ignored and rejected. They have shown complete insensitivity, he charged,
to all expressive behavior, emotions, sentiment, symbolic gestures of greeting,
and drama. In short, "none of the aesthetic sensibility of Latin culture has found
lodgment in the Chan Kom people."[67]

Further support that Redfield was dismayed rather than pleased at the long-
term implications of change in Chan Kom appears in his private correspondence.
In a letter in which he discussed his draft for *A Village That Chose Progress*
with his friend and University of Chicago colleague John Nef, Redfield expressed the fear that his text might sound too pessimistic regarding the consequences of the villagers' refusal to adopt only practical aspects of modernity and
none of the artistic or expressive aspects of Latin civilization. The villagers, in
their indifference to any aesthetic concerns coupled with their solitary focus
upon practical, commercial concerns, he suggested "seem to be making, in a
small way, the characteristic mistakes of Western civilization."[68]

Redfield characteristically understated his ideas, and his style in *A Village
That Chose Progress* is no exception to this pattern. At the heart of this book,
however, lies his conviction that art is the saving grace of civilization—technical
progress alone is sterile. Redfield should thus be seen as profoundly ambivalent
over the coming of modernity to Chan Kom. While he admired the villagers'
iron work ethic and strong-willed dedication to improving their lives through
introduction of new tools and techniques, he feared that their coherent belief
structure would be rent by the subtle introduction of new modes of thought and
new social attitudes. And without a sense of values for aesthetic aspects of civi-

lization, for artistic pursuits that can re-create meanings which have been fragmented through "progress," modernity thus loomed, in Redfield's view, as more
dangerous than helpful to a village such as Chan Kom.

Notes

1. Although Redfield published his article "The Folk Society" in 1947, he actually wrote this much earlier. He wrote it first as a lecture for delivery at the College of the University of Chicago; Sol Tax translated it into Spanish and had it published as "La Sociedad Folk," *Revista Mexicana de Sociología* 4, no. 4 (1942); Redfield finally published it at the request of the editors in the *American Journal of Sociology* 52 (January 1947): 293-308.

2. "Anthropology, A Natural Science?" *Social Forces* (June 1926): 715-721; "Culture Changes in Yucatan," *American Anthropologist* 36 (January-March 1934): 57-69.

3. Harry S. Ashmore, *Unseasonable Truths: The Life of Robert Maynard Hutchins* (Boston: Little, Brown and Company, 1987); Mary Ann Dzuback, *Robert M. Hutchins, Portrait of an Educator* (Chicago: University of Chicago Press, 1992); Benjamin McArthur, "A Gamble on Youth: Robert M. Hutchins and the Politics of Presidential Selection," *History of Education Quarterly* (Summer 1990): 161-186.

4. Hutchins's complex relationship with faculty members at Chicago is best covered by William McNeill in *Hutchins' University: A Memoir of the University of Chicago, 1929-1950* (Chicago: University of Chicago Press, 1991), and Edward Shils, "Robert Maynard Hutchins," *American Scholar* (January 1990): 211-235; see also Dzuback, *Robert M. Hutchins.*

5. When Hutchins arrived on campus, over fifty individuals and committees reported directly to the president, including five professional school deans and thirty-nine department heads. Hutchins drastically simplified the Chicago structure by clustering the graduate departments into four separate divisions: biological sciences, physical sciences, social sciences, and humanities. For each division he appointed a dean who reported directly to him and represented all departments within the division. He then no longer had to deal with thirty-nine separate departments but rather only four divisional deans. When Hutchins first created the four graduate divisions in 1930, he appointed senior established figures as deans. He dramatically altered the character of his top administrative circle in the mid-1930s, though, by replacing three of his four divisional deans with men of his own generation—men who were almost half the age of most of the Chicago professors. He selected Robert Redfield to be the first member of this new younger set in his administration. Redfield was a newly appointed associate professor in 1934 when Hutchins selected him to be dean. The deanship carried automatic promotion to full professor; thus, during the first six years of his career, Redfield advanced from the position of assistant to full professor and dean. See McNeill, *Hutchins' University,* 67, 79, 89-90; Dzuback, *Robert M. Hutchins,* 171, 179, 182.

6. On Hutchins as a secular moralist, see Dzuback, *Robert M. Hutchins,* 103-108.

7. Robert M. Hutchins, "University Education," *Yale Review* 25 (June 1936): 665-682; Robert M. Hutchins, *The Higher Learning in America* (New Haven, Conn.: Yale University Press, 1936).

8. Robert Redfield to Robert M. Hutchins, 30 September 1936, box 121, folder 13, Robert Maynard Hutchins Papers, Addenda, Special Collections, Joseph Regenstein Library, University of Chicago, Chicago.

9. Some sense of the friendship between Hutchins and Redfield can be gained from the eulogy Hutchins delivered at Redfield's funeral. "Remarks by Robert M. Hutchins," in "Robert Redfield: A Memorial Service," 16 November 1958, pp. 13-15, box 5, folder

2, Robert Redfield Papers, Addenda, Special Collections, Joseph Regenstein Library, University of Chicago, Chicago (hereafter cited as RRA-UC).

10. While the "New Plan" quickly came to be known as the "Hutchins Plan," Hutchins was merely the one who implemented this curriculum, not the one who designed it. A movement for change in the Chicago undergraduate curriculum had been under way long before Hutchins came to Chicago. The two presidents who had preceded Hutchins, Ernest DeWitt Burton (1923-1927) and Max Mason (1927-1929), had each appointed committees to redesign the existing curriculum. Chauncey Boucher, dean of arts, sciences, and literature under Mason, had led the Mason-era curriculum project and had completed a plan for a far-reaching redesign of the Chicago curriculum just at the time Max Mason left. Hutchins reviewed the curricular reform efforts undertaken during the 1920s and initiated plans for immediate implementation of the Boucher plan. Thus, even though the plan came to be called the "Hutchins Plan," in design it was truly the "Boucher Plan." Several excellent accounts provide in-depth information on the origins and extended development of undergraduate curricular reform at Chicago during the Hutchins era. I found these particularly useful: F. Champion Ward, ed., *The Idea and Practice of General Education: An Account of the College of the University of Chicago* (Chicago: University of Chicago Press, 1950); Donald N. Levine, "Challenging Certain Myths about the 'Hutchins' College," *University of Chicago Magazine* 77 (Winter 1975): 36-39, 51; McNeill, *Hutchins' University*; Dzuback, *Robert M. Hutchins*; and John J. MacAloon, ed., *General Education in the Social Sciences: Centennial Reflections on the College of the University of Chicago* (Chicago: University of Chicago Press, 1992).

11. The 1931 initiative had passed while Hutchins was still in the "honeymoon period" of his administration. His close associate Mortimer Adler, furthermore, had not yet offended numerous faculty members who might have remained at least partially sympathetic to Hutchins's ideas. See McNeill, *Hutchins' University*, and Shils, "Robert Maynard Hutchins" for insightful comments on the relationship between Hutchins and Adler and on the consequences this relationship had for Hutchins.

12. McNeill, *Hutchins' University*, 110-120; Dzubeck, *Robert M. Hutchins*, 130-131.

13. The list of those who have served as instructors reads almost like a "who's who" of mid-twentieth-century American sociology and includes, among many others, Louis Wirth, Edward Shils, Robert Redfield, Daniel Bell, David Riesman, Milton Singer, Lewis Coser, Philip Rieff, and Reinhard Bendix. See the excellent "festschrift" to the Soc 2 course edited by John MacAloon, *General Education in the Social Sciences*.

14. In a recent autobiographical essay, Joseph Gusfield, a member of the Soc 2 teaching staff during the late forties, described his experience as a Soc 2 instructor. "The staff itself and the weekly staff meetings, or seminars, were a feast of intellectual energy and joy that has remained for me an ideal of academic talk; one whose level I have never since been able to find or to recreate. The erudition, incisiveness, and originality were great and exciting spurs to my developing interests in academic work. That high flow of conversation was also a noisy battlefield of competing egos seeking an acclaim they had yet to receive elsewhere. It was intimidating to a young and unsure scholar, but it was also immensely fruitful as a period of learning." Joseph Gusfield, "The Scholarly Tension: Graduate Craft and the Undergraduate Imagination," in MacAloon, *General Education in the Social Sciences*, 168. See also David Riesman's essay in the same volume, "My Education in Soc 2 and My Efforts to Adapt It in the Harvard Setting," and Daniel

Bell's autobiographical remarks in *The Reforming of General Education: The Columbia College Experience in Its National Setting* (New York: Columbia University Press, 1966), 26-38.

15. Redfield published a number of essays on social science education from the 1930s through the early 1950s. Most obvious in these essays are the numerous references he makes to the Chicago social science survey courses—an indirect indication of the enormous effect these courses had upon him. See Robert Redfield, "The Place of the Social Sciences in a General Education," in *Growth and Development: The Basis for Educational Programs* (New York: New York Progressive Education Association, 1936), 141-151; "Research in the Social Sciences: Its Significance for General Education," *Social Education* 5 (December 1941): 568-574; "The Study of Culture in General Education," *Social Education* 11 (October 1947): 259-264; "Social-Science Research in General Education," *Journal of General Education* 6 (January 1952): 81-91.

16. For an extended exploration of Redfield's role as a public intellectual, see Kathryn Jean Kadel, "Little Community to the World: The Social Vision of Robert Redfield, 1897-1958" (Ph.D. diss., Northern Illinois University, DeKalb, Ill., 2000), 141-304.

17. Two government actions, in particular, had angered newspaper owners. First, the Roosevelt administration had greatly expanded the use of press agents to channel official information to the press. These press agents—"spin doctors" in today's parlance—played an important advocacy role in packaging government information so that it would appeal to the public. Newspaper owners perceived their power being undercut; not only had their reporters lost access to actual policy-makers, but also government had institutionalized an alternative channel for distributing information. The line between propaganda—a powerful force in European nations during World War II—and government press relations was becoming less obvious. Second, government officials and owners of the press had clashed over compliance with federal legislation. The Roosevelt administration had attempted to force publishers to abide by federal wage and union laws in the same way as other businesses. Newspaper owners insisted that imposition of such laws upon them violated constitutional protection of freedom of the press. The perception that American publishers had of this "erosion" of press freedom is aptly discussed in Margaret A. Blanchard, "The Hutchins Commission, the Press, and the Responsibility Concept," *Journalism Monographs* 47 (May 1977): 3-10, and Michael Schudson, *Discovering the News: A Social History of American Newspapers* (New York: Basic Books, 1982), 164-167.

18. Blanchard, "The Hutchins Commission," 11-13; Ashmore, *Unseasonable Truths*, 272; Schudson, *Discovering the News*, 166-167.

19. James Boylan, "The Hutchins Report: A Twenty-Year View," *Columbia Journalism Review* 6 (Summer 1967): 5-8.

20. I am indebted to Benjamin MacArthur for this phrase.

21. Alice K. Smith, *A Peril and a Hope: The Scientists' Movement in America, 1945-47* (Chicago: University of Chicago Press, 1965), 27-34; Dzuback, *Robert M. Hutchins*, 216-218; Paul L. Boyer, *By the Bombs' Early Light: American Thought and Culture at the Dawn of the Atomic Age* (New York: Pantheon, 1985), 49-64.

22. Wesley T. Wooley, *Alternatives to Anarchy: American Supranationalism since World War II* (Bloomington: Indiana University Press, 1988): 41-44; Lawrence S. Wittner, *The Struggle against the Bomb*, vol. 1: *One World or None: A History of the World Nuclear Disarmament Movement through 1953* (Stanford, Calif.: Stanford University Press, 1993), 67; Boyer, *Bomb's Early Light*, 38.

23. For an excellent treatment of the history of the NAACP's legal battle against segregation, see Richard Kluger, *Simple Justice: The History of Brown v. Board of Education and Black America's Struggle for Equality* (New York: Alfred A. Knopf, 1976; reprint, New York: Vintage Books, 1977).

24. Franz Boas led the way during the first two decades of the twentieth century in challenging assumptions of black inferiority. His students, in particular, Otto Klineberg and Melville Herskovits, greatly extended the scientific critique of racist ideology. Harvard psychologist Jerome Bruner also wrote extensively on the negative effects segregation inflicted upon the learning process; Bruner took an active part, furthermore, in the NAACP desegregation effort, serving as an expert witness in several trials. On the efforts of social scientists to combat racial discrimination, see George W. Stocking, Jr., *Race, Culture, and Evolution: Essays in the History of Anthropology* (New York: Free Press, 1968), 110-132, 161-194, 270-307; Carl N. Degler, *In Search of Human Nature: The Decline and Revival of Darwinism in American Social Thought* (New York: Oxford University Press, 1991), 59-83, 176-211; and Kluger, *Simple Justice*, 308-314.

25. Gunnar Myrdal, *An American Dilemma* (New York: Harper and Row, 1944).

26. The two men who were largely responsible for committing the NAACP to the sociological approach, Howard Law School professor William H. Hastie and Thurgood Marshall, realized that social science had been used to justify segregation from its inception in the late nineteenth century. A revolution in the social scientific conception of race had occurred in the 1910s and 1920s, though, and Hastie and Marshall were anxious to bring these new perspectives to bear on the segregation issue. For a very useful account of the earlier usages of social science race theory, see Herbert Hovenkamp, "Social Science and Segregation before *Brown*," *Duke Law Journal* 1985 (June-September): 624-672.

27. This phrase is Mark Tushnet's. See Mark V. Tushnet, *The NAACP's Legal Strategy against Segregated Education* (Chapel Hill: University of North Carolina Press, 1987), 118-121.

28. See "Remarks by William R. Ming, Jr.," in "Robert Redfield: A Memorial Service," 16 November 1958, pp. 9-11, box 5, folder 2, RRA-UC. For information on Redfield's contributions to the NAACP's battle against restrictive covenants, see Clement Vose, *Caucasians Only: The Supreme Court, the NAACP, and the Restrictive Covenant Cases* (Berkeley: University of California Press, 1959).

29. Heman Sweatt did matriculate in the University of Texas Law School. He did not have sufficient academic background, however, to succeed (he had received his collegiate education in an unaccredited Jim Crow college), and he left after three terms. He went on to obtain a degree in social work and pursued a successful career in this field. See Michael L. Gillette, "Heman Marion Sweatt: Civil Rights Plaintiff," in *Black Leaders for Their Times*, ed. Alwyn Barr and Robert A. Calvert (Austin: Texas State Historical Collections, 1981), 157-188.

30. Chapter 12 of Richard Kluger's *Simple Justice* offers an excellent treatment of the *Sweatt* case that includes a detailed description of Redfield's contribution as expert witness. Jonathan Entin's "*Sweatt v. Painter*, the End of Segregation, and the Transformation of Education Law," *Review of Litigation* 5 (Winter 1986): 3-71, and Mark Tushnet's *The NAACP's Legal Strategy against Segregated Education* provide critical assessments of the importance of *Sweatt v. Painter* to the overall NAACP fight to overturn *Plessy v. Ferguson*. Useful information on the context and ramifications of the

Sweatt case at the University of Texas can be found in Michael L. Gillette, "Blacks Challenge the White University," *Southwestern Historical Quarterly* 86 (October 1982): 321-344.

31. Robert Redfield to Lisa Redfield Peattie, (August 1945), box 1, folder 9, RRA-UC.

32. Robert Redfield, "Consequences of Atomic Energy," *Phi Delta Kappan* 27 (April 1946): 221-224. Representative articles by Redfield's colleagues include William F. Ogburn's "Sociology and the Atom," *American Journal of Sociology* 51 (January 1946): 267-275, and Louis Wirth's "Responsibility of Social Science," *Annals of the American Academy of Social and Political Science* 249 (January 1947): 143-151. See the excellent discussion of social scientists' contributions to the postwar nuclear discourse in Boyer's *By the Bomb's Early Light*, 166-177.

33. Robert Redfield, "Social Science in the Atomic Age," *Journal of General Education* 1 (January 1947): 120-124.

34. Redfield, "Social Science in the Atomic Age," 122.

35. On the efforts by social scientists in the immediate postwar years to achieve new standing for their disciplines, especially their attempt to gain recognition by the National Science Foundation, see Samuel Z. Klausner and Victor M. Lidz, eds., *The Nationalization of the Social Sciences* (Philadelphia: University of Pennsylvania Press, 1986).

36. The full name of this institution is the Johann Wolfgang Goethe-Universität Frankfurt located in Frankfurt-am-Main.

37. German higher education had not only been ideologically corrupted by the Nazis, but most institutions had lost the majority of their faculty members and, in some cases, much of their facilities during the war. Allied bombing destroyed over 60 percent of the buildings at the University of Frankfurt and by the end of the war, the institution was struggling to survive. Hutchins campaigned to bring American assistance to German higher education and committed University of Chicago resources to bolster the depleted professorial ranks at Frankfurt. Harvard followed the Chicago lead and initiated a similar program called "Harvard-at-Heidelberg." See "Chicago in Frankfurt," *Time* 51 (12 April 1948): 85; "Chicago in Frankfurt," *Newsweek* 31 (12 April 1948): 83. James F. Tent, *Mission on the Rhine: Reeducation and Denazification in American-Occupied Germany* (Chicago: University of Chicago Press, 1982).

38. "The Art of Social Science," *American Journal of Sociology* 54 (November 1948): 181-190.

39. Robert Redfield to Everett C. Hughes (January 1949); Hughes to Redfield, 24 January 1949; Redfield to Hughes, 28 February 1949; Redfield to Hughes, 11 March 1949, box 14, folder 13, Robert Redfield Papers, Special Collections, Joseph Regenstein Library, University of Chicago, Chicago.

40. Redfield presented the following lectures at Frankfurt: (1) "The Logic and Functions of Social Science"; (2) "Social Science among the Humanities"; (3) "Social Science as an Art"; (4) "Social Science and Values"; and (5) "Social Science as Morality." He based the third lecture closely on "The Art of Social Science," which he had published the previous year in the *American Journal of Sociology*. Redfield also published the first lecture as "Social Science in Our Society," *Phylon* 11, no. 1 (1950): 31-41, and the second lecture as "Social Science among the Humanities," *Measure* 1 (Winter 1950): 60-74. All five of the Frankfurt essays appear as a unit in *Human Nature and the Study of Society: The Papers of Robert Redfield*, vol. 1, ed. Margaret Park Redfield (Chicago: University of Chicago Press, 1962).

41. Redfield, "The Logic and Functions of Social Science," in *Human Nature and the Study of Society*, 33-37.

42. Redfield, "Logic and Functions of Social Science," 35.

43. See Redfield's review of George A. Lundberg's *Social Research: A Study in Methods of Gathering Data* (New York: Longmans, Green and Co., 1929) in *American Anthropologist* 33 (January-March 1931): 106-107.

44. Redfield cited two recent articles that elaborated on the similarities between the natural and social sciences: Lewis White Beck, "The Natural Science Ideal in the Social Sciences," *The Scientific Monthly* 68 (June 1949): 386-394, and Donald G. Marquis, "Scientific Methodology in Human Relations," *Proceedings of the American Philosophical Society* 87 (December 1948): 411-416. Redfield also acknowledged that he was not the first to call attention to the bonds between the humanities and social sciences; he cited Ruth Benedict's "Anthropology and the Humanities," *American Anthropologist* 50 (October-December 1948): 585-593 to this effect.

45. Redfield, "Social Science among the Humanities," in *Human Nature and the Study of Society*, 49-50.

46. Redfield, "Social Science as an Art," in *Human Nature and the Study of Society*, 62.

47. Redfield, "Social Science as an Art," 63.

48. Redfield, "Social Science among the Humanities," in *Human Nature and the Study of Society*, 47.

49. Redfield, "Social Science among the Humanities," 55-57.

50. Redfield acknowledged that personal values could conflict with scientific judgment, and he cited the conflict he faced in evaluating research on racial differences. Shortly before Redfield had gone to Frankfurt, Henry E. Garrett had published an article entitled "Negro-White Differences in Mental Ability in the United States," *Scientific Monthly* 65 (October 1947): 329-333. Garrett argued that blacks were inherently inferior to whites; he rebutted the claims of psychologists, like Otto Klineberg, furthermore, who argued that observed differences between blacks and whites derived from environmental factors. Garrett was not a minor figure in the American social scientific establishment. Indeed, he was chairman of the Columbia psychology department, and he represented a formidable challenge to the NAACP and the social scientists who were aligned with the organization in the effort to demonstrate that no differences could be proved to exist between blacks and whites, a strategy designed to deprive segregationists of the "scientific" basis they claimed. As soon as Garrett's article appeared in print, Thurgood Marshall appealed to Redfield to muster a social scientific rebuttal to Garrett (Thurgood Marshall to Robert Redfield, 6 February 1948, box 23, folder 4, RR-UC). Redfield admitted to his Frankfurt audience that he had experienced no small conflict upon reading Garrett's paper: "If a paper is published that reaches the conclusion that intelligence tests have proved the mental inferiority of the Negro and I see that the writer is from some state in the deep South [Garrett had begun his capsule biography, which was printed prominently right beneath the title of the article, by stating that he was a "native of Virginia"], I am aware," Redfield acknowledged, "that I anticipate that I will find something faulty in the work or the reasoning. Then, when I read the article, do I judge it by its internal evidence as to scientific worth? It is certainly my duty so to judge it." "Social Science and Values," in *Human Nature and the Study of Society*, 74. On Garrett's role in opposing the NAACP's desegregation effort, see Kluger, *Simple Justice*, 480-507.

51. Robert Redfield, "Social Science as Morality," in *Human Nature and the Study of Society*, 85-86. Several authors have since produced much fuller treatments of the sociology of social science. See Leon Bramson, *The Political Context of Sociology* (Princeton, N.J.: Princeton University Press, 1961); Robert W. Friedrichs, *A Sociology of Sociology* (New York: Free Press, 1970), and David M. Ricci, *The Tragedy of Political Science: Politics, Scholarship, and Democracy* (New Haven, Conn.: Yale University Press, 1984).

52. Mark C. Smith, *Social Science in the Crucible: The American Debate over Objectivity and Purpose, 1918-1941* (Durham, N.C.: Duke University Press, 1994), 5-9.

53. Robert Bierstedt, "Sociology and Humane Learning," *American Sociological Review* 25 (February 1960): 3-9. Other similar humanistic conceptions of social science can be seen in the following texts from the late 1950s and early 1960s: C. Wright Mills, *The Sociological Imagination* (New York: Oxford University Press, 1958), Peter L. Berger, *Invitation to Sociology: A Humanistic Perspective* (Garden City, N.Y.: Anchor Books, 1963), and Eric R. Wolf, *Anthropology* (Princeton, N.J.: Princeton University Press, 1964). The American Sociological Association even featured a session at its 1966 annual meeting entitled "Sociology as a Field of the Humanities." See Friedrichs, *A Sociology of Sociology*, 125-128.

54. Redfield and his assistant, Alfonso Villa Rojas, conducted the fieldwork for the first Chan Kom study in 1931; they published their monograph on Chan Kom in 1934. Robert Redfield and Alfonso Villa Rojas, *Chan Kom: A Maya Village* (Washington, D.C.: Carnegie Institution of Washington, 1934).

55. Robert Redfield, *A Village That Chose Progress: Chan Kom Revisited* (Chicago: University of Chicago Press, 1950), 1-20.

56. Redfield, *Village That Chose Progress*, 23-24.

57. Redfield, *Village That Chose Progress*, 86-87.

58. Redfield, *Village That Chose Progress*, 88-92.

59. Redfield, *Village That Chose Progress*, 92-112.

60. Redfield, *Village That Chose Progress*, 113-138.

61. Redfield, *Village That Chose Progress*, 175.

62. Redfield, *Village That Chose Progress*, 174-178.

63. Redfield, *Village That Chose Progress*, 178.

64. Howard Cline, *Hispanic American Historical Review* 30 (November 1950): 521-525; Ralph L. Beals, *American Anthropologist* 53 (January-March 1951): 93-94; Edward Spicer, *Annals of the American Academy of Political and Social Science* 273 (January 1951): 298-299.

65. When the villagers decided to build a road in the early 1930s to connect their isolated settlement with Chichén Itzá, the nearest center of "civilization" and connection point for the road to the city of Mérida, they had referred to their little road as "the road to the light." Redfield, *Village That Chose Progress*, 152-153.

66. Students who used the text in the Social Science II course at the University of Chicago during the 1950s used to refer to it as "The Little Village that Could." Ralph W. Nicholas, afterword, in MacAloon, *General Education in the Social Sciences*, 284.

67. Redfield, *Village That Chose Progress*, 154.

68. Redfield's concern over being perceived as too pessimistic or deterministic is quite obvious in his remarks to Nef. "Your second comment will cause me to read the last pages more carefully to see if I have suggested to the reader any apparent conviction on my part that absorption of values of art and faith is impossible. I do not want to give that

suggestion. At the same time I have to report that in Chan Kom there seems to me little evidence that the people there are absorbing such. The mood and the interest are practical, commercial. They seem to be making, in a small way, the characteristic mistakes of Western civilization. Surely, I do not want to suggest that I like that, or that I think it inevitable. But there it is." Robert Redfield to John Nef, 21 September 1948, box 36, folder 5, John U. Nef papers, Special Collections, Joseph Regenstein Library, University of Chicago, Chicago.

Chapter 4

From Folk Societies to Civilizations

Although Redfield enjoyed wide renown among anthropologists almost from the moment he entered the profession—owing largely to the instant success of *Tepoztlán*—most anthropologists in the 1930s and 1940s did not regard his work as belonging to the mainstream of the discipline. Sociologists, being more accustomed to working with comparative studies and theoretical generalizations, accepted Redfield's work more readily during these decades than did anthropologists. Nevertheless, even though sociologists utilized his theoretical notions, particularly the folk-urban construct, most did not regard Redfield as one of their own. Indeed, he spent the majority of his career located somewhat uncomfortably on the margins of both anthropology and sociology.

Yet following World War II, the intellectual agenda of American anthropology shifted, and many of the issues that Redfield had pursued in relative isolation during the 1930s moved to the center of disciplinary focus. In particular, American anthropologists began to turn their attention toward the study of complex societies, social and cultural evolution, and universal cultural values. Redfield not only had spent his career studying social transformation in a scheme that accorded closely with postwar considerations of social evolution, but also had been one of the pioneers in extending anthropology toward study of complex societies. Moreover, the study of values, especially as reflected in villager's worldviews, had held a prominent role in his Latin American community studies. Therefore, as these concerns became central within postwar anthropological practice, Redfield emerged as something of an elder statesman, a seasoned explorer of the new terrain. Redfield undertook teaching and research, moreover, with renewed interest during the late forties and the fifties, and the postwar era proved to be one of the most productive periods of his career, a period in which he both reinterpreted much of his earlier work as well as contributed much that was new.

The Transformation of Postwar American Anthropology

World War II marks a distinct divide in the history of American anthropology. Three developments, in particular, intersected to change the character of the discipline during the postwar era: (1) the generation of a cluster of powerful new ideas by anthropologists who came of age intellectually during the late 1920s and early 1930s and were anxious to push beyond Boasian disciplinary traditions; (2) the influx of a large number of new students into anthropology, many of them veterans, who swelled department enrollments and greatly increased disciplinary momentum; and (3) the emergence of anthropology as a "policy science"; anthropology thus achieved parity with other branches of the social sciences in assisting government officials in the formation of national and international policies.[1]

The first of these developments, the formation of new intellectual directions within the discipline, represented a diversified effort by several anthropologists to confront and reconsider many of the foundational ideas of twentieth-century American anthropology. For the first three decades of the twentieth century, thought and practice within American anthropology had conformed largely to the approach advanced by Franz Boas. In the late nineteenth century, Boas had challenged the widespread reliance on speculative, often racist, evolutionary perspectives within anthropology and had firmly established the empirical historical method as the standard disciplinary approach. By insisting that anthropologists adhere to empirical methods, Boas was mounting a campaign to drive the use of "armchair" methods out of the discipline. Nineteenth-century anthropologists had derived almost all of their information about other cultures from accounts made by travelers and missionaries. Anthropology according to this method consisted of selectively weaving together various traveler's accounts, often embellishing the narrative with notions based upon conjectural history, to produce sweeping syntheses, such as Sir James Frazer's *The Golden Bough*. Boas regarded this approach as not only unscientific, but also as blatantly biased toward celebration of civilized life at the expense of primitive life.

Anthropologists needed to go to the field, Boas maintained, to collect their own data, as did scientists in other disciplines. Moreover, Boas pushed anthropologists to abandon their attempts to view development of individual tribes and villages through the lens of a grand evolutionary scheme. Instead, Boas urged that anthropologists pursue a strictly historical method. Where use of the evolutionary perspective had masked individual differences in favor of constructing an all-embracing developmental scheme, the historical method focused upon differences, the unique aspects of each tribe and village. For much of his career, Boas suggested that after sufficient historical characterization of particular peoples had been accomplished, larger generalizations could be drawn from the collected data. But in his later years, he reversed himself on this point and concluded that the immense amount of historical data collected on different peoples throughout the world was so complex that it defied drawing generalizations.[2]

Boasian anthropology readily lent itself, however, to one broad generalization—the notion of cultural relativism. Boas developed the general principles upon which this notion rested through his decades of research among North American Indians. His students, however, produced the clearest formulations of cultural relativism as a doctrine. Two students, in particular, Ruth Benedict in *Patterns of Culture* (1934) and Melville J. Herskovits in *Man and His Works* (1948), offered the classic expressions of cultural relativism. Benedict and Herskovits argued that modern empirical anthropology had demonstrated the existence of a multiplicity of different cultures, each of which was organized around a unique constellation of values. Since each of these value systems was culturally determined, no absolute evaluations could be made about any of these different moral systems; all moral systems must therefore be regarded as relative. Recognition of the relativity of value systems obligates us, furthermore, to respect and tolerate each separate way of life. Virtually all American anthropologists during the 1930s and 1940s embraced this doctrine of benevolent tolerance as articulated by Benedict and Herskovits. Their formulation of cultural relativism came to stand, moreover, as the essence of Boasian cultural criticism and provided American anthropology much of its disciplinary identity from the 1920s through the mid-1940s.[3]

Yet this prevailing sense of tolerance failed to survive World War II. The rise of Nazism and other forms of totalitarianism during the 1930s, and, especially, revelations of the atrocities committed during World War II under the banner of culture, shattered the faith most American anthropologists had placed in the doctrine of cultural relativism. And following the war, anthropologists fell into acrimonious dispute among themselves over the continuing viability of the notion of cultural, particularly ethical, relativism. The Nazis had provided a chilling demonstration of how ideas of cultural uniqueness could lend themselves to grotesque expression and be used to justify monstrous behavior. Most American anthropologists began to de-emphasize, therefore, the unique aspects of each culture and focused instead on uniformities, especially shared moral and ethical values, existing among cultures. Rather than celebrating the relativism of cultural value systems, many turned instead toward the search for universal cultural values.[4]

The postwar reaction against cultural relativism represented the most obvious attempt to deviate from the Boasian disciplinary tradition. Nevertheless, during the late thirties and early forties, a handful of younger anthropologists had also begun to chafe at other strictures inherent in Boas's approach to anthropology, especially the rigid emphases he had placed upon use of the historical particularist method and avoidance of broad cultural generalizations.[5] And following the war, many members of the discipline chose to push beyond Boasian constraints.

The intellectual agenda for anthropology expanded rapidly under the stimulus of these younger anthropologists. In separate essays, Robert F. Murphy and Eric R. Wolf have identified the primary new themes that came to dominate postwar American anthropology.[6] In addition to the de-emphasis upon cultural relativism, the most prominent among these themes were: (1) a renewal of interest in social evolution; (2) a shift in concern with cultural particularities to cultural uniformities; (3) a change in focus from study of primitive tribes to study of more complex societies, such as peasant villages, towns and cities, and even nations and civilizations; (4) an increase in concern with the dynamics of cultural and social change; and (5) a continuation in interest in the relationship between culture and personality. Significantly, all these issues reflected a new concern with the development of a more theoretically sophisticated approach to anthropological practice than that which had prevailed during the previous few decades.

Complementing these intellectual trends, powerful demographic and institutional trends also greatly affected anthropology during the postwar era. Before the war, anthropology had been one of the smallest disciplines in the academy. After the war, though, growth in anthropology surged. Classes which had previously only attracted a few students suddenly filled to capacity. "The growth of the student population required such an increase in faculty," anthropologist Walter Goldschmidt remembered, "that it was impossible to keep up with the teaching demand, and faculty were recruited from among students fresh back from the field, before their dissertations were complete."[7] And where before the war, most institutions had offered instruction in anthropology only through combined departments, after the war, most American colleges and universities organized independent anthropology departments. Membership in the American Anthropological Association increased twentyfold, furthermore, between 1941 and 1964.[8]

Yet the cohort of students who entered anthropology during the mid-1940s to early 1950s was distinguished by qualitative as well as quantitative measures. Not insignificantly, a very high proportion of these students were veterans. Supported by the GI Bill, millions of veterans returned from being stationed overseas and enrolled in institutions of higher education.[9] For almost a decade, these veterans exerted a distinct intellectual influence upon American college and university campuses. The combination of their maturity in years and experience coupled with their diverse class and ethnic backgrounds enabled them to look at issues quite differently from traditional students. War service had provided most veterans with extensive experience in living overseas among peoples of different nationalities and cultures. For many veterans, these experiences whetted their appetites for further study of culture and international issues. Accordingly, a high proportion of veterans chose to study social sciences, particularly anthropology, to pursue interests awakened during their years of military service. Yet anthropology professors who taught these classes filled with veterans faced a challenging situation. Not only were many of the students older than the professors, but also many of the students had lived among peoples of whom the professors had only read. Nevertheless, the combination of classes filled to capacity with mature, motivated students made the mid-1940s to mid-1950s an exciting time to be both a professor and a student in anthropology.[10]

The third development that strongly influenced the direction of postwar anthropology was the emergence of the discipline as one of what Harold Lasswell called the "policy sciences." In Lasswell's usage, this term was "not another way of talking about the 'social sciences' as a whole, nor of the 'social and psychological sciences.' Nor [were] the 'policy sciences' identical with 'applied social science.'" Instead, the expression "policy sciences" embraced all the social sciences, but most important, it captured the intimate connection that had come to exist, particularly during World War II, between the social scientific establishment and government officials. A new outlook had emerged in the postwar era, which Lasswell referred to as the "policy orientation," an outlook that reflected an awareness of the relevance of developments in the social sciences to the intelligence and policy concerns of the national government.[11]

Of all the social sciences, economics had been the first to demonstrate its relevance to government policy-makers. Economists had proved invaluable during World War I in forecasting facilities and resources required to produce the necessary munitions and in helping to coordinate the distribution of men and materiel in the battlefield. Psychologists also demonstrated their utility during World War I by administering intelligence tests and assisting in selecting personnel for various assignments. Following the war, moreover, psychologists gained an even greater foothold within the policy-making community by linking intelligence testing to the eugenics movement. Significantly, economists and psychologists both relied heavily upon quantitative techniques. Other social sciences lagged behind economics and psychology in finding acceptance among policy-makers largely because the methods they employed were not quantitative and did not appear to yield crisp objective results. Anthropology and sociology, for example, stood on the margins during World War I and made only slow progress in joining the policy elite during the 1920s and 1930s.

But with the advent of World War II, anthropology burst into its own and anthropologists demonstrated the power to contribute meaningfully to national intelligence and policy-making needs. Anthropologists, particularly through the national character studies pioneered by Ruth Benedict and Margaret Mead, proved they could produce results that no other discipline could provide. And by the end of World War II, anthropology had earned its place among the policy sciences.[12]

Anthropology secured an even firmer foothold among policy-makers during the postwar era, moreover, as the United States turned from national defense toward promotion of world development. In his 1949 inaugural address, President Truman announced his Point Four Program in which he promised "a bold new program for making the benefits of our scientific advances and industrial progress available for the improvement and growth of underdeveloped areas."[13] Through this program, Truman committed the United States to provide wide-ranging economic assistance to virtually every underdeveloped nation throughout Asia, Africa, and Latin America. American policy-makers quickly turned toward academic social scientists for help in designing and implementing the Point Four directives. Since anthropologists had the greatest experience in dealing with peoples in lesser developed nations, they assumed a prominent advisory role from the very beginning of the Point Four program.[14]

While anthropologists' contributions to the Point Four program raised the profile of anthropology among the policy elite and government officials, this connection did not bring much additional financial support into anthropology departments. In the late forties and early fifties, the federal government had not yet begun to fund social science research to any extent.[15] What government did not fund, however, major foundations did. Indeed, by the 1920s, philanthropic foundations had come to represent an important sector in the national policy-making establishment, and their actions complemented the government's on multiple levels. The Rockefeller and Carnegie Foundations began to provide substantial funding for academic social science research in the early 1920s; and in the late forties, the Ford Foundation joined the effort and began to channel millions of dollars into support of social science research, particularly research directed toward international or "area" studies. Anthropology was one of the prime beneficiaries of the Ford Foundation area studies funding, and research in the discipline expanded enormously during the 1950s through this support. Thus, from the early years of World War II into the 1950s, anthropology came to be recognized by both government decision makers and foundation officials as a strategic and useful field of study. This new distinction brought both money and prestige to the discipline, factors which helped to fuel the explosive growth anthropology experienced during the postwar era.[16]

Rise of the Civilizations Dialogue at Chicago

Anthropology at Chicago clearly reflected the intellectual and demographic shifts that transformed the discipline as a whole during the postwar era. From 1946 to 1948, enrollment in the department soared, and most of the new students were veterans.[17] Faculty members had anticipated this growth and had launched an effort shortly before the war ended to revamp the graduate curriculum and to design a course of study especially oriented toward returning GIs. In February 1945, Redfield, as social sciences dean, and Fay-Cooper Cole, as chairman of anthropology, had arranged to have Sol Tax promoted from research associate to associate professor of anthropology and had charged him with preparation of this new curriculum.[18] Tax, who had been struggling since the mid-1930s to establish himself academically—he had been thwarted first by the depression and then the war—approached the task of revising the curriculum with great enthusiasm. By the fall quarter of 1945, Tax announced three new courses designed to serve as the introductory sequence for anthropology graduate students. Anthropology 220, "Human Origins," would provide a year-long introduction to the anthropological view of humanity; Anthropology 230, "Peoples of the

World," would offer a panoramic survey of world cultures; and Anthropology 240, "Culture, Society, and the Individual," would present a thorough treatment of the principles of social anthropology. Only the first of these courses, "Human Origins," was actually offered in fall 1945; "Peoples of the World" debuted the following fall, "Culture, Society, and the Individual" in fall 1947.[19]

To assist him in designing the "Human Origins" course, Tax, a cultural anthropologist, enlisted the help of his departmental colleagues William Krogman, a physical anthropologist, and Robert Braidwood, an Old World archaeologist. Together these three developed a course strongly oriented around the new thinking in anthropology. Most particularly, this course emphasized the evolutionary perspective—both biological and social—that had recently reemerged within the discipline.[20] In order to facilitate teaching, Tax, Krogman, and Braidwood designed a comprehensive syllabus and a bound, two-volume set of readings. The first volume contained reprints of published papers, the second volume original papers. While this practice would hardly raise an eyebrow today, it represented an innovative attempt during the mid-1940s to put the most current literature into the hands of students and to ground an introductory course on the cutting edge of a discipline. In addition to the three course designers, several other members of the Chicago anthropology faculty actively took part in this course. Taught around a large round table always with two, three, sometimes more professors present, "Human Origins" came to have the atmosphere of a department seminar, a forum in which both students and professors worked out new research directions.[21]

One of the primary research directions to emerge among professors active in the "Human Origins" circle concerned the origins of civilizations. Braidwood and Tax both shared a strong interest in exploring the origins of civilizations, and they gave this issue a prominent place in their course. Each brought a different perspective for thinking about civilizations, and these differences provided the basis for a provocative contrast in ideas. Robert Braidwood—who had earned his Ph.D. under Henri Frankfort, the renowned historian of the Near East affiliated with Chicago's Oriental Institute—approached the study of civilizations from a distinctly historical perspective. Sol Tax, by contrast, who had been trained in cultural and social anthropology and had spent several years working in Guatemala with Redfield, approached the study of civilizations from a processual, sociological view.

Tax and Braidwood served as the nucleus for a cluster of Chicago scholars interested in civilizations. Braidwood brought several of his Oriental Institute colleagues, such as the Egyptologist John Wilson and the Assyriologist Thorkild Jacobsen, into the "Human Origins" group; and Robert Redfield also quickly became a regular participant in the circle. The combination of Braidwood and his colleagues plus Tax and Redfield provided for a critical mass of scholars interested in studying the origins of civilizations. The disciplinary differences between the two groups proved to be complementary, moreover, and stimulated fruitful collaboration among these scholars from the mid-1940s through the mid-1960s.

Interest in civilizations was not limited, of course, to scholars at the University of Chicago. Indeed, consideration of the origins and destinations of civilizations constituted one of the major themes in transatlantic intellectual discourse during the middle decades of the twentieth century. From the 1920s through the 1940s, numerous thinkers—including Oswald Spengler, Pitirim Sorokin, A. L. Kroeber, F. S. C. Northrop, V. Gordon Childe, and Arnold J. Toynbee—had published extensively and had raised great interest among both academic scholars and members of the public in the consideration of civilizations. While the Chicago "Human Origins" circle read and discussed the works of all these authors, none exerted more influence among them than V. Gordon Childe (1892-1958). The Australian-born British archaeologist and prehistorian Childe not only lent personal assistance in constructing Braidwood and Tax's course syllabus and readings (he was a close friend of Braidwood), but Childe also provided through his writings a powerful body of work that served as one of the primary sources of intellectual direction for the Chicago civilizations group.[22]

Childe, who had received his formal education in classical philology, first at Sydney University then at Oxford, had established himself during the mid-1920s to early 1930s as one of the world's leading students of European and Near Eastern prehistory. Through such works as *The Dawn of European Civilization* (1925), *The Most Ancient East* (1928), *The Danube in Prehistory* (1929), and *New Light on the Most Ancient East* (1934), he demonstrated a powerful ability not only to synthesize existing philological, historical, and archaeological research, but also to provide compelling new interpretative frameworks for viewing this research. It was as a theorist, clearly, that Childe most influenced the Chicago "Human Origins" circle.

During the 1930s, Childe turned his attention toward consideration of cultural evolution on a grand scale, and he produced two widely read books addressing this theme. In *Man Makes Himself* (1936) and *What Happened in History* (1942), he explored the long course of human development from the distant prehistoric past during which humans existed as hunter-gatherers—a period extending from about 10,000 to several hundred thousand years ago—through the emergence of settled village existence and eventually development of urban civilizations in the ancient world. In these two books, Childe introduced a series of ideas that fundamentally changed the way archaeologists and prehistorians thought about early human history.

Childe focused predominantly on two events in human prehistory: the emergence in the Old World of agriculture and the first cities. Previous archaeologists had presented the transition from the Old Stone Age (Paleolithic era), in which humans existed as hunter-gatherers, to the New Stone Age (Neolithic era), in which humans became food producers, largely as a transition in tool types. The emphasis in these earlier accounts had been upon the change from the use of stone knives, spear heads, and hide-scrapers to stone hoe-blades. Childe focused, however, not on the details of shift in tools, but rather on the social significance of these changes. The transition from the Paleolithic to the Neolithic ages, he argued, was not simply a change in toolmaking techniques. Instead it constituted a social and economic revolution. As humans moved from being hunter-gatherers to food producers, they not only asserted a new control over nature, but also radically altered their fundamental pattern of social organization. Childe proposed that this transformation swept through the Old World in a sudden fashion around 7,000 years ago, and he referred to it as the "neolithic revolution."

The Neolithic revolution resulted in the emergence of a multitude of small, self-sufficient communities scattered throughout Mesopotamia and Egypt. During the next few thousand years, the Neolithic villagers built upon the innovation of agriculture by mastering several other technologies. Not only did they assiduously devote themselves to implementing controlled irrigation and mastering the flood-prone Nile and Tigris-Euphrates Rivers, but also they developed competency in mining, metallurgy, simple architecture, and ceramics. Development of these new technologies led quickly to the invention of wheeled carts, sailing ships, and oxen-drawn plows. This explosion in technology resulted in profound changes in the social and economic structure in the neolithic Near East. Most particularly, the isolation of the small communities gave way to increasing contacts—first trade, then immigration and conquest—among the myriad of villages. Conquest led to capital accumulation, centralization, and eventual formation of cities which functioned as the control points for rudimentary states. Childe identified the emergence of these first cities around 3000 B.C.E. as the second seminal transformation in early human history, and he named it the "urban revolution."

The Neolithic and urban revolutions represented in Childe's panoramic vision the two axial transformations of prehistory. Before Childe, archaeologists and prehistorians had constructed a multiplicity of regional—mostly racially based—schemes of prehistory. No one had attempted a grand vision encompassing the full sweep of prehistory. Childe not only offered this vision, but he presented a structured, processual account. His notion of two climactic revolutions lent a powerful narrative simplicity to what had previously been a collection of unrelated individual histories. Moreover, in Childe's hands, what had previously been chronological ages in archaeology became technological ages. Tools, as implements reflecting the means of production, became indicators of changing social and economic structures. In short, in Childe's work, archaeology became not merely an antiquarian, museum-oriented pursuit, but a social science.[23]

Childe's work deserves extended consideration, because he provided the basic framework within which the Chicago civilizations discourse operated, and his work served as the point of departure for much of the subsequent research undertaken by members of the "Human Origins" circle. The Chicago responses to Childe fall into two distinct categories. The first of these consists of direct refutations of Childe's claims as well as efforts to address obvious lacunae in Childe's synthesis of prehistory. The work of both Robert Braidwood and

Robert McCormick Adams belongs in this first category. Braidwood rejected Childe's notion that agriculture first emerged in the riverine valleys of Egypt and Mesopotamia and dedicated his entire career to pursuing his own hypothesis that agriculture emerged instead on the more arid "hilly flanks" above the rivers.[24] Adams spent much of the early portion of his career attempting to redress the almost complete neglect of New World civilizations apparent in Childe's scholarship. Braidwood and Adams drew, of course, on other theorists, including Julian Steward and, later, Gordon Willey. But Childe's work served as the immediate and primary catalyst for their research directions.

The second category of response to Childe focused not on addressing specific claims or omissions in Childe's interpretations but challenged, instead, Childe's ideological perspective. Childe was a Marxist, and his historical accounts reflect a strongly materialist bias. The driving force behind historical change in his work is clearly technological innovation; as new technology is introduced into a society, so the mode of production—the socioeconomic order—of that society changes. All senior civilizations students at Chicago rejected Childe's materialistic approach to history.

Thorkild Jacobsen led the ideological challenge against Childe through his 1946 essay "Appraisal of Breasted and Childe on Mesopotamia," which was included in the "Human Origins" course syllabus. Jacobsen criticized Childe for his portrayal of both the psychological and religious dimensions of life in ancient Mesopotamia. Childe's depiction of human behavior fell short, he charged, because Childe's explanations "operate[d] almost exclusively with motives which are fully conscious and narrowly utilitarian-rationalistic." This "tendency to look for rational-utilitarian motives" rendered Childe's explanations of the development of writing or irrigation all too mechanistic. In discussing religion, Jacobsen complained that Childe spoke in such deterministic terms that Mesopotamian religion became little more than "a conspiracy of priests hoodwinking the laity."[25] In separate works, Braidwood, Redfield, Frankfort, and Adams also challenged Childe's pronounced materialist emphasis.[26] It seems plausible that some of the Chicago opposition to Childe's ideological perspective stemmed from Cold War perspectives. Yet Jacobsen wrote in 1946, before the marked rise in Cold War-McCarthyite tensions. Moreover, the Chicago challenges to Childe reflected perspectives long characteristic of the social sciences at Chicago—specifically, the emphases on social psychological determinants of behavior and the importance of symbolic aspects of existence—and thus seem more in keeping with Chicago's intellectual tradition than mere displays of knee-jerk anti-Marxism. Nevertheless, despite ideological differences between Childe and the Chicago group, the scope of Childe's synthesis and the strength of his conception of process and pattern in prehistory won Childe a strong and loyal following at Chicago throughout the 1940s and 1950s.[27]

Rethinking the Folk-Urban Continuum

For much of his career, Robert Redfield served as dean of social sciences at Chicago. Selected by Robert Hutchins in 1934, Redfield held the deanship until 1946. Like other Chicago administrators, Redfield continued to function as an active scholar during his years as dean. In addition to conducting his Yucatan research, each year he co-led the anthropology department's research seminar and taught his folk society and anthropological methods courses. Redfield suffered, nevertheless, under his heavy administrative, research, and teaching load, and he held the deanship for as long as he did only out of devotion to Hutchins.[28] By early 1946, Redfield realized, however, that he had to lighten his obligations. While on a camping vacation in the New Mexico wilderness Redfield wrote to Sol Tax and described his need for a change of pace:

> I am realizing something that I was beginning to understand, under all the hurry of my life in Chicago. From now [on] I shall have to get along with doing about half as much as I have been doing in these past years. I had come to the point where I was doing so much more than my poor powers allowed that my inefficiency and impatience were becoming a positive public menace. If I am to be at all useful, I must do less. . . .
>
> I have given so little attention to anthropology teaching this year that I am ashamed. I believe, however, that with 1947 my arrangements will be such as to cause me to devote most of my time again to the department and to teaching.[29]

The "arrangements" Redfield referred to were his planned resignation at the end of the year as dean of social sciences and assumption of the chairmanship of the anthropology department. The position as chair, furthermore, was only a temporary measure; by 1949, Redfield had shed all administrative responsibilities and was able to devote himself solely to teaching and writing.

Redfield approached this return to teaching, moreover, with a desire to move beyond his earlier thinking. Writing again to Tax, Redfield outlined his intentions for his new directions:

> I am pretty clear about another thing: I should not continue to give courses that I have been giving. They are dangerously like routine. I know I don't have more to say than I have been saying. But I think the only hope of getting something more to say is to commit myself to work on fresh topics. . . .
>
> I think I should like to spend what energies I have in working on Human Nature as a topic. . . . In the summer, I might give a similar small course, or seminar, on "Culture and Civilization."[30]

Redfield proceeded to develop an entire body of new courses that he gave during the 1950s. This decade proved to be, furthermore, the most creative and productive period in his entire career.

The civilizations discourse that developed at Chicago following the war profoundly affected the direction Redfield's thinking took during the late forties and the fifties. This discourse provided him the opportunity to return to some of the major problems surrounding the nature of social change that he had attempted to deal with in his decade-long Yucatan project. The new interpretations and approaches Redfield encountered through the Chicago civilizations discourse, particularly the ideas of Gordon Childe, challenged Redfield to rethink his own ideas about civilization as both entity and process. For most of his career, Redfield had considered the work of archaeologists and historians to be of little relevance to his processual studies. But Childe's approach to prehistory, based upon a judicious mixture of archaeology, ethnological inference, and historical reconstruction, had convinced Redfield that archaeology and history could be effectively used to study social processes. Redfield was also greatly influenced by his collaboration with the classical archaeologists from the Oriental Institute, especially Henri Frankfort, Robert Braidwood, and Thorkild Jacobsen, who further demonstrated to him how the historical perspective could illuminate issues he had previously examined only from a sociological point of view.[31]

Beginning in the late forties, Redfield began to discuss publicly his revised conceptions about civilization processes. One of the first formal occasions in which he advanced these new notions was a symposium on the "Birth of Civilization" held during March 1947 at the Oriental Institute. This faculty symposium grew out of the "Human Origins" seminar. The prime initiators were Braidwood and Tax, and they guided its development so as to create a forum in which professors could debate and discuss problems surrounding the origins of civilizations on a level beyond that possible in the student-faculty seminar. Redfield served as the moderator of the three-day "Birth of Civilization" symposium, offering both the leadoff "Statement of the Problem" paper and conclusions at the end of the event.[32]

Redfield's opening lecture dealt with the problem of defining civilization. Civilization—as entity and process—is notoriously difficult to define, and any conference focused solely on discussion of its origin needed to have its starting definitions made clear. Redfield began by reviewing approaches commonly taken to delimiting and defining civilization, and he suggested that of all the approaches available, the use of an ideal-typical scheme offered the most conceptual power. For this purpose, he proposed a somewhat modified version of his folk-urban typology. He presented a synopsis of the imaginary type of society he had previously defined as "folk society" and advanced the notion that civilization, rather than urban society, represented the polar opposite of folk or primitive society. Arguing that all human societies that existed twenty-five thousand years ago could be generally represented by the typology of folk society, Redfield proposed that "'civilization' then becomes the extent to which this imagined society was left behind."[33]

In suggesting the shift from a folk-urban to a folk-civilization construct, Redfield introduced two important changes in his thinking. First, the substitution of "civilization" for "urban" greatly expanded the scope of social transformation embraced by his dichotomy and allowed for consideration of broader political and cultural developments than possible in his earlier schema. This was especially pertinent in thinking about such phenomena as the rise of states and complex religious systems. This shift can be seen as a change in the spatial dimension of his dichotomy; the idea of civilization as the polar opposite of the folk community simply placed more emphasis on the geographic dimensions of the transformation than had been suggested by the folk-urban construct.

While the first shift in Redfield's thought concerned space, the second shift concerned time. The folk-urban notion operated largely in the present; the folk-civilization notion included, however, an important temporal dimension. The urban or metropolitan idea had represented the actualization of modernity—it was a functional notion with no historical referent. Yet the notion of civilization could not be so easily emptied of historical content. Civilizations stretched across time and space and could not be conceptualized unless both spatial and temporal dimensions were taken into account. In shifting from a folk-urban to a folk-civilization construct, therefore, Redfield made a major switch from a comparative sociological to a historical sociological perspective.

In his contribution to the "Birth of Civilization" symposium, Redfield only briefly considered the historical aspects of the emergence of the first civilizations. Over the next few years, though, he dedicated himself to exploration of this issue, especially as illuminated by his folk-civilization notion. In the spring of 1952, he offered in a set of lectures at Cornell University an in-depth treatment of the grand process of human social evolution. These lectures served as the basis for his *The Primitive World and Its Transformations* (1953).[34]

Gordon Childe's *Man Makes Himself* and *What Happened in History* provided Redfield with a point of departure for *The Primitive World*. Specifically, Redfield recognized that Childe's Neolithic and urban revolutions described the same general transformation he had been working with in his folk-urban notion. He recognized, moreover, that despite Childe's somewhat poorly developed sense of anthropological sensibility, Childe's characterization of the culture of Neolithic villages resembled his own ideal description of folk culture. Yet because Childe had based his constructs on hard archaeological evidence, they had a specific historical claim that Redfield's more abstract typological models did not have. Redfield's intention in *The Primitive World* was to move beyond the strictly functional scope of his own model and to consider the origins of civilization from a historical as well as processual or sociological perspective. He borrowed Childe's chronological framework, therefore, and combined it with his own ideas about cultural dynamics of village communities in order to produce an approach that featured the anthropological richness of his own work and the historical and archaeological strengths of Childe's work.

By discussing the transformation of folk societies into urban civilizations within a specific historical context, namely, as a development which took place in concerted fashion first in the ancient Near East from about 7000 to 3000

B.C.E., Redfield was able to clarify issues that had been poorly conceptualized in his earlier formulations of the folk-urban transition. Most specifically, Redfield resolved the ambiguity attached to his usage of the term "folk." In his previous use of the term, from the mid-1920s through the 1940s, he had used it sometimes to describe primitive tribal peoples and sometimes primitive peoples as well as peasants. Critics, especially Oscar Lewis, had drawn attention to this inconsistency and cited it as a significant factor detracting from the overall power of Redfield's continuum notion.[35] The historical framework required Redfield to distinguish between tribal and peasant ways of life according to not only sociological characteristics—the essential terms of his folk-urban continuum—but also according to chronological precedence. In constructing a chronological view of the transformation of human social organization from its earliest tribal village structures to the level defined as civilization, Redfield found it necessary to distinguish peasantry from primitive tribal life. In *The Primitive World*, he clearly stated that "folk" applied only to primitive tribal forms of association while the peasantry represented, by contrast, a form of association that developed historically through the action of cities upon folk societies.

The macrohistorical view Redfield assumed in *The Primitive World* allowed him to historicize his conception of peasantry. Peasantry became in this perspective not an evolutionary stage, folk-to-peasantry-to-civilization, but a historical development that actually followed emergence of the first cities. Indeed, peasantry stood as an accommodation or response to city life rather than a stage on the way toward urbanization. As such, peasantry represented a stable intermediate form of social organization between primitive or folk and urban civilized life and deserved consideration as a distinct social-historical entity. Accordingly, Redfield directed much of his subsequent work during the 1950s to exploration of the historical and social anthropological significance of peasants.

Although Redfield accepted much of Childe's analysis and methodology, he disagreed with the priority Childe placed upon material over ideational change in the overall process of human social evolution. Redfield developed his argument in *The Primitive World* largely in opposition to Childe's materialist interpretation. Where Childe portrayed the grand narrative of human development as a series of technological revolutions, Redfield showed it to be a fundamentally moral-intellectual transformation. Redfield did not advance his interpretation as a refutation of Childe, however, but rather as a complementary view. Thus, the reader senses in *The Primitive World* that Redfield attempted a dialogue with Childe by pitting the idealistic view of historical causation against the materialistic-technological view.

At the crux of this dialogue lay two strikingly different views of the social and cultural nature of Neolithic communities. In *Man Makes Himself*, Childe had described Neolithic communities as having been bound together by "social and political institutions" that were "consolidated and reinforced by magico-religious sanctions, by a more or less coherent system of beliefs and superstitions, by what Marxists would call an ideology."[36] In "The Urban Revolution" (1950), a widely read article in which Childe summarized the basic ideas from

Man Makes Himself and *What Happened in History*, Childe had claimed that the solidarity that characterized the precivilized community was "really based on the same principles as that of a pack of wolves or a herd of sheep."[37] Redfield found these comments by Childe to reveal a profound insensitivity to the sociological complexity of primitive communities. Childe had essentially depicted the Neolithic community as a superstition-bound village, a village whose members were bound together by a herd mentality, or worse, a brow-beating ideology. Redfield reacted strongly to this image of the Neolithic community, to this "comparison of precivilized society with that of animals," and argued that "[e]ven the little glimpses of religion and sense of obligation to do right which are accorded the archaeologist show us that twenty-five thousand years ago the order of society was a moral order."[38]

Redfield suggested, however, that in order to grasp fully the moral nature of early human communities, the archaeological record needed to be complemented by ethnographic studies of contemporary folk communities. Childe had frequently utilized ethnographic data to gain insight into several facets of primitive village life, such as tool manufacture and usage and social organization. Indeed, Childe had been a pioneer among archaeologists in attempting to use anthropological studies to assist in construction of a functional interpretation of archaeological artifacts.[39] Redfield welcomed Childe's efforts in this direction and pushed to extend the interchange between archaeology and anthropology even further. In *The Primitive World*, Redfield drew upon his ethnographically derived understanding of surviving folk societies to produce a more sociological view of Neolithic village life than Childe had offered in his synthetic treatments of prehistory. From this sociological perspective, Redfield advanced an interpretation of the Neolithic and urban transformations that emphasized social and moral change over technological change—an idealistic account to complement Childe's materialistic account.[40]

While the dialogue with Childe provided Redfield with a point of departure and a major organizing theme for *The Primitive World*, Redfield also maintained a second dialogue within this text which extended far beyond his exchange with Childe. This second dialogue was with Robert E. Park and, more largely, the entire tradition of nineteenth-century sociology. Here Redfield undertook a sustained examination of the sociological ideas that underlay his folk-urban construct. In the process of this examination, moreover, he offered a dramatically modified view of the sociological processes associated with the general folk to civilization transformation.

In developing his folk-urban continuum construct, Redfield had drawn most directly upon Robert E. Park's theory of urban ecology. Indeed, the folk-urban continuum can by seen as an attempt by Redfield to systematize ideas expressed only incompletely in Park's work. Park's theory of urban ecology had exerted enormous influence in American sociology during the first few decades of the twentieth century. At Chicago, Louis Wirth, Robert Redfield, and Everett Hughes all used it as the cornerstone of their systematic thinking about the meaning of urbanism and the process of urbanization. Redfield and Wirth, in particular, devoted great effort toward refining, systematizing, and extending Park's complex and sometimes vague and contradictory notions.

In the process of bringing greater coherence and systematization to Park's urban theory, however, Wirth and Redfield subtly changed the overall complexion of Park's ideas. Whereas Park relied almost exclusively upon Simmel, Durkheim, and Maine for his conceptions of urban social order and social evolution, Redfield and Wirth drew heavily from Ferdinand Tönnies as well as Simmel, Durkheim, and Maine. While Park's writings displayed a certain ambivalence toward the city and urban modernity, Park expressed in the main a robust receptivity to the urban way of life. Here Park echoed both Simmel and Durkheim. By drawing upon the ideas of Tönnies, however, Wirth and Redfield introduced a distinct antiurban theme into Chicago urban theory. Specifically, Wirth and Redfield borrowed from Tönnies the constructs of Gemeinschaft and Gesellschaft. These two concepts denoted not only distinct forms of human association, but also a grand theory of social evolution. Tönnies' schema, which depicted the transformation of the communal Gemeinschaft of the village into the cash-nexus Gesellschaft of the metropolis, bore the unmistakable sensibility of tragedy. Redfield and Wirth borrowed heavily from Tönnies throughout the late 1920s and the 1930s, and the works they produced during these years reflect the tragic pathos associated with Tönnies' ideas.

In their reworking of Park's thought, Redfield and Wirth wove ideas drawn from Tönnies directly into Park's general scheme of urban theory. They equated the social bonds of a Gemeinschaft with what Park had characterized as the cultural or moral order of a society; the bonds of the Gesellschaft they equated with Park's symbiotic or technical order. They argued, moreover, that the transformation of a village into a town and then into a city represented a process in which the Gemeinschaft or moral order of the village declined as the Gesellschaft or technical order of the city expanded. Such a zero-sum perspective lent an inescapable sense of decline to the urbanization process. While Wirth and Redfield never produced any works that could be characterized as blatantly antiurban—indeed their writings were nuanced and displayed a decided ambivalence toward urban modernity—the trope of declension appeared in most of the works they wrote during the late twenties through the early forties on urbanization.[41]

Over the course of the 1940s, Redfield's colleagues and students subjected his theory of urbanization, in particular his notion of the folk-urban continuum, to severe criticism.[42] Redfield was himself aware, moreover, that his folk-urban construct failed to capture adequately much of the dynamic associated with the processes of urbanization and civilization. His labored conclusion to *The Folk Culture of Yucatan* reflected this awareness as did the articles he and Sol Tax published during the late 1930s to the mid-1940s on the secular folk traders of Guatemala.[43] *The Primitive World* provided Redfield, however, an opportunity not only to introduce a historic dimension into his ideas about the general folk-civilization transformation, but also to reinterpret his notions about the sociology of this process. Here he advanced a thorough reinterpretation of the concepts he and Louis Wirth had developed out of ideas inherited from Robert E. Park and the nineteenth-century European social theorists. Most significant, in this new interpretation of the processes of urbanization and civilization, Redfield clearly transcended the limitations of the trope of declension which had so colored his earlier works.

Civilization and the Moral Order

In his works up through the early 1940s, Redfield had presented the folk to urban transformation as a process in which the moral order of the folk society declined as the technical order of urban society expanded. In *The Primitive World*, he continued to conceptualize civilization as a process involving a shifting balance between the moral and technical orders. He suggested, however, the need to revise his previous unidirectional interpretation of the transition between these orders:

> In folk societies the moral order predominates over the technical order. It is not possible, however, simply to reverse this statement and declare that in civilizations the technical order predominates over the moral. In civilization the technical order certainly becomes great. But we cannot truthfully say that in civilization the moral order becomes small. There are ways in civilization in which the moral order takes on new greatness. In civilization the relations between the two orders are varying and complex.[44]

By critically analyzing his previous interpretation of the interaction between the moral and technical orders in the civilization process, Redfield was attempting to come to terms with the sociological determinism that had informed much of his earlier work as well as the work of many of his colleagues at Chicago. Furthermore, by using the general abstract terms of moral and technical orders, Redfield was able to subsume into a single comprehensive analysis the ideas of the most prominent theorists of development active in the 1920s through the 1940s, including the Parkian Chicago sociologists as well as Gordon Childe and William F. Ogburn. While the Chicago sociologists' construct of the technical order did not equate exactly with the notion of technology—as used, for example, by Childe and Ogburn—the resemblance was close enough to afford comparison. From a general view, therefore, the view of development advanced in the 1920s and 1930s by Wirth, Redfield, Ogburn, and Childe had identified technological innovation as the engine of social change. Culture, the locus of the moral order, was but a passive victim in the face of technology and most often responded slowly to technical change, resulting in Ogburn's famous "cultural lag." Redfield's driving purpose in *The Primitive World*, was to go beyond this technological determinism and to recognize the agency of culture, especially ideas, in exerting a mutually important force, along with that of technology, in developing civilized society.

While Redfield accepted the notion that technological innovations played the initiating role—the catalyst—in the civilization process, as Childe had so convincingly argued in his discussion of the origins of the Neolithic revolution, Redfield argued that technological innovations generated multiple counter-responses which could not simply be regarded as lagging, secondary reactions. Instead, he proposed, these cultural responses also had the power to initiate social change and indeed to exert reciprocal effects upon the technical order:

> It is not enough to say that the technical order is destroyer of the moral order. It is not enough to identify civilization with development in the technical order alone. It is also to be recognized that the effects of the technical order include the creation of new moral orders. Through civilization people are not only confused, or thrown into disbelief and a loss of will to live. Through civilization also people are stimulated to moral creativeness. . . . Civilization is creator to the moral order as well as destroyer.[45]

Thus, Redfield introduced the notion of historical contingency into his discussion of the civilization process. Instead of a unidirectional view of the interaction between moral and technical orders, Redfield had come to espouse a dialectical view. Drawing upon Toynbee, Redfield portrayed the dynamic of civilization as a challenge-response pattern. Moreover, rather than seeing challenge as inevitably stemming from change in the technical order, he had come to see both the technical and moral orders as capable of driving civilization forward.

The primary means by which the moral order exerted influence, Redfield advanced, came through generation of visionary ideas—ideas of social reform and utopian invention. These ideas demonstrated a distinct agency, a potency extending beyond the sources of their creation. Indeed, in Redfield's conception, ideas once generated passed into a public sphere of discourse and operated almost as if they had a life of their own. Thus a reform notion held the power to haunt society, to continue to present itself as an alternative, as an ideal representing a different way of life. Here Redfield reflected the influence of Alfred North Whitehead. In *The Adventure of Ideas* (1933), Whitehead offered a sweeping account of the intellectual history of the West, one that emphasized the influence of a few signal ideas, in particular, the increasing recognition of the worth of the individual human. This rising valuation of humanity expressed itself most powerfully in the progressive expansion from antiquity to the late nineteenth century of notions of human freedom and equality. The "growth of the idea of the essential rights of human beings, arising from their sheer humanity," Whitehead proposed, "affords a striking example in the history of ideas. Its formation and its effective diffusion can be reckoned as a triumph—a chequered triumph—of the later phase of civilization."[46]

While Whitehead exercised a powerful philosophical-historical influence upon Redfield's *Primitive World*, A. L. Kroeber, the doyen of mid-twentieth-century American anthropology, provided an important anthropological-historical influence. In his encyclopedic text *Anthropology* (1948), Kroeber had advanced a spirited defense of the history of progress. Human culture, when seen from a grand view, Kroeber argued, clearly demonstrated progressive change.[47] Most important of those manifestations of cultural progress identified by Kroeber, Redfield judged, was the gradual rise of "prohumane" values within virtually all cultures that had developed into historic civilizations. These values, such as those expressed by the censure of slavery, human sacrifice, and torture, became codified, moreover, in the great religions that developed within these civilizations. In summarizing this grand trend in human ethical development, a trend described in similar fashion by both Kroeber and Whitehead, Redfield stated, "[t]he moral canon tends to mature."[48] Here Redfield was not denying the existence of evil or willfully ignoring countless violations of these ethical norms. Rather, he was stating that the evolution and increasing acceptance of these humanistic standards as ethical *ideals* constituted progress (apart from their actual realization) and represented a force for good in the dialectical play between moral and technical orders within human societies.

Discussion of innovation within the moral order, however, raised difficult philosophical issues—issues not encountered when considering innovation within the technical order. Namely, the focus on innovation, within either the technical or moral order, forced discussion of the issue of progress. While recognition of *technological* progress in human societies hardly generated controversy, the attempt to assess *moral* progress represented a highly controversial issue. The problem of progress had occupied a central position within anthropology during the nineteenth century, but it had virtually fallen off the disciplinary agenda after the turn of the century. Rejection of the concept of progress had resulted chiefly from the spread of the idea of cultural relativism. To think in terms of progress, of the advancement of one culture's moral system over another, had come to be seen by anthropologists during the first half of the twentieth century as one of the most egregious forms of ethnocentrism.

Redfield recognized that his ideas about progress within the moral order represented a challenge to mid-century anthropological orthodoxy. He chose to confront his theoretical opponents directly, therefore, and in the last chapter of *The Primitive World*, he launched a vigorous reconsideration of the notions of cultural relativism and progress. Redfield began his consideration of cultural relativism by examining the logical underpinnings of the theory, particularly as formulated by Ruth Benedict and Melville Herskovits. Benedict and Herskovits argued that all cultural values, according to the findings of contemporary empirical anthropology, were relative and therefore were deserving of tolerance and respect. While Redfield easily accepted the first proposition, he found the second proposition in this formulation of cultural relativism to be logically untenable. No "therefore" existed, he argued, between the two propositions; simply recognizing the existence of multiple value systems did not compel automatic respect and tolerance. Indeed, "we might just as well hate them all." The notion that all cultures and value systems were equally deserving of respect and tolerance was not a logical consequence of the relativity of cultural values, Redfield concluded, but rather a moral judgment advanced by Benedict and Herskovits.[49]

Yet Redfield did not fault Benedict and Herskovits for allowing value judgments to creep into their anthropology. Instead, he directed his criticism toward their failure to recognize that moral commitments influenced their scientific work. For neither Benedict nor Herskovits acknowledged the doctrine of tolerance to be a value judgment; instead they both insisted upon the value-free objectivity inherent in their anthropological practice. "A basic necessity of ethnographic research," Herskovits proclaimed in his magnum opus, *Man and His Works*, "is the exercise of scientific detachment, which in turn calls for a rigid exclusion of value-judgments."[50] Redfield challenged this extreme emphasis upon value-free social science and, building upon the ideas he had introduced in his Frankfurt lectures, suggested that a middle road existed between objectivity and interest. "It is not quite realistic," Redfield remarked, "to conceive of the ethnologist's objectivity as excluding all valuing, or as permitting only universal benevolence toward all cultures."[51] Thus, by confronting the necessity, indeed the ineluctability, of valuing in ethnographic practice, Redfield argued, anthropologists would not only come closer to grasping the inner experiences of those they observed, but also would be able to come to terms with the dilemma of cultural relativism.

The solution to the relativism quandary lay, moreover, in recognizing that what Kroeber described as "progress," the evolution of "prohumane" values, represented a standard anthropologists could use to judge value systems in other cultures. But anthropologists needed to draw a distinction between precivilized and civilized cultures. For civilization, conceived as a grand worldwide process, has produced a more highly developed moral sense in civilized than in precivilized cultures. "On the whole the human race has come to develop a more decent and humane measure of goodness—there has been a transformation of ethical judgment which makes us look at noncivilized peoples not as equals, but as people on a different level of experience." Consequently, our expectations for behavior in civilized cultures should be higher. We should not expect, for example, the Siriono of Bolivia to conform to the same standards of behavior as we hold for people in China or the United States. We should not judge the Siriono husband who leaves his sick wife to die in the jungle by the same standard therefore as we would judge a suburban husband who leaves his wife to die in a snowdrift. "We do not expect a people to have a moral norm that their material conditions make impossible."[52]

In essence, Redfield proposed a double standard for judging human behavior. On the one hand, he observed, "[w]e judge the conduct of primitive peoples—as of other people—by their success in acting in accordance with the ideals they have chosen." On the other hand, "we also judge the conduct of a primitive people by the degree to which they conform to the conceptions that have developed in history as to what human beings ought to be." These transcultural conceptions or values, furthermore, have been developed through the course of human civilization and refined and articulated in all the world's great traditions. To look at other cultures in an evaluative sense, moreover, did not constitute an option for anthropologists. Rather, anthropologists in the postwar world had the "responsibility to look at the cultures of other peoples in the light of civilized ethical judgment." Here Redfield clearly stated that civilization and not the folk society stood as the moral arbiter for human society. Folk society is governed by mores, which Redfield termed "automatic morality." Civilization, by contrast, represented a conscious attempt by humankind to articulate a moral order, and it is this intentionally constructed order, Redfield believed, that represented the culmination of human ethical striving.[53]

Redfield understood that he was moving well beyond the bounds of anthropological practice as defined during the first half of the twentieth century. He believed, however, that the postwar world demanded anthropologists to take such a step, especially to recognize the subjectivity that underlay all ethnographic practice. He closed *The Primitive World* with a personal confession in which he described his own coming to terms with the subjectivity of anthropology:

> In me, man and anthropologist do not separate themselves sharply. I used to think I could bring about that separation in scientific work about humanity. Now I have come to confess that I have not effected it, and indeed to think that it is not possible to do so. All the rules of objectivity I should maintain: the marshaling of evidence that may be confirmed by others, the persistent doubting and testing of all important descriptive formulations that I make, the humility before the facts, and the willingness to confess oneself wrong and begin over. I hope I may always strive to obey these rules. But I think now that what I see men do, and understand as something that human beings do, is often with a valuing of it. I like or dislike as I go. This is how I reach understanding of it. The double standard of ethical judgment toward primitive peoples is a part of my version of cultural relativity. It is because I am a product of civilization that I value as I do. It is because I am a product of civilization that I have both a range of experience within which to do my understanding-valuing and the scientific disciplines that help me to describe what I value so that others will accept it, or, recognizing it as not near enough to the truth, to correct it. And if, in this too I am wrong, those will correct me here also.[54]

While Redfield clearly pushed the limits of anthropological theory in *The Primitive World*, critics and readers received the book well. Both social scientists and philosophers reviewed it and it received attention in academic as well as literary journals.[55] Clyde Kluckhohn observed:

> The book is a most significant contribution to the anthropological study of values and 'universals.' It also not only draws from philosophy (most notably Whitehead) but builds solid bridges from anthropology to philosophy, overlapping, for instance, with many aspects of Northrop's work.[56]

Elvin Hatch, in his important work on cultural relativism, *Culture and Morality: The Relativity of Values in Anthropology* (1983), uses Redfield's transcultural "humanistic principle" as the starting point in his carefully reasoned case for a revised approach to cultural relativism. Hatch faults Redfield for not stating clearly the "criterion he used in judging bad and good (and in distinguishing between primitive and civilized values)," but he praises Redfield's overall effort to articulate a workable postwar approach to relativism.[57] Readers also accepted *The Primitive World* well, and a paperback edition of the book, which has undergone multiple reprintings, has been maintained in print by Cornell University Press continuously up to the present.

In sum, *The Primitive World* represents an extremely important text in Redfield's overall output. It was a transitional work that linked two distinct but related periods of his life. In it he offered both a sweeping reinterpretation of his earlier ideas about the directions and dynamics of civilization—conceived as both process and historical entity—and a preview of the new directions he was to take during the 1950s in the comparative study of civilizations. Most important, Redfield offered a new conception of the role of anthropology in post-World War II society. By urging anthropologists to go beyond their cherished notion of cultural relativity, and to attempt to draw distinctions among various human practices and ideologies based upon conceptions of universal human morality, he was pushing anthropologists out onto an existential ledge. He was demanding, in essence, that anthropologists recognize the value connotations implicit in their knowledge and, furthermore, that they use their comparative studies of human societies to assist in construction of a more inclusive and just moral order for modern humanity.

Notes

1. George Stocking has described the years c. 1920 to c. 1965 as the "classical period" in American anthropology. "Die Geschichtlichkeit der Wilden und die Geschichte der Ethnologie," *Geschichte und Gesellschaft* 4, no. 4 (1978): 520-535; "Anthropology in Crisis? A View from between the Generations," in *Crisis in Anthropology: View from Spring Hill, 1980*, ed. E. Adamson Hoebel, Richard Currier, and Susan Kaiser (New York: Garland, 1982), 407-419. Stocking characterizes this period as being unified through the shared devotion of practitioners to fieldwork and the broad acceptance of the functional perspective. By suggesting that World War II stands as an important watershed within twentieth-century American anthropology, I am not rejecting Stocking's notion that the larger period from c. 1920 to c. 1965 represents a unified era. Rather, I am proposing that the postwar period marked a distinct moment within this era. As Eric R. Wolf stated, "The experience of World War II certainly altered both the social organization and the intellectual materials of the anthropological profession in the United States. Many of the trends were already under way before the war; but most of them showed a qualitative change, as well as a quantitative increment, after it." *Anthropology* (New York: W. W. Norton, 1964), 6-7. Recently, moreover, Stocking has also remarked that he is "more inclined to see World War II as perhaps a significant break within the classical period." "Paradigmatic Traditions in the History of Anthropology," in George W. Stocking, Jr., *The Ethnographer's Magic and Other Essays in the History of Anthropology* (Madison: University of Wisconsin Press, 1992), 345.

2. On Boas's views of comparative studies in anthropology, see his "The Limitations of the Comparative Method in Anthropology," *Science*, n.s. 4 (18 December 1896): 901-908; *Anthropology: A Lecture Delivered at Columbia University, December 18, 1907* (New York: Columbia University Press, 1908); "Some Problems of Methodology in the Social Sciences," in *The New Social Science*, ed. Leonard D. White (Chicago: University of Chicago Press, 1930), 84-98; and "History and Science in Anthropology: A Reply," *American Anthropologist* 38 (January-March 1936): 137-141.

3. Ruth Benedict, *Patterns of Culture* (Boston: Houghton Mifflin, 1934); Melville J. Herskovits, *Man and His Works: The Science of Cultural Anthropology* (New York: Alfred A. Knopf, 1948). On Boasian anthropology as cultural critique, see Richard Handler, "Boasian Anthropology and the Critique of American Culture," *American Quarterly* 42 (June 1990): 252-273.

4. Elvin Hatch, *Culture and Morality: The Relativity of Values in Anthropology* (New York: Columbia University Press, 1983), 85-101; Eric R. Wolf, *Anthropology* (New York: W. W. Norton, 1964), 20-22.

5. See Clyde Kluckhohn, "The Place of Theory in Anthropological Studies," *Philosophy of Science* 6 (July 1939): 328-344; Alexander Lesser, "Problem versus Subject Matter as Directives of Research," *American Anthropologist* 41 (October-December 1939): 574-582; and Leslie White, "A Problem in Kinship Terminology," *American Anthropologist* 41 (October-December 1939): 566-573.

6. Wolf, *Anthropology*, 6-32; Robert F. Murphy, "A Quarter Century of American Anthropology," in *Selected Papers from the American Anthropologist, 1946-1970*, ed. Robert F. Murphy (Washington, D.C.: American Anthropological Association, 1976), 4-10.

7. Walter Goldschmidt, "The Cultural Paradigm in the Post-War World," in *Social Contexts of American Ethnology, 1840-1984, 1984 Proceedings of the American Ethnological Society*, ed. June Helm (Washington, D.C.: American Ethnological Society, 1984), 167.

8. Wolf, *Anthropology*, 8.

9. It is hard to underestimate the impact of the GI Bill upon American higher education during these years. The number of veterans who rushed to take advantage of this legislation far exceeded all expectations. By 1947, the peak year for veterans on campus, veterans represented almost one-half of the entire enrollment in American institutions of higher education. Beyond merely causing a transitory explosion in enrollment, though, the GI Bill permanently changed the demographics of American higher education. This legislation cut across class and racial lines. It provided the means for multitudes of students to attend elite institutions, which they could never have afforded on their own, and facilitated access to higher education for ethnic minorities, many of whom had previously been both formally and informally excluded from the best American colleges and universities. The democratization of higher education that resulted from passage of this legislation proved most dramatic because it transpired primarily at the finest American institutions. Veterans chose overwhelmingly to attend elite private and public schools, and they distinguished themselves by dominating the honor rolls at these institutions. Early critics of the GI Bill, like Robert Maynard Hutchins, who predicted that veterans would lower the quality of American higher education by their clamoring to enroll in a bevy of vocational courses, were proved wrong in dramatic fashion, moreover, as the academically minded veterans predominantly chose to pursue education in the traditional liberal arts disciplines. See Joseph F. Kett, *The Pursuit of Knowledge under Difficulties: From Self-Improvement to Adult Education in America, 1750-1990* (Stanford, Calif.: Stanford University Press, 1994), 416-423, and Keith W. Olson, *The GI Bill, the Veterans, and the Colleges* (Lexington: University Press of Kentucky, 1974).

10. On the choice of veterans to enter the social sciences, see Robert A. McCaughey, *International Studies and Academic Enterprise: A Chapter in the Enclosure of American Learning* (New York: Columbia University Press, 1984), 118-119; Murphy, "Introduction: A Quarter Century of American Anthropology," 4-5; and Goldschmidt, "The Cultural Paradigm in the Post-War World," 166. Robert Murphy also provides an interesting portrayal of the postwar intellectual environment among Columbia anthropology graduate students, most of whom were sponsored by the GI Bill, in his essay "Julian Steward" in *Totems and Teachers: Perspectives on the History of Anthropology*, ed. Sydel Silverman (New York: Columbia University Press, 1981), 177, and "Anthropology at Columbia: A Reminiscence," *Dialectical Anthropology* 16, no. 1 (1991): 72-73. Eric R. Wolf, who attended Columbia on the GI Bill with Murphy, corroborates Murphy's account in his "Reply" to Alan R. Beals's, "On Eric Wolf and the North Berkeley Gang," *Current Anthropology* 29 (April 1988): 307. Interviews I conducted with anthropologists who were students at Chicago during the mid-forties indicate that the environment created by veterans at Chicago closely resembled that at Columbia as described by Murphy. McKim Marriott, interview by author (Chicago, 22 February 1994); Charles M. Leslie, interview by author (Newark, Delaware, 1 August 1994).

11. Harold D. Lasswell, "The Policy Orientation," in *The Policy Sciences: Recent Developments in Scope and Method*, ed. Daniel Lerner and Harold D. Lasswell (Stanford, Calif.: Stanford University Press, 1951), 3-4.

12. On the development of anthropology and psychology as policy sciences during World War II, see Ellen Herman, *The Romance of American Psychology: Political Culture in the Age of Experts* (Berkeley: University of California Press, 1995), 17-47; Virginia Yans-McLaughlin provides an especially good account of the development of wartime national character studies in "Science, Democracy, and Ethics: Mobilizing Culture and Personality for World War II," in *History of Anthropology*, vol. 4, *Malinowski, Rivers, Benedict, and Others: Essays on Culture and Personality*, ed. George W. Stocking, Jr. (Madison: University of Wisconsin Press, 1986), 184-217.

13. David A. Baldwin, *Foreign Aid and American Foreign Policy: A Documentary Analysis* (New York: Praeger, 1966), 61.

14. Robert A. Packenham provides a good description of the initiation of the Point Four program in *Liberal America and the Third World: Political Development Ideas in Foreign Aid and Social Science* (Princeton, N.J.: Princeton University Press, 1973), 25-49.

15. On the development of federal government support for the social sciences, see Samuel Z. Klausner and Victor M. Lidz, eds., *The Nationalization of the Social Sciences* (Philadelphia: University of Pennsylvania Press, 1986).

16. See Robert McCaughey, *International Studies and Academic Enterprise*, 141-196, on the Ford Foundation and the growth of area studies in the 1950s.

17. Charles M. Leslie, interview by author (Newark, Delaware, 1 August 1994).

18. Fay-Cooper Cole to Ralph W. Tyler, 10 February 1945, box 35, folder 2, Robert Redfield Papers, Special Collections, Joseph Regenstein Library, University of Chicago, Chicago (hereafter cited as RR-UC).

19. *Official Publications of the University of Chicago, Announcements, The College and the Divisions* 45 (Chicago: University of Chicago, 1945-1946), 204; *University of Chicago, Announcements* 46 (1946-1947), 209; *University of Chicago, Announcements* 47 (1947-1948), 217.

20. Sherwood Washburn replaced Krogman in physical anthropology at Chicago in 1947. Washburn proceeded to bring an even more pronounced emphasis on biological evolution to the "Human Origins" course as well as to the entire Chicago program.

21. Robert J. Braidwood, "Prehistoric Investigations in Southwestern Asia," *Proceedings of the American Philosophical Society* 116 (August 1972): 311-312; Braidwood, "Robert J. Braidwood," in *The Pastmasters: Eleven Modern Pioneers of Archaeology*, ed. Glyn Daniel and Christopher Chippindale (London: Thames and Hudson, 1989), 92-93; Interviews, Charles Leslie, Robert Braidwood, Sherwood Washburn. See also the excellent discussion on the postwar reorganization of the Chicago anthropology program by George W. Stocking, Jr., in *Anthropology at Chicago: Tradition, Discipline, Department* (Chicago: The Joseph Regenstein Library of the University of Chicago, 1979), 33.

22. On Childe's influence upon and contributions to the Chicago civilizations group, see Braidwood's "Prehistoric Investigations in Southwestern Asia," 310-312, and "Robert J. Braidwood," in *Pastmasters*, 90-93.

23. Numerous excellent discussions of Childe's work and career have recently appeared. I have relied heavily upon Bruce G. Trigger, *Gordon Childe: Revolutions in Archaeology* (New York: Columbia University Press, 1980); Trigger, *A History of Archeological Thought* (Cambridge: Cambridge University Press, 1989), 244-288; David R. Harris, ed. *The Archaeology of V. Gordon Childe* (London: UCL Press, 1994); Andrew Sherratt, "V. Gordon Childe: Archeology and Intellectual History," *Past and Present* 125

(November 1989): 159-185; and William J. Peace, "Vere Gordon Childe and American Anthropology," *Journal of Anthropological Research* 44 (Winter 1988): 417-433.

24. Braidwood clearly acknowledges Childe as the point of departure for his research; see Robert J. Braidwood and Linda Braidwood, "Jarmo: A Village of Early Farmers in Iraq," *Antiquity* 24 (December 1950): 189; Robert J. Braidwood, "Prehistoric Investigations in Southwestern Asia," 311-312; and "Robert J. Braidwood," in *Pastmasters*, 90-93.

25. Thorkild Jacobsen, "Appraisal of Breasted and Childe on Mesopotamia," in *Human Origins: An Introductory General Course in Anthropology. Selected Readings, Series 2*, 2d ed. (Chicago: University of Chicago Bookstore, 1946), 250-255; see also the briefer but similar comments by Richard A. Parker in "Appraisal of Breasted and Childe on Egypt," *Human Origins*, 256-257.

26. Robert J. Braidwood, *Courses toward the Urban Life* (Chicago: Aldine, 1962); Henri Frankfort, *Birth of Civilization in the Near East* (Bloomington: Indiana University Press, 1951); Robert Redfield, *The Primitive World and Its Transformations* (Ithaca, N.Y.: Cornell University Press, 1953); Robert McCormick Adams, *The Evolution of Urban Society* (Chicago: Aldine, 1966).

27. On the important, but different, reception Childe received at Columbia and Berkeley, see Joan Vincent, *Anthropology and Politics: Visions, Traditions, and Trends* (Tucson: University of Arizona Press, 1990), 190-191, and William Peace, "Vere Gordon Childe and American Anthropology."

28. Redfield was intent upon resigning the deanship in 1939 but allowed himself to be persuaded by Hutchins and University of Chicago vice president, William Benton, to stay on (William Benton to Robert Hutchins, 6 June 1939, President's Papers, 1925-1945, box 110, folder 1, Special Collections, Joseph Regenstein Library, University of Chicago, Chicago). On Redfield's sense of dedication to Hutchins, see Redfield's comments in the tribute article published upon Hutchins's departure from Chicago, "The Hutchins Influence," *University of Chicago Magazine* 43 (June 1951): 9.

29. Robert Redfield to Sol Tax (February 1946), box 56, folder 3, Sol Tax Papers, Special Collections, Joseph Regenstein Library, University of Chicago, Chicago (hereafter ST-UC).

30. Robert Redfield to Sol Tax, 1 March 1949, box 56, folder 3, ST-UC.

31. Archaeologists who studied with Redfield in the late 1930s and early 1940s have commented on the low opinion Redfield held of archaeology during these decades. See the autobiographical accounts: Richard MacNeish, *The Science of Archaeology?* (North Scituate, Mass.: Duxbury Press, 1978), and Paul S. Martin, "Early Development in Mogollon Research," in *Archaeological Researches in Retrospect*, ed. Gordon R. Willey (Cambridge, Mass.: Winthrop, 1974), 3-32.

32. "Birth of Civilization" symposium agenda, 4, 6, and 11 March 1947, box 5, folder 15, RR-UC.

33. Robert Redfield, "The Birth of Civilization: A Definition of the Problem," March 1947, box 72, folder 9, RR-UC.

34. Redfield, *Primitive World*, v.

35. Oscar Lewis, *Life in a Mexican Village: Tepoztlán Restudied* (Urbana: University of Illinois Press, 1951), 432.

36. Childe, *Man Makes Himself*, 97-98.

37. Childe, "The Urban Revolution," *Town Planning Review* 21 (April 1950): 7; Redfield mistakenly cites this as appearing in Childe's *Prehistoric Migrations in Europe* (Oslo: Ascheboug; Cambridge: Harvard University Press, 1950).

38. Redfield, *Primitive World*, 16.

39. See V. Gordon Childe, "Archaeology and Anthropology," *Southwestern Journal of Archaeology* 2 (Autumn 1946): 243-251.

40. "The great transformations of humanity," Redfield explained, "are only in part reported in terms of the revolutions in technology with resulting increases in the number of people living together. There have also occurred changes in the thinking and valuing of men which may also be called 'radical and indeed revolutionary innovations.' Like changes in the technical order, these changes in the intellectual and moral habits of men become themselves generative of far-reaching changes in the nature of human living. They do not reveal themselves in events as visible and particular as do material inventions, or even always as increasing complexity in the systems of social relationships. Nor is it perhaps possible to associate the moral transformations with limited periods of time as we can associate technological revolutions with particular spans of years. Yet the attempt to identify some of the transformations in men's minds can be made." *Primitive World*, 24-25.

41. This declension perspective is especially obvious in Wirth's work in two articles he published in the *American Journal of Sociology*, "Urbanism as a Way of Life," *AJS* 44 (July 1938): 1-24, and "The Urban Society and Civilization," *AJS* 45 (March 1940): 743-755. In Redfield's writings, it is most prominent in *The Folk Culture of Yucatan* and "The Folk Society and Culture," *AJS* 45 (March 1940): 731-742, an article he published as a companion piece to Wirth's "Urban Society" essay.

42. See chapter 2 for a detailed discussion of the debates that developed over the validity and utility of Redfield's folk-urban continuum.

43. Sol Tax, "Culture and Civilization in Guatemalan Societies, *Scientific Monthly* 48 (May 1939): 463-467; Tax, "World View and Social Relations in Guatemala," *American Anthropology* 43 (January-March 1941): 27-42; and Robert Redfield, "Primitive Merchants of Guatemala," *Quarterly Journal of Inter-American Relations* 1 (October 1939): 42-56.

44. Redfield, *Primitive World*, 24.

45. Redfield, *Primitive World*, 77-81.

46. Alfred North Whitehead, *The Adventure of Ideas* (New York: Macmillan, 1933), 15.

47. A. L. Kroeber, *Anthropology* (New York: Harcourt, Brace and Company, 1948), 296-304.

48. Redfield, *Primitive World*, 163.

49. Redfield, *Primitive World*, 146-147.

50. Herskovits, *Man and His Works*, 80.

51. Redfield, *Primitive World*, 154.

52. Redfield, *Primitive World*, 163.

53. Redfield, *Primitive World*, 163-164.

54. Redfield, *Primitive World*, 165.

55. Examples include Clyde Kluckhohn, *American Anthropologist* 56 (April 1954): 295-297; Gideon Sjoberg, *American Journal of Sociology* 59 (November 1953): 277-278;

Frank E. Hartung, *Ethics* 64 (April 1954): 234-236; and Stephen W. Reed, *Yale Review* 43 (Autumn 1953): 152-154.

56. Kluckhohn, "Review of *The Primitive World and Its Transformations*," *American Anthropologist* 56 (April 1954): 297.

57. Hatch, *Culture and Morality*, 136, 109. My discussion of cultural relativism is greatly indebted to Hatch's excellent work.

Chapter 5

Comparative Civilizations Studies: Explorations in Theory and Methodology

The active interest in civilizations studies that emerged at the University of Chicago following World War II not only stimulated the growth of a lively intellectual community, but also provided impetus for several new institutional developments. Redfield played a leading role in these developments, particularly through his establishment at Chicago of a cross-disciplinary program for civilizations study. With the assistance of Robert M. Hutchins, Redfield secured one of the first Ford Foundation grants to higher education and in 1951 launched a program dedicated to the comparative study of world cultures and civilizations.

Redfield believed the comparative study of world civilizations offered a powerful means to transcend the dilemmas of cultural relativism that had received such attention in the years following World War II. Specifically, he regarded the comparative evaluation of the world's major civilizations as a promising method for the determination of universal human values. An understanding of these human universals was essential, Redfield thought, for establishing a harmonious world community—a community that recognized and protected differences among the various peoples and cultures of the world.

Redfield held a rather abstract notion of civilizations. He was wary of exacting objective definitions. Instead, he saw civilizations as constructs, "formed things of the mind," that allowed one to perceive and think about large cultural or social systems that endured through time. His conception of civilizations was thus a largely mentalist view—a view that focused on value constellations that lay at the base of a culture or civilization.

Of course Redfield was but one of many during the 1940s and 1950s interested in the comparative study of civilizations. Numerous scholars, most notably Arnold J. Toynbee, had directed their efforts toward the consideration of civilizations. Little consensus existed, however, among scholars over how to approach the study of civilizations or even how to define civilizations. Redfield recognized that little progress would be made in comparative civilizations studies unless scholars adopted a more uniform approach to these studies. He chose to focus his project on civilizations studies specifically on the development of methodologies and theoretical approaches that would better facilitate the comparative study of civilizations. Redfield and his colleague Milton Singer thus worked together closely throughout the 1950s to elevate the level of practice among comparative civilizations scholars.

The University of Chicago Comparative Civilizations Project

Through the 1940s, the focal point for the University of Chicago civilizations discourse had been in the anthropology department and at the Oriental Institute. But in 1949, a handful of faculty members from the Institute and the social sciences division proposed to Robert Hutchins the creation of a more formal organization dedicated to the study of complex societies, cultures, and civilizations. Hutchins reacted positively to this idea, and he charged Redfield with the tasks of developing a plan for the organization and a proposal to obtain outside funding to underwrite the project.[1]

During the summer of 1949, Redfield prepared a preliminary plan for an "Institute of Cultural Studies" and submitted it to Hutchins. Redfield proposed that its purpose be the "comparative study of the principal systems of values of the societies that have mattered most in history," and added that these "systems of values" could be reasonably described as "cultures." He then elaborated four specific objectives for the institute: (1) the study of "ultimate" values—those pertaining to ethics and religion—in the major cultures and civilizations of the world; (2) the integration of the work of humanists and social scientists in their studies of humanity; (3) the comparative analysis of world civilizations and development of "a knowledge of other cultures comparable with that we have of Western Europe"; and (4) the study of human nature. This final objective subsumed the first three, moreover, and reflected the ultimate purpose of the project. "In advancing the comparative study of the systems of values of the world's peoples," Redfield observed, "we move toward better understanding of that humanity which is widespread or universal, and on which a world community must rest."

Redfield then briefly described how the Institute of Cultural Studies might be organized. He proposed that the institute be composed primarily of faculty members drawn from already established departments in the divisions of the social sciences and humanities. Yet participation in the institute would not require withdrawal from these departments; rather, involvement in the institute would complement faculty members' normal academic duties and affiliations. The institute would have the authority to appoint a small number of faculty whose only university affiliation would be the institute. While this organization would largely be devoted to research, it would also admit to the university and supervise a small group of doctoral students. A separate Committee on Cultural Studies would be established to handle these academic matters. This committee would take over and expand the work of similar committees already in existence at the university, such as the Committee on Social Thought and the smaller, less active Committee on the History of Culture. Finally, Redfield commented on the effects he expected the founding of such a cross-disciplinary institute to exert on the university as a whole: "I think the growth of committees and institutes is a good thing for one reason that it weakens Departments, for Departments preserve routine at the expense of creativeness and integration, and they are trade associations."[2]

Yet Redfield anticipated trouble arising from his proposal, particularly in regard to his suggestion that the Committee on Cultural Studies subsume the Committee on Social Thought. Redfield had not based his suggestion, however, merely upon whim or the bureaucratic desire to simplify and rationalize an organizational chart. Instead, his proposal reflected a profound conflict that had developed at Chicago during the late 1940s over the Committee on Social Thought. This conflict derived largely from the founder of the committee, economic historian John U. Nef.[3]

John Nef had founded the Committee on Social Thought in 1941 with the assistance of Robert Redfield, Frank H. Knight, and Robert Hutchins. Nef established this committee with the intention of providing an alternative to the standard course of graduate education at Chicago. The committee offered a chance for a small group of carefully chosen students to work outside narrow departmental guidelines and to adopt a cross-disciplinary approach to study in the social sciences and humanities. In many ways, Nef implemented on a small scale the reform ideas that Hutchins had been trying to instill in the Chicago graduate school since the early 1930s. While the Chicago faculty had allowed Hutchins to reform the undergraduate curriculum, few were willing to allow him to influence graduate training. Hutchins found in Nef, though, a supporter who was interested in constructing a semiautonomous faculty committee to implement on a small scale the reforms he had advocated for graduate education. Nef brought more than merely the interest in establishing such a committee; he also brought the resources. Nef had come into great wealth through his marriage to Elinor Castle, who underwrote the cost of the committee—faculty salaries and, frequently, student stipends—for the first several years of its existence.[4]

Nef saw the committee as an agent of moral, even spiritual reform. Here he echoed Hutchins, who just a few years before the founding of the committee had published his manifesto, *The Higher Learning in America* (1936). Indeed, Nef came to see himself as the anointed interpreter of Hutchins's ideas, and he regarded the Committee on Social Thought as the actualization of the Hutchins reform vision. During the mid-thirties, Hutchins had urged American universities to assert moral and cultural leadership over a materialistic and philistine society. By the end of the decade, though, Hutchins had come to view the mission of the university in broader terms. As Europe edged toward yet another world war, Western civilization itself appeared to be on the brink of moral and spiritual crisis, and Hutchins called, accordingly, for American universities to commit themselves to allaying this crisis.[5] Nef also threw himself with great vigor into the popular crisis-of-civilization discussion, publishing from 1939 through 1943 a flurry of articles as well as a hefty book entitled *The United States and Civilization* (1942). Nef argued that in the face of the collapse of Western civilization, the United States needed to provide the moral, intellectual, and spiritual direction that had previously come from Europe. Like Hutchins, Nef believed that universities were the core cultural and intellectual institutions in American society and thus needed to serve as command posts in the struggle to preserve and advance the course of Western civilization.[6]

Nef believed the mission of the Committee on Social Thought was to provide moral leadership for all American higher education. Significantly, he had called his committee during its first year of existence the "Committee on the Study of Civilization" and only changed it to the more neutral Committee on Social Thought to obtain official acceptance at the university.[7] Nef argued fervently, moreover, that the truths and values that should constitute a moral education existed as absolutes. These values were to be known, he asserted, through study of the philosophical and humanistic classics of the Western tradition. Redfield and Knight, both dyed-in-the-wool pragmatists, argued vehemently with Nef during the early days of the committee and pressed the case for the social contingency of truths and knowledge. The committee reflected these divergent perspectives during its first few years of existence.[8] But by the mid-1940s, Nef had asserted such control over the committee that it came to reflect largely his philosophical outlook. Nef came to be so domineering, though, that many professors who had once eagerly devised programs to fit within the province of the committee began to distance themselves from Nef. Frank Knight quit the committee altogether in the early forties, Redfield drifted away in the mid-forties, and by the end of the decade, a handful of the participants began to call for creation of a new organization—the Institute of Cultural Studies—within which faculty members could pursue their work free from the domination of Nef.[9]

The Institute of Cultural Studies thus represented a reform movement initiated by faculty members associated with the Committee on Social Thought. As Redfield worked to develop a plan for the Institute of Cultural Studies, he labored over how the new institute should relate to the Committee on Social Thought. Redfield and Nef were close friends; indeed, they had been friends since boyhood—they had both attended the Laboratory School at the University of Chicago and had been on the faculty together since the late twenties. Redfield and Hutchins had also remained nominally active throughout the forties on the Committee on Social Thought and supported the spirit of the venture even if they disapproved of Nef's heavy-handed style. But Redfield believed that the Committee on Social Thought had become an obstacle to cooperative work at Chicago and recommended in his first proposal that Nef's committee be folded into the institute. In the end, though, Redfield and Hutchins decided not to make any heavy-handed moves of their own and suggested that the new institute should simply coexist with the Committee on Social Thought. The reform impulse that gave rise to the proposal for an Institute of Cultural Studies died quietly therefore in the planning stages for the new institute. It was easier simply to establish an additional committee than to try to resolve thorny issues related to such a high profile unit as the Committee on Social Thought.

In November 1949, Redfield submitted a brief and understated proposal to both the Carnegie Corporation and the Rockefeller Foundation requesting support for the University of Chicago Institute of Cultural Studies. In a description that closely resembled the preliminary proposal he had submitted earlier to Hutchins, Redfield outlined the purpose and objectives of the institute. He did not belabor the justification for such a project in the comparative study of world cultures and civilizations. He simply observed that American scholars were quite parochial in their almost exclusive focus on the study of the Western tradition and argued that the contemporary world situation demanded that American intellectuals develop a broader, more inclusive view of the world. He concluded by offering a short description of the proposed organization and personnel plan for the institute and presented an estimated five-year budget. Redfield projected that the institute would support sixteen professors and nine postdoctoral fellows, and he requested $1,000,000 to underwrite their activities over the course of five years. Both the Carnegie Corporation and the Rockefeller Foundation found the aims of the Institute of Cultural Studies to be too vague and ambitious and chose not to support the venture.[10]

The proposal Redfield submitted does not appear to be the type likely to attract the attention of action-oriented philanthropists. Not only was it extremely brief—only five pages long—but also, Redfield wrote it in a restrained, almost terse, tone and carefully avoided even the slightest degree of hyperbole. Nowhere did he mention tangible benefits that might ensue from the project, nor did he make any grand promises of securing world peace or cooperation. Indeed, Redfield promised virtually nothing. At most he suggested the value of working to create a less parochial, more cosmopolitan intellectual community within American academia. Furthermore, he treated the justification for creation of such a community as self-evident. His proposal, in short, was not a "pitch." Rather, it was a statement of modest aims—despite the decidedly immodest amount of financial support requested—by a man who was accustomed to obtaining support for his ideas without ever having to hardsell them in the academic and philanthropic marketplace.

A few months after Redfield received rejection notices from the Rockefeller and Carnegie officials, Robert M. Hutchins accepted a position as an associate director at the Ford Foundation. Suddenly, funding for Redfield's project became easily available. As a director of the foundation, Hutchins was granted wide-ranging authority and was easily able to persuade foundation trustees to underwrite Redfield's civilizations studies project.[11] In August 1951, the board approved the first grant toward Redfield's "Project on Intercultural Studies," as it came to be called by the Ford officials, a program the foundation continued to underwrite for the entire decade of the 1950s at a total cost of $375,000.[12]

The amount of money that Robert Redfield received from the Ford Foundation was close to what he would have received had the Carnegie Corporation or Rockefeller Foundation approved his Institute of Cultural Studies proposal. Yet the project Redfield developed using the Ford grant differed markedly from the proposed Institute of Cultural Studies. Most important, Redfield did not obtain any institutional status at the University of Chicago for the Ford-sponsored Project on Intercultural Studies. The Institute of Cultural Studies was to have been an official body that financed and supervised a recognized interdisciplinary academic committee—a committee capable of hiring and granting tenure to faculty members as well as awarding graduate degrees to students. But with Robert Hutchins leaving the university in December 1950, Redfield lost the executive support he needed to establish such a committee. Hutchins's successor, Lawrence Kimpton, disapproved of the committees already in existence, especially the Committee on Social Thought, and certainly would not have brooked an initiative to form another similar committee.[13] Thus although Hutchins was able to secure a large grant of money for Redfield to establish an interdisciplinary program in civilizations studies, the program Redfield established had much less institutional standing than when originally conceived—a limitation that was to affect the outcome of the project dramatically.

While Redfield was forced to abandon his institutional goals for his civilizations project, he retained the general intellectual and ideological goals for comparative civilizations study that he had advanced in his Institute of Cultural Studies proposal. Redfield intended to use his Ford-sponsored program to stimulate and develop interest in the study of the world's great civilizations, particularly their systems of core values, for the express purpose of helping to create "an intellectual basis for a world community."[14] Yet up until 1951, Redfield had not developed any specific plans and objectives to guide such studies. Thus when he heard from Hutchins in early 1951 that Ford funding would be forthcoming, he was forced to devise quickly a plan of action that could be presented to Ford trustees.

Redfield sent Hutchins a preliminary plan in March 1951 and followed with a more detailed version in June. Shortly after Redfield submitted this plan, the trustees of the Ford Foundation granted Redfield $75,000 to initiate his project. Redfield then submitted reports to Hutchins on an annual basis in which he summarized work accomplished over the year, described future plans, and requested additional funding. From 1951 through 1953, Hutchins shepherded the Redfield project through official channels at the foundation and secured additional grants of $100,000 for Redfield in both 1952 and 1953.[15] But in 1953, Hutchins was forced out of the organization by the new president, Rowan Gaither, who replaced Paul Hoffman, and Redfield lost his only supporter at the foundation.[16]

After Hutchins left the foundation, responsibility for overseeing the Redfield-Singer project shifted to the foundation's Overseas Research and Training Section. And during the spring and summer of 1954, members of this section attempted to familiarize themselves with the Chicago project and to render a decision as to whether funding should be continued. Upon reviewing the project file Hutchins had left behind, foundation officials began to voice skepticism about the direction of the program. In an inter-office memorandum, one official observed pointedly that "terms of reference, progress reports, and future plans have been somewhat diffuse; grants have been made largely as investments in outstanding men engaged in important undertakings, it would seem." Foundation officials thus decided that before granting Redfield additional funds, they would need to conduct an intensive appraisal of the project. They asked Redfield to submit a comprehensive status report, and they enlisted external consultants to review the entire Chicago project. The consultants judged the Redfield-Singer program to be a strictly academic project with little chance for contributing "directly to the early realization of a world community." Foundation officials had also come to regard the program as insufficiently practical, and they decided in the fall of 1954 to discontinue their support. The foundation thus notified Redfield in October 1954 that he was to receive a "terminal" grant of $100,000 to assist him in bringing project activities to a close. With careful management, however, Redfield and Singer were able to stretch funds they had already received to support project activities until the early sixties.[17]

Holistic Methods: Critique and Development

The plans and reports that Redfield submitted to Hutchins provide a documentary trail that allows us to see the progressive evolution of Redfield's civilizations project. Above all, these documents make clear that this project did not spring into action immediately upon his receiving funding. Rather, it took Redfield and his colleagues almost two years to forge a coherent direction for the project. Almost as soon as he heard from Hutchins that the project would receive support from the Ford Foundation, Redfield recruited a small group of colleagues to help him establish the program at Chicago. Most important of these was his colleague from the College at the University of Chicago, Milton Singer.[18]

Milton Singer had come to Chicago in 1936 and had earned a Ph.D. in philosophy under Rudolph Carnap. Beginning in 1941, he had taught the core social science courses in the College. In 1947, he had become chair of the "Soc 3" course; and from 1948 through 1950, he had served as chair of the entire College social science staff. During the mid-1940s, Singer and his colleagues engaged in a thorough revision of the Soc 2 course and introduced a version of the course organized around the general theme of culture and personality. David Riesman, who joined the Soc 2 staff in 1946, provided the major impetus for pushing the course in this direction. His Soc 2 lectures during these years constituted the material that he was to publish in 1950 as *The Lonely Crowd*.[19] Singer found the notion of national character especially intriguing, and he began to collaborate with Riesman and his associates on the study of American civilization.[20]

Singer's turn toward the study of American civilization also brought him into Robert Redfield's circle of associates. Redfield and Singer had known each other since the forties through their collaboration in the College social science courses. Their association became closer in late 1949 when Redfield undertook to establish the Institute for Cultural Studies. Redfield was aware of Singer's growing interest in the study of American culture and civilization; and when Redfield received the grant from the Ford Foundation, he invited Singer to help him establish the project at Chicago. Singer's explorations in American culture quickly led, moreover, to a broader interest in cultural studies, and he found himself quite at home intellectually with the speculative, philosophical anthropology that Redfield engaged in. Redfield welcomed his interest and invited him in the fall of 1951 to co-teach courses with him in cultural anthropology. Within a few years, Singer came to identify himself as an anthropologist and, in 1955, he accepted a formal position within the Department of Anthropology at Chicago.

What brought Singer and Redfield together? Each came from extremely different cultural and intellectual backgrounds. Yet each found a powerful common interest in the comparative study of civilizations and cultures—so powerful, indeed, that they worked closely together on joint projects through almost the entire decade of the 1950s, halted only by Redfield's death in October 1958. A quick survey of the works which Singer wrote from the 1950s through the 1980s indicates that while Singer had an active and capacious intellect, he was neither a highly original nor overly systematic thinker. However, a survey of Singer's works also reveals that his learning was immense. He was well-read in a number of fields, especially philosophy and the human sciences. Students and colleagues of Singer affirm, moreover, that he was a powerful reader and an insightful critic.[21] It appears, therefore, that Singer and Redfield complemented each other in valuable ways. Where Redfield was the more original thinker, Singer was a scholar of greater breadth. Together, they were able to sustain a dialogue over civilizations studies that extended across almost an entire decade and launched between the two of them half a dozen different books.

Although Redfield and Singer were sure from the start about the overall strategic goals for the Chicago Project on Intercultural Studies, they arrived at the more tactical goals only through a process of trial and error. They spent most of the first year after receiving the initial Ford grant familiarizing themselves with the work of other scholars in the United States and Europe who were pursuing similar comparative civilizations studies. After this first exploratory year, they established a practical direction for the Chicago program. They chose to focus their efforts on two primary objectives. First, Redfield and Singer elected to use funds from the Ford grant to stimulate and support comparative civilizations research at a number of different American universities. Second, they undertook a comprehensive survey of existing methods for comparative civilizations analysis intended, especially, to enable them to develop more sophisticated and robust approaches for the study of civilizations.

Over the course of the 1950s, Redfield and Singer supported a number of different projects in civilizations research at other universities. They concentrated most of their efforts, however, toward sponsoring various conferences in specialized aspects of civilizations studies; they published the proceedings of most of these conferences, moreover, in a book series entitled "Comparative Studies of Cultures and Civilizations." Between 1953 and 1956, Redfield and Singer sponsored a series of symposia on Chinese and Islamic studies and comparative linguistics.[22] Redfield and Singer were especially influential in shaping the direction of Chinese studies in the United States during the 1950s and 1960s. In the years immediately following the Chinese Revolution, Chinese studies in America had fallen victim to acrimonious ideological factionalism. Redfield and Singer introduced a social scientific orientation into American Chinese studies that served to minimize the ideological conflict that had characterized the earlier literary-philosophical approach to Chinese studies.[23]

Redfield and Singer also channeled support into pedagogical efforts, supporting, especially, the introduction of non–Western civilization courses into the undergraduate curriculum. They supported, in particular, Bernard Cohn's 1957 efforts to develop and implement in the University of Chicago College an introductory course in Indian civilization. Cohn's initiative led to similar courses being developed for Chinese and Islamic civilization and for the implementation at Chicago during the 1960s of a comprehensive set of undergraduate courses in non–Western civilizations.[24]

Despite the efforts they made to stimulate and support research and pedagogical initiatives in the study of civilizations among other scholars, Redfield and Singer devoted most of their attention to the methodology aspect of the Chicago civilizations project. They established three distinct directions in their methodology efforts: (1) the construction of a critique and assessment of existing methods for study of total cultural patterns, such as national character or ethos studies; (2) the demonstration of the utility of worldview studies for holistic cultural comparison; and (3) the writing of a comprehensive manual on the aims and methods of comparative civilizations studies.[25]

Milton Singer undertook the first phase of the methodology project by conducting a critical survey of the major methods available for study of total cultural patterns. Singer had become interested in total cultural analysis through his work in the College at Chicago with David Riesman. Singer and Redfield were sympathetic in a general sense to the various methods used for total cultural analysis, such as national character, ethos, and modal personality analysis. They both shared grave reservations, however, about the basic philosophical assumptions on which these methods rested as well as the sampling techniques employed for conducting these analyses. Singer spent almost three years during the early fifties trying to develop a composite approach to the various total cultural methods. He found this composite method, however, to be an elusive goal, and he never published his full study of the various methods he examined. Nevertheless, Singer did publish in 1961 his descriptive survey of the available methods of total cultural analysis. This survey stands today as one of the best overviews of the 1950s culture and personality movement.[26]

Redfield led the second phase of the methodology agenda with his studies on worldview. The worldview of a people, in Redfield's definition, encompassed the totality of ideas that people within a culture shared about the self, human society, and the natural and spiritual worlds. Most important, worldview offered an insider's view; it constituted a deliberate attempt by an observer to construct a representation of how individuals within a culture conceptualize the world they looked out upon. Redfield had begun to develop his notion of worldview in the late 1930s as he wrote the summary volume for his Yucatan work, *The Folk Culture of Yucatan* (1941). When he and Villa Rojas had first described the intellectual and spiritual dimensions of life for the Maya villager in *Chan Kom: A Maya Village* (1934), they had presented the villagers' views of nature and the gods in separate chapters. This approach corresponded with standard ethnographic practice during the thirties. But in *The Folk Culture of Yucatan*, Redfield broke with this conventional approach, because he had come to regard accounts that separated various dimensions of the villagers' inner worlds, such as his earlier *Chan Kom*, as distortions. He had come to believe, furthermore, that anthropologists needed to present the body of beliefs about the self, nature, and the gods held by members of a folk culture as an integrated system and not merely a collection of disjointed ideas. In chapter 5 of *The Folk Culture of Yucatan*, "The Villager's View of Life," he presented an initial conception for such an integrated inner view.[27]

It was not until the early fifties, however, after he had received the Ford Foundation grant, that Redfield advanced a theoretical conceptualization of worldview studies and began to urge others to pursue such investigations. Redfield's major contribution was to construct a formal definition of the notion of worldview.[28] In a 1952 article, "The Primitive World View," he proposed that all cultures held a distinct worldview that could be used as a category of cross-cultural comparison. "To use the concept" of worldview, Redfield advanced, "is to assume certain human universals." Most important, it implied that in every society, each member was conscious of a self. Persons within all societies distinguished themselves from all else. The self stood therefore as the "axis of world view." Redfield drew upon the ideas of George Herbert Mead to develop his conception of how persons within different societies drew distinctions between self and others. The worldview of all peoples also allowed for some way to discriminate between the human and not human—in short, worldviews invariably implied some notion of human nature. Finally, every worldview embraced a distinction between "God" and "nature." The worldview of a people— the idea system of the average person not the product of reflective intellectuals—thus represented, Redfield proposed, a characteristic quality of a people, as distinct as other group constructs, such as national character, ethos, or mode of thought. Redfield further elaborated on his definition of the concept of worldview, especially on the transformation worldviews underwent as peoples shifted from traditional to modern orientations, in chapter 4 of *The Primitive World and Its Transformations*.[29]

Redfield enlisted two of his graduate students—E. Michael Mendelson and Charles M. Leslie, as well as a colleague, Calixta Guiteras-Holmes, a well-established Cuban anthropologist—to assist him in his worldview explorations. In the early fifties, Redfield arranged support for them to study worldviews held by peoples in three different Latin American villages. Mendelson elected to go to Atitlan, a Maya Indian village in Guatemala, Guiteras-Holmes to Chenalhó, a Tzotzil Indian village in the Chiapas Highlands of Mexico, and Leslie to the Zapotec Indian town of Mitla, Oaxaca, in southern Mexico. Redfield's intention was for each to produce an account of the worldview of these different peoples. He was then going to publish these three accounts together in a single volume; this set of accounts would thus provide an insightful view of these different peoples, but it would also demonstrate the utility of worldview for cross-cultural comparative studies. All three completed their studies by the mid-fifties. The studies turned out to be rather different from one another, though, and it would have required substantial editing to join them together in the composite volume Redfield had first envisaged. Redfield had been diagnosed with lymphatic leukemia in late 1955, and his failing health prevented him from working to fashion a single volume out of these studies before his death in 1958. Guiteras-Holmes and Leslie published their studies as individual monographs; Mendelson never published his complete study. However, Mendelson did publish a collection of articles based upon his dissertation as well as a condensed Spanish version of his work.[30]

The studies by these anthropologists revealed, however, several basic methodological limitations in Redfield's worldview approach. Most glaring of these limitations was the problem of hearsay evidence. Guiteras-Holmes, in particular, based her account largely on the description provided by a single informant. She did not attempt to cross-check his information with other informants or to verify if his descriptions accurately reflected the actions of the people. Both Leslie and Mendelson used multiple informants to minimize this weakness. Leslie's study provided a striking example, nevertheless, of the ultimate weakness in Redfield's worldview construct. Namely, Leslie's work, which resembled a "myth and symbol" study of the people of Mitla, was too much of an impressionistic study—it was more a work of art than a scientific analysis that could lend itself to comparative study. In short, the concept of worldview as defined by Redfield was a provocative one that offered a unique view of the structure of ideas within individual cultures; however, it was too diffuse and loose to provide an effective guide to comparative study.[31]

The third phase of Redfield and Singer's methodology agenda represented their most ambitious undertaking. Shortly after they received the Ford grant, Singer and Redfield decided to write a comprehensive manual on the comparative study of cultures and civilizations. They planned to divide this book into three parts: part I, "Methods for characterizing and comparing wholes," was to justify the need for comparative study of cultures and civilizations and present a guide to methods useful for such studies; part II, "Methods of characterizing and comparing cultures through their ingredients," was to address the use of studies of language, literature, philosophy, cultural history, and history of civilizations as techniques for comparative analysis; and part III, "The Great Traditions," was to demonstrate application of the techniques advanced in parts I and II for characterization of major world cultures and civilizations extending from prehistoric human cultures, to ancient (extinct) civilizations, to preeminent contemporary civilizations such as Confucianism and Taoism, Buddhism, Hinduism, Judaism, Christianity, and Islam.[32] Despite the investment of several years of effort in this manual, though, it became obvious by the mid-fifties that Singer and Redfield had devised too ambitious a plan for themselves. They were able to make progress in certain areas, particularly in defining a methodology for the anthropological exploration of the oral traditions encompassed within the world's major civilizations. Nevertheless, partly because of Redfield's failing health in the mid-fifties and partly because of the magnitude of the project, Redfield and Singer were unable to complete this book before Redfield's death in 1958.[33]

Theorizing Connections: Little and Great Traditions

In the process of working on the civilizations manual, Redfield concentrated his efforts on elaborating a theoretical justification for the role of anthropologists in the study of complex cultures and civilizations. Prior to the 1950s, most scholarly work on civilizations had focused on high culture. Redfield argued, however, that the world's major civilizations embraced a vast number of people who had little connection with high culture. In India and China, for example, the majority of the population lived in peasant and tribal villages. Most people in these villages were not literate and played little part in the high culture that was seen as the definitive aspect of Indian or Chinese civilization. Redfield proposed that these traditional peoples had a distinctive culture that was as much a part of Indian or Chinese civilization as the high culture of the literati or intelligentsia. Indeed, these great civilizations embraced two distinct levels of culture—a "great tradition of the reflective few" and a "little tradition of the unreflective many"—that could only be adequately studied if attention were directed to both. In a series of articles and finally a short book, which he wrote from late 1953 through 1956, Redfield advanced a theoretical description of the dynamic relationship that existed between these two traditions.[34] He suggested that anthropologists, furthermore, were most prepared to deal with nonliterate cultures and were thus best suited for studying the lower level or "little traditions" within the major civilizations.

While "the great tradition is cultivated in schools or temples," Redfield observed, "the little tradition works itself out and keeps itself going in the lives of the unlettered in their village communities." Yet these two traditions, he argued, do not operate independently of each other. The great tradition reaches outward constantly from the centers of power and exerts pressure upon the little traditions of the villages in the hinterland. "If we enter a village within a civilization we see at once that the culture there has been flowing into it from teachers and exemplars who never saw that village, who did their work in intellectual circles perhaps far away in space and time." This influence, moreover, is not unidirectional. The great tradition arose in part, Redfield argued, from the refinement and development of elements derived from the folk cultures of peoples indigenous to a civilization. Great and little traditions could thus be thought of, Redfield suggested, "as two currents of thought and action, distinguishable, yet ever flowing into and out of each other."[35]

Redfield recognized that anthropologists were newcomers when it came to studying the ancient but still-living civilizations of India, Islam, and China. Studies of these cultures had "long been cultivated by historians and other humanistic scholars."[36] Yet in their work, these students had concentrated almost exclusively on examination of the great traditions in these civilizations. Trained in philosophy, philology, history, and literary analysis, these scholars had focused on written texts produced by the urban elite and generally ignored the traditional oral culture—the little traditions—of the masses who lived in the myriad of rural villages. Redfield noted this imbalance and proposed that a more comprehensive understanding of these civilizations could be obtained through examination of both the little and great traditions. Yet the same mode of study could not be used to study both traditions; the same scholars could not attempt both studies. Redfield suggested therefore a division of scholarly labor. While the humanists continued in their studies of great traditions, he urged, anthropologists needed to slip into the "back entrance" of civilizations and study the little traditions of the villages. The composite of these two approaches—of the "textual" studies of the humanists and the "contextual" studies of the anthropologists—could then yield a deeper understanding of civilizations than obtained through previous examinations. Redfield's theory of connections both explained the internal cultural dynamics of civilizations and justified the value of ethnographic community studies in the larger field of civilizations studies.[37]

Although Redfield introduced the notion of Great and Little Traditions into anthropological discourse, his colleagues, particularly Milton Singer and McKim Marriott, took the lead during the mid-1950s in elaborating the construct and applying it to actual field studies. Singer greatly extended the reach of the Great and Little Traditions construct by applying Redfield's abstract ideas in the study of Indian civilization. In the fall of 1953, Singer began to pursue seriously a study of Indian civilization, undertaking postdoctoral studies at the University of Pennsylvania with the renowned Sanskritist W. Norman Brown. After working a term with Brown, Singer then moved to Berkeley to continue his studies with the social anthropologist and Indologist David G. Mandelbaum. Upon returning to Chicago in the spring of 1954, Singer led the way in establishing the pronounced focus on the study of India that came to characterize the Chicago civilizations project during the mid- to late fifties.

Singer's most direct contribution toward the extension of Redfield's theory lay in his demonstration of the compatibility of Redfield's ideas with those of the Indian social anthropologist M. N. Srinivas. Srinivas, who had been trained by Radcliffe-Brown at Oxford, published in 1952 a masterful social analysis of Hinduism, *Religion and Society among the Coorgs of South India.*[38] Singer had read this book while he was at Berkeley and discussed it with Mandelbaum and members of his research seminar. After careful reading, Singer had come to the conclusion that Srinivas's description of the interaction between pan-Indian Brahmanic Hinduism and the local village rituals of the Coorgs represented a specific example of the process Redfield had described abstractly as the interaction between Great and Little Traditions.

Srinivas had conducted an in-depth study during the 1940s of the social and religious structure of Coorg society. The Coorgs are a people who live in a number of small villages in a mountainous remote province located on the southwestern edge of the southern Indian state of Mysore. Srinivas focused especially on the sociocultural dynamics of caste. Significantly, he found evidence indicating that the local village customs of the Coorgs, which had derived from ancient non-Hindu rituals, had gradually changed over a period of centuries to become more like Brahmanic Hindu practices. Srinivas labeled this process in which local village rites were replaced by Sanskritic Hindu practices "Sanskritization." The effect of Sanskritization, he argued, was to raise the caste level of the Coorgs, to narrow the social distance between the Brahmins and them. He proposed, furthermore, that the process of Sanskritization was not limited to the Coorgs, but represented a widespread practice in India that provided a general mechanism of caste mobility within Hindu society.

Srinivas's study exercised a powerful impact during the postwar era among Indian, British, and American social scientists. Singer found his work particularly stimulating because it seemed to be a natural extension of Redfield's theoretical efforts. Redfield provided a basic "framework of ideas for a social anthropology of civilizations," and Srinivas's work offered an on-the-ground example of "how to extend the methods and concepts of social anthropology to a complex historic civilization." Synthesizing Srinivas's and Redfield's ideas, Singer devised a plan for field studies in India and subsequently embarked upon two decades of sustained research and publication in the study of Indian civilization.[39]

Immediately upon returning to Chicago in the spring of 1954, Singer began to orient the Chicago civilizations project toward the study of India. Project activities had slowed considerably during the fall of 1953 and winter of 1954 while Singer was at Pennsylvania and Berkeley and Redfield was in Sweden delivering a series of lectures at the University of Uppsala. But with Singer's return in April 1954, the Chicago project again began to move forward.

While Singer had been at Berkeley, he and Redfield had planned a special version of their Comparison of Cultures seminar, which they called "The Indian

Village," to consider methodological issues related to the study of Indian civilization. Specifically, they intended this seminar to provide a forum in which investigators who were engaged in actual field research in India could evaluate the utility of Redfield's ideas about village community studies and Great and Little Traditions for the study of Indian civilization. Singer and Redfield organized this seminar with the assistance of two Berkeley faculty members, David Mandelbaum and McKim Marriott.[40] Together they convened a group of eight social anthropologists who were engaged in conducting village research in India to join several Chicago graduate students in considering the study of India in the light of two specific questions: (1) "To what extent is the Indian village an isolated and self-sufficient 'little community'?" (2) "What can be learned from village studies about Indian civilization as a whole?" To provide theoretical background for seminar participants, the organizers circulated an outline of Redfield's "Little Community" lectures.

McKim Marriott not only helped organize the Village India seminar, but he also presented one of the research papers and edited for publication each of the other papers presented. In the year following the seminar, he published these papers as *Village India: Studies in the Little Community* (1955), a volume in Redfield and Singer's Comparative Studies of Cultures and Civilizations series.[41] This collection gained immediate attention and exerted a seminal influence during the 1950s and 1960s among anthropologists interested in the study of Indian civilization.[42]

This volume marked a turning point in the conceptualization of the Indian village among anthropologists and other social scientists. For almost two centuries, Westerners had viewed the Indian village as the locus of "traditional India." The village represented, in short, a baseline that could be regarded as the primitive or essential India. Accordingly, village studies were regarded as useful for recovering precolonial India (as a kind of salvage ethnology). Such a view of the Indian village necessarily regarded it as an isolate, a distinct element within the universe of Indian civilization.[43] The eight researchers who presented papers at the Chicago Village India seminar rejected this view. Each presented evidence that convincingly demonstrated that the Indian village could not be considered a self-sufficient isolate. Instead, they placed the village within a complex network of connections that linked it to neighboring villages, towns, and cities. This network derived from connections based upon kinship, caste, marriage, occupation, trade, religion, and politics. No village could be understood, therefore, without taking into account this wider, historically conditioned, sociocultural matrix.

Each of the papers in *Village India* spoke directly to the first question Singer had posed for the seminar, but only a few papers addressed his second question. Indeed, only one author attempted to deal in depth with Singer's question regarding the utility of village studies for characterization of the larger whole of Indian civilization. In "Little Communities in an Indigenous Civilization," McKim Marriott undertook to describe some of the ways in which the North Indian village of Kishan Garhi was "articulated within the Indian universe." Marriott based his paper on field research he had conducted in India from 1950 to 1952. He had conducted this research as a doctoral student at Chicago working under the direction of W. Lloyd Warner. Although Marriott had taken some courses with Redfield, he had not been strongly influenced by Redfield in the design and conduct of his dissertation research. Yet Marriott encountered Redfield's ideas through Milton Singer who came to Berkeley in January 1954 to undertake a quarter of postdoctoral work in Indian studies with David Mandelbaum. In his contribution to the Village India seminar, Marriott attempted to use Redfield's notion of Great and Little Traditions as well as Srinivas's Sanskritization construct as a set of analytical lenses to reevaluate the data he had collected earlier on Kishan Garhi. In the process of doing this, Marriott demonstrated that Redfield's and Srinivas's ideas offered powerful tools for conceptualizing cultural dynamics within a village such as Kishan Garhi. He greatly extended Redfield's work by taking ideas that Redfield had dealt with on a strictly theoretical level and applying them to actual ethnographic data. Marriott provided, in short, the first case study analysis that tested the explanatory power of Redfield's Great and Little Traditions construct.[44]

Marriott focused his analysis on the annual cycle of religious festivals in Kishan Garhi. He determined that the village celebrated both Sanskritic Hindu and local pagan festivals. The Hindu festivals, he argued, reflected the influence in the village of the pan-Indian Great Tradition, while the local pagan festivals reflected the influence of the Little Tradition. These cultural traditions, however, did not operate independently of each other. Rather, Marriott offered evidence that indicated the pan-Indian Sanskritic tradition acted to modify local practices and, through a process he termed "universalization," progressively shaped these practices to become more like the ways of the Great Tradition. He also provided evidence that suggested this interaction was reciprocal. To this effect, he offered several examples that showed how the local traditions exerted force upon the more universal tradition to transform it, through a process he called "parochialization," into a form more congenial with the unique environment of the individual village.[45]

Because the village served as a locus of interaction for both the Great and Little Traditions, Marriott argued, it offered a unique vantage point for the study of Indian civilization. Although the effort to develop a holistic understanding of Indian civilization demanded investigation at the village level, village studies could never constitute the sole level of analysis. For the village did not exist as a sociocultural isolate, an entity understandable—in functionalist fashion—in its own terms. Instead, the village needed to be understood in a dualistic context— one that embraced both its local parochial identity as well as its larger universal identity. "A focus upon the small half-world of the village and a perspective upon the universe of Indian civilization thus remain mutually indispensable for whole understanding," Marriott concluded, "whether of Hinduism or of the traditional forms of India's social structure." With this conclusion, Marriott addressed both of Milton Singer's leadoff questions and effectively summarized the entire Village India seminar.[46]

The Cultural Role of Cities

Although Redfield and Singer invested much of their time exploring the sociocultural roles of rural villages within civilizations, they also directed their attention toward considering the roles of cities within civilizations. Cities were not, of course, a new interest with Redfield. His Yucatan project had included a major urban component; the theory of change implied in his folk-urban construct, moreover, rested upon the view of cities—the centers of capitalism, industry, and mass communications—as the agents of social change. Redfield's notion of the Great and Little Traditions also raised issues about the relationship between cities and villages. Redfield and Singer explored the urban-rural dimensions of the Great/Little Traditions notion at length in a jointly written article, "The Cultural Role of Cities" (1954).[47]

They wrote this article at the invitation of Bert F. Hoselitz, an economic historian at Chicago who focused in his studies upon the relationship between social and cultural factors and economic growth. Hoselitz was a leading figure during the 1950s and 1960s among Western social scientists who were studying "modernization" factors in the "developing" nations. In 1951, Hoselitz had founded the journal *Economic Development and Cultural Change* to foster and disseminate scholarship on sociocultural and economic development, a journal he continued to edit with only minor interruptions for the next thirty-five years. This journal became, moreover, one of the major outlets for the modernization theorists of the fifties and sixties.[48]

Hoselitz also periodically sponsored conferences to bring together social scientists and government policy-makers to discuss various aspects of development. In the fall of 1953, he proposed to several of his colleagues that they hold a conference to explore the role of cities in economic development and cultural change. Hoselitz, who had recently published an article, "The Role of Cities in the Economic Growth of Underdeveloped Countries,"[49] wanted to stimulate his colleagues to look further into the relationship between urbanization and development. He suggested that they look at this issue from five distinct perspectives—the demographic, sociological, cultural, historical, and economic—and he solicited leadoff papers from various colleagues to address each separate perspective. Hoselitz approached Singer and Redfield, with whom he had collaborated closely for several years, and asked them to contribute the article on the cultural aspects of cities and development. In response to Hoselitz's request, Redfield and Singer wrote "The Cultural Role of Cities," an article that came to exercise much influence among development theorists and urban anthropologists.[50]

In "The Cultural Role of Cities," Redfield and Singer attempted to complement the view of urban centers that Hoselitz had advanced. Hoselitz had discussed distinctions made by economic historians between cities that functioned as political-intellectual centers and those that functioned as economic centers. Redfield and Singer, however, proposed, a different typological distinction for towns and cities, one that emphasized the role cities played in cultural rather than political or economic processes.

Cities played two distinct and contrasting roles, they argued, in interacting with and shaping the cultural traditions of a civilization. They referred to these two forms of interaction as the "orthogenetic" and "heterogenetic" functions of cities. No city in their scheme accorded entirely with one function or the other; rather, the terms orthogenetic and heterogenetic referred simply to predominating tendencies. Orthogenetic cities emerged, they proposed, only in "primary" civilizations, like India or China. Cities that functioned in this role, for example, Banares or ancient Beijing, were dominated by "literati" and an "indigenous bureaucracy." These cities fulfilled a largely sacred and administrative role. Indeed, the activities of the learned but religiously orthodox literati provided the major purpose and definition of orthogenetic cities. In these centers, literati transformed the local ways—preserved and transmitted through oral culture—of the indigenous Little Tradition into the codified textual Great Tradition. Heterogenetic cities, however, fulfilled a much different role. These were not centers of the orthodox; instead, foreigners and cosmopolitans dominated these cities. The intellectuals in these cities, moreover, were not literati but heterodox secular "intelligentsia." And here, the dominant intellectual activity was not elaboration of an orthodox tradition into sacred texts and formalized rituals, but rather development of secular knowledge in science, law, and commercial-entrepreneurial practice.[51]

Redfield had long portrayed the city as a locus of cultural change. In "The Cultural Role of Cities," however, he and Singer advanced a crucial distinction in the types of change a city may foster. The city served as a center of change, they emphasized, in both its orthogenetic and heterogenetic roles. The roles differed, they explained, only according to the nature of change:

> Insofar as the city has an orthogenetic role, it is not to maintain culture as it was; the orthogenetic city is not static; it is the place where religious, philosophical and literary specialists reflect, synthesize, and create out of the traditional material new arrangements and developments that are felt by the people to be outgrowths of the old. What is changed is a further statement of what was there before. Insofar as the city has a heterogenetic role, it is a place of conflict of differing traditions, a center of heresy, heterodoxy, and dissent, of interruption and destruction of ancient tradition, or rootlessness, and anomie.[52]

Thus, while the orthogenetic transformation led to a perpetuation of the Little Tradition in the more refined and elaborated Great Tradition, the heterogenetic transformation led to a decisive break with the Little Tradition. This break freed "the intellectual, aesthetic, economic, and political life from the local moral norms," and "developed" both "an individuated expediential motivation" and "a revolutionary, nativistic, humanistic, or ecumenical viewpoint, now directed toward reform, progress, and designed change."[53]

"The Cultural Role of Cities" demonstrates how far Redfield's thinking had come regarding the processes of urbanization since he wrote *The Folk Culture of Yucatan* in 1941. Then, he had depicted the city as bringing only disorganization to folk culture. He revealed in *The Primitive World and Its Transformations* a greatly modified view of the cultural effects of urbanization. But it was in "The Cultural Role of Cities" that he articulated his most sophisticated conceptualization of urbanization, demonstrating that he had gone far beyond regarding the city merely as an agent of disorganization—as he had argued in all his work up through *The Folk Culture of Yucatan*.

During the early 1950s, urban anthropology had just begun to emerge as a subspecialty. Redfield served as one of the founding fathers of this new field through his investigations of the city of Mérida during the 1930s and through his continuing efforts to theorize the relationship between cities and culture. Redfield and Singer's "Cultural Role of Cities" served as a pivotal essay for the new urban anthropology, especially through its introduction of the "orthogenetic" and "heterogenetic" typology and its provocative suggestions regarding the cultural processes involved in different forms of urbanism. Shortly after writing this article, moreover, Milton Singer undertook field research on his own in urban anthropology by initiating a study of cultural traditions within metropolitan Madras. Singer established himself through this line of research as one of the central urban anthropologists of the fifties and sixties.[54]

In his research in Madras, Singer investigated the cultural dynamics of Sanskritic Hinduism within the urban environment. Employing the Redfieldian Great Tradition/Little Tradition notion as the basic organizing principle for all his studies, Singer devoted himself throughout his "second career" of anthropology to promoting acceptance and use of the construct by other social anthropologists and scholars of comparative civilizations. Students of Indian and Buddhist civilizations proved most receptive to the notion. From the mid-fifties through the early seventies, Redfield's ideas exercised an important influence in these fields.[55]

Singer brought together the first body of work treating Indian civilization from the Great Tradition/Little Tradition perspective. In a collection entitled *Traditional India: Structure and Change* (1959), he presented the work of twenty different Indologists—including European, Indian, and American scholars—all of whose work reflected Redfieldian influence. Several of those who contributed to *Traditional India*, furthermore, such as M. N. Srinivas, Surajit Sinha, and Bernard S. Cohn, went on in the sixties to produce additional studies informed by Redfield's dual tradition notion. Clearly most important, though, of the studies of Indian civilization organized around the Great Tradition/Little Tradition construct was Singer's magnum opus, *When a Great Tradition Modernizes: An Anthropological Approach to Indian Civilization* (1972). Singer presented here the results of his seventeen years of research in Madras, in which he extended and significantly modified the framework of ideas he had derived from Redfield. Especially notable in Singer's modifications to Redfield's ideas was his demonstration of the coexistence in India of modern and traditional ways—in short, Singer asserted that becoming modern did not constitute a zero-sum process.

Singer worked longer than most students of Indian civilization within the Great Tradition/Little Tradition framework. Indeed, among Indologists, Redfield's construct enjoyed its greatest popularity in the late fifties and early sixties. In the early to mid-sixties, however, students of Buddhist civilization began to use the idea, and the Great Tradition/Little Tradition construct came to exercise an even broader influence within Buddhist studies than it had in Indian studies. The Redfield influence in Buddhist studies continued to be felt throughout the sixties and into the early seventies. During these years, many of the leading scholars in the field, such as Gananath Obeyesekere, Michael Ames, Hans-Dieter Evers, Melford Spiro, and Stanley J. Tambiah, all worked to a lesser or greater extent within Redfieldian terms.[56]

Nevertheless, while Redfield's Great Tradition/Little Tradition idea attracted numerous proponents, it also attracted multiple critics. Much of the criticism that emerged centered on the vagueness of Redfield's terminology and on the complexities and confusion that arose in situations in which multiple Great Traditions coexisted in the same geographic area. Most important, many found that the ideas did not work in the field where distinctions between two traditions often appeared negligible or nonexistent. Critics charged, furthermore, that Redfield's ideas were too structural and did not sufficiently acknowledge the role of historical factors in the shaping of complex cultures and civilizations.[57]

Those who criticized the Great Tradition/Little Tradition notion for its ambiguity or lack of precision were faulting Redfield, essentially, for not having constructed a model with predictive capabilities. Redfield acknowledged, however, that his idea held no predictive value. Speaking to a group of anthropologists at the Center for Advanced Study in the Behavioral Sciences but a few months before his death, Redfield explained that his idea was a heuristic device, a "concept of cogitation," and not an operational model.[58]

Redfield's construct provided a set of terms that facilitated discussion of the operation of symbolic and ideological process within civilizations. His conceptual terminology filled a void, moreover, in the discourse of American social scientists. During the first half of the twentieth century, social theorists had largely ignored macrosociological issues and had focused, instead, on the micro level—on social interactions within neighborhoods and cities. Thus, few theories existed in the late forties and early fifties that could provide terms useful for discussing social dynamics on a grand scale.[59] Redfield not only provided this conceptual apparatus, but also he anticipated several more sophisticated theoretical developments. In particular, his ideas foreshadowed the center-periphery theory of Edward Shils, the structuralism of Claude Lévi-Strauss, and the axial-age constructs of Karl Jaspers and S. N. Eisenstadt.[60] While Redfield's ideas gave way during the mid- to late sixties to these broader and more powerful theories, Redfield's Great Tradition/Little Tradition construct served as a pioneering idea in the development of modern macrosociological theory.

Notes

1. Thorkild Jacobsen, "Preliminary Outline of a Proposed Institute of Cultures," 9 May 1949, no box, folder 1, President's Papers, Appointments & Budgets, 1950-1955, Special Collections, Joseph Regenstein Library, University of Chicago, Chicago (hereafter cited as PP-UC, 1950-55).

2. Robert Redfield, "What is the Institute concerned with?" c. May 1949, no box, folder 1, PP-UC, 1950-55 (draft memorandum Redfield to Hutchins; earlier version of same memorandum in box 4, folder 16, Robert Redfield Papers, Special Collections, Joseph Regenstein Library, University of Chicago, Chicago (hereafter cited as RR-UC); Robert Redfield to Robert M. Hutchins and Everett C. Hughes, 30 June 1949, no box, folder 1, PP-UC, 1950-55.

3. Redfield to Hutchins and Hughes, 30 June 1949, no box, folder 1, PP-UC, 1950-55; Everett C. Hughes to Robert M. Hutchins and Robert Redfield, 19 July 1949, no box, folder 1, PP-UC, 1950-55.

4. On John Nef and the founding of the Committee on Social Thought, see Harry S. Ashmore, *Unseasonable Truths: The Life of Robert Maynard Hutchins* (Boston: Little, Brown and Company, 1989), 190-191, 229-232, 270-272; William H. McNeill, *Hutchins' University: A Memoir of the University of Chicago, 1929-1950* (Chicago: University of Chicago Press, 1991), 119-121; Mary Ann Dzuback, *Robert M. Hutchins, Portrait of an Educator* (Chicago: University of Chicago Press, 1992), 111, 208, 214-216, and 282.

5. Robert M. Hutchins, *The Higher Learning in America* (New Haven, Conn.: Yale University Press, 1936). A good sense of the change that Hutchins underwent during the 1930s can be gained by comparing the optimistic dedicatory speech Hutchins gave in 1929 at the opening of Chicago's "1126" Social Science Research Building with his grim, apocalyptic address a decade later at the ten-year commemoration for the building. Robert M. Hutchins, "Address of Dedication," in *The New Social Science*, ed. Leonard D. White (Chicago: University of Chicago Press, 1930), 1-3; Hutchins, "Address," in *Eleven Twenty-Six: A Decade of Social Science Research*, ed. Louis Wirth (Chicago: University of Chicago Press, 1940; reprint, New York: Arno Press, 1974), 1-4. On Hutchins's conception of the moral purpose of the university, see Dzuback, *Robert M. Hutchins*, 100-108).

6. A selection of Nef's early forties civilizations writings includes: John U. Nef, "The American Universities and the Future of Western Civilization," *Review of Politics* 1 (July 1939): 241-260; "A Social Science Objective," *University of Chicago Magazine* 31 (November 1939): 10-11, 27-28; "On the Future of American Civilization," *Review of Politics* 2 (July 1940): 261-282; "Civilization at the Crossroads," *Review of Politics* 3 (July 1941): 283-299; "Civilization at the Crossroads-II," *Review of Politics* 3 (October 1941): 451-478; *The United States and Civilization* (Chicago: University of Chicago Press, 1942); Nef offered a retrospective view of his joint efforts with Robert Hutchins in "The University of Chicago and the World, 1929-1951," *Review of Politics* 13 (October 1951): 399-429; see also Nef's *The Universities Look for Unity: An Essay on the Responsibilities of the Mind to Civilization in War and Peace* (New York: Pantheon, 1953), and his autobiography, *Search for Meaning: The Autobiography of a Nonconformist* (Washington, D.C.: Public Affairs Press, 1973), 173-189.

7. The Executive Committee of the Division of Social Sciences allowed formation of the Committee on the Study of Civilization in early 1942. However, the Executive Committee did not approve of the name or field of study described by the civilization

committee and refused to authorize degree-granting powers for the committee until it changed its name and focus. During the summer of 1942, Redfield (then dean of the social sciences division) wrote and submitted to the Executive Committee a proposal for a "Committee on Social Thought." The Executive Committee approved Redfield's proposal, and the Committee on Social Thought became a degree-granting committee in the fall of 1943. Robert Redfield to John U. Nef, Robert M. Hutchins, and Frank H. Knight, 17 August 1942, box 1, folder "Correspondence [Study of Civilization] 1941-42," Committee on Social Thought Papers (hereafter cited as CST), Special Collections, Joseph Regenstein Library, University of Chicago, Chicago; Redfield, "The Committee on Social Thought," 19 August 1942, CST, box 1, folder "Correspondence [Study of Civilization] 1941-42".

8. From late fall in 1941 through the winter of 1942, Nef, Hutchins, Redfield, and Knight met weekly for sumptuous lunches at the Shoreland Hotel—all at Nef's expense—to discuss the purpose and direction for the new committee. These lunches, which often went on for hours, were given over to long discussions about the direction of the committee and, more generally, about the aims of education itself. All four frequently continued their discussion between meetings, moreover, by writing heated letters to each other. This collection of letters provides a record of an extraordinary extended argument over the philosophy and purpose of education as well as the nature of truth and values— an argument that captures in microcosm much of the debate over education that charged Chicago during the thirties and forties. Several dozen of these letters have survived and are located in box 59, folders 5 and 6, Frank H. Knight Papers, Special Collections, Joseph Regenstein Library, University of Chicago, Chicago and box 1, folder "Correspondence [Study of Civilization] 1941-42," CST, and box 1, folder "Faculty Correspondence, 1942-1951," CST.

9. Jacobsen, "Preliminary Outline of a Proposed Institute of Cultures."

10. Robert Redfield, "An Institute of Cultural Studies," 25 November 1949, no box, folder 1, PP-UC, 1950-55; Robert M. Hutchins to Charles Dollard, 23 November 1949, no box, folder 1, PP-UC, 1950-55; Robert M. Hutchins to Chester Bernard, 23 November 1949, no box, folder 1, PP-UC, 1950-55.

11. When Henry Ford died in 1947, his heirs realized that they would lose control of the Ford Motor Company because of the inheritance taxes they would be required to pay unless they found a way to shelter their inheritance. They found that they were able to lighten the tax burden significantly and still retain control of the company by giving most of their stock in the company to the Ford Foundation. Previous to that, the Ford Foundation had been a small, local charity that had supported the arts in Detroit and given generously to the Henry Ford Hospital and the Henry Ford Museum. After the Ford heirs donated their stock to the foundation, it became the richest philanthropic organization in the world. Dwight Macdonald, *The Ford Foundation: The Men and the Millions* (New York: Reynal & Company, 1956); Francis X. Sutton, "The Ford Foundation: The Early Years," *Daedalus* 116 (Winter 1987): 41-92.

12. The Redfield-Singer project received its name almost by default. Because Redfield never submitted a formal proposal for the program—Hutchins handled initial negotiations orally—the program came to be known by the first name Ford Foundation officials assigned to it. In Redfield's early correspondence with Hutchins, Redfield spoke of a program for the "comparative study of cultures" and a "program for the stimulation of cultural studies." But when the foundation first approved funds for Redfield, foundation

director Paul G. Hoffman spoke of Redfield's "studies in the general field of intercultural relations." This name came to hold increasingly official status in foundation memoranda; and by the fall of 1954, foundation personnel had begun to refer to the program as the "Project in Intercultural Relations." At the University of Chicago, however, the program came to be known more descriptively as the "Redfield project" or the "Comparative Civilizations Project." Robert Redfield to Robert M. Hutchins, 21 March 1951, Ford Foundation Archives, New York, Microfilm reel 0505; Grant no. 519-50 (hereafter cited as FORD), Section 4; Redfield to Hutchins, 7 June 1951, FORD, Section 1.2; Paul G. Hoffman to Redfield, 1 August 1951, FORD, Section 1.6; docket entry, Board of Trustees meeting, 29-30 October 1954, FORD, Section 1.4; Richard H. Davis, *South Asia at Chicago: A History* (Chicago: Committee on Southern Asian Studies, 1985), 29-40.

13. On Kimpton's view of educational innovations implemented by Hutchins, see Ashmore, *Unseasonable Truths*, 305-310.

14. Redfield to Hutchins, 21 March 1951, FORD, Section 4.

15. Redfield to Hutchins 21 March 1951, FORD, Section 4; Redfield to Hutchins, 7 June 1951, FORD, Section 1.2; Redfield to Hutchins, 21 December 1951, FORD, Section 3.2; Redfield to Hutchins, 14 February 1952, box 5, folder 10, Robert Redfield, Ford Foundation Papers, Special Collections, Joseph Regenstein Library, University of Chicago, Chicago (hereafter cited as RRFF); Hutchins to Redfield, 19 February 1952, box 5, folder 10, RRFF; Redfield to Hutchins, 7 March 1952, FORD, Section 1.9; Redfield to Hutchins, 16 January 1953, box 5, folder 10, RRFF.

16. Hutchins's difficulties at the Ford Foundation are described in Dzuback, *Robert M. Hutchins*, 231-253.

17. John Howard to Don K. Price, 24 May 1954, FORD, Section 4; Cleon O. Swayzee to Robert Redfield, 7 June 1954, box 5, folder 16, RRFF; Redfield to Swayzee, 5 July 1954, FORD, Section 1.9; Clarence E. Thurber to Paul Appleby, 30 August 1954, FORD, Section 4; Paul Appleby to Clarence E. Thurber, 14 September 1954, FORD, Section 4; docket excerpt, Board of Trustees meeting, 29-30 October, 1954, FORD, Section 1.4.

18. Redfield also enlisted the help of another philosopher, Eliseo Vivas, of Northwestern University. Vivas contributed on a limited basis during the first year of the project but drifted away after that.

19. David Riesman with Nathan Glazer and Reuel Denney, *The Lonely Crowd: A Study of the Changing American Character* (New Haven, Conn.: Yale University Press, 1950). See David Riesman, "Becoming an Academic Man," in *Authors of Their Own Lives: Intellectual Biographies by Twenty American Sociologists*, ed. Bennett M. Berger (Berkeley: University of California Press, 1990), 22-74; Riesman, "My Education in Soc 2 and My Efforts to Adapt It in the Harvard Setting," in *General Education in the Social Sciences: Centennial Reflections on the College of the University of Chicago*, ed. John J. MacAloon (Chicago: University of Chicago Press, 1992), 178-216.

20. In 1949, Singer published the first article of his scholarly career, a critical essay on the notion of American character. "How the American Got His Character," *Ethics* 60 (October 1949): 62-66. Up until that point, he had devoted himself solely to teaching in the College. Collaboration with Riesman and his associates, however, opened up a new scholarly avenue for Singer. And from the late 1940s onward, he began to shift his focus away from undergraduate teaching toward research, writing, and the guidance of graduate students. Singer wrote several essays on the development of the Chicago civilizations project in which he briefly discussed his own career shift. Milton Singer, "Robert Red-

field's Development of a Social Anthropology of Civilizations," in *American Anthropology: The Early Years*, 1974 Proceedings of the American Ethnological Society, ed. John V. Murra (St. Paul, Minn.: West Publishing, 1976), 197-198; Singer, "Symbolism of the Center, the Periphery, and the Middle," in *Center: Ideas and Institutions*, ed. Liah Greenfeld and Michel Martin (Chicago: University of Chicago Press, 1988), 210-212.

21. Joseph Gusfield, telephone interview with author, 11 August 1995; Murray Wax, telephone interview with author, 17 June 1995.

22. Redfield and Singer published the papers presented at the conferences in the following "Comparative Studies of Cultures and Civilizations" series volumes: *Studies in Chinese Thought*, ed. Arthur Wright (Chicago: University of Chicago Press, 1953); *Unity and Variety in Muslim Civilization*, ed. Gustave E. von Grunebaum (Chicago: University of Chicago Press, 1955); *Chinese Thought and Institutions*, ed. John King Fairbank (Chicago: University of Chicago Press, 1957), and *Language in Culture*, ed. Harry Hoijer (Chicago: University of Chicago Press, 1954).

23. On Redfield's influence on Chinese studies in the United States, see John King Fairbank, *Chinabound: A Fifty-Year Memoir* (New York: Harper & Row, 1982), and Paul M. Evans, *John Fairbank and the American Understanding of China* (New York: Basil Blackwell, 1988).

24. Singer first mentioned these courses in his 1957 project status report (Milton Singer to John Howard, 17 June 1957, FORD, Section 1.9). See also Milton Singer, ed., *Introducing India in Liberal Education* (Chicago: University of Chicago Press, 1957); McKim Marriott, "Anthropology Courses in Regions and Civilizations: An Indian Civilization Course," in *The Teaching of Anthropology*, ed. David G. Mandelbaum, Gabriel W. Lasker, and Ethel M. Albert (Berkeley: University of California Press, 1963), 203-216; Davis, *South Asia at Chicago: A History*, 45-51; and Milton Singer, "A Conversation of Cultures: The United States and Southern Asia," in *Semiotics of Cities, Selves, and Cultures: Explorations in Semiotic Anthropology* (Berlin: Mouton de Gruyter, 1991), 169-188.

25. The single best expression of Redfield and Singer's methodological goals is the foreword they wrote for Arthur Wright's *Studies in Chinese Thought*, the first volume in their "Comparative Studies of Cultures and Civilizations" series (Robert Redfield and Milton Singer, foreword to *Studies in Chinese Thought*, ed. Wright, v-viii).

26. Milton Singer, "A Survey of Culture and Personality Theory and Research," in *Studying Personality Cross-Culturally*, ed. Bert Kaplan (New York: Harper & Row, 1961), 9-90.

27. Robert Redfield, *The Folk Culture of Yucatan* (Chicago: University of Chicago Press, 1941); Robert Redfield and Alfonso Villa Rojas, *Chan Kom: A Maya Village* (Washington, D.C.: Carnegie Institution of Washington, 1934; reprint, Chicago: University of Chicago Press, 1962).

28. Redfield also channeled some of the funds from the Ford Foundation grant to support completion of an English translation of one of the seminal studies of worldview, Marcel Griaule's *Dieu d'Eau*, which appeared in English as *Conversations with Ogotemmeli: An Introduction to Dogon Religious Ideas* (London: Oxford University Press, 1965).

29. Robert Redfield, "The Primitive Worldview," *Proceedings of the American Philosophical Society* 96 (February 1952): 30-36; Robert Redfield, *The Primitive World and Its Transformations* (Ithaca, N.Y.: Cornell University Press, 1953).

30. Calixta Guiteras-Holmes, *Perils of the Soul: The Worldview of a Tzotil Indian* (New York: Free Press of Glencoe, 1961); Charles M. Leslie, *Now We Are Civilized: A Study of the Worldview of the Zapotec Indians of Mitla, Oaxaca* (Detroit: Wayne State University Press, 1960); E. Michael Mendelson, "Religion and World-view in Santiago Atitlan." Ph.D. diss., University of Chicago, 1957; Mendelson, "The King, the Traitor, and the Cross: An Interpretation of Highland Maya Religious Conflict," *Diogenes* 21 (Spring 1958): 1-10; Mendelson, "A Guatemalan Sacred Bundle," *Man* 58 (August 1958): 121-126; *Los Escandalos de Maximon*, Seminario de Intregracion Social, Publication no. 19 (Guatemala City: Ministerio de Educacion, 1965).

31. I am indebted here to E. Michael Mendelson's insightful discussion of world-view research in his article "World View" in the *International Encyclopedia of Social Science*, ed. David L. Sills (New York: Macmillan and Free Press, 1968); see also, Michael Kearney, *Worldview* (San Francisco: Chandler and Sharpe Publishers, 1984), 1-106.

32. The initial description of the Redfield-Singer book on civilizations appears in Robert Redfield to Robert M. Hutchins, 7 March 1952, Document F, "The Comparative Study of Cultures and Civilizations," FORD, Section 1.9. Redfield also lists the book as an active project in his 1954 report to the Ford Foundation (Redfield to Cleon O. Swayzee, 5 July 1954, FORD, Section 1.9). See also Milton Singer to Redfield, 7 January 1952, box 3, folder 6, RRFF.

33. During the last year of his life, Redfield was working on writing a smaller, less comprehensive book on civilizations than the earlier work he and Singer had projected. He spent the spring of 1958 at the Center for Advanced Study in the Social Sciences, and there he wrote and presented three essays that were to be part of his shorter work on civilizations: "Civilizations as Things Thought About," "Civilizations as Cultural Structures," and "Civilizations as Societal Structures." He died before he could publish these essays or complete his short book on civilizations studies. These essays were published, however, in the first volume of Redfield's collected papers, *The Papers of Robert Redfield,* ed. Margaret Park Redfield, vol. 1, *Human Nature and the Study of Society* (Chicago: University of Chicago Press, 1962).

34. Robert Redfield, "The Natural History of the Folk Society," *Social Forces* 31 (March 1953): 224-229; Redfield, "Community Studies in Japan and China: A Symposium," *Far Eastern Quarterly* 14 (November 1954): 3-10; Redfield, "The Social Organization of Tradition," *Far Eastern Quarterly* 15 (November 1955): 13-21; Redfield, *Peasant Society and Culture: An Anthropological Approach to Civilization* (Chicago: University of Chicago Press, 1956).

35. Redfield, *Peasant Society and Culture*, 42-43.

36. Redfield was referring here to the long tradition of civilizations scholarship extending from such humanists as Jacob Burckhardt, James Henry Breasted, and Oswald Spengler to Arnold Toynbee, Henri Frankfort, and F. S. C. Northrop.

37. Redfield, *Peasant Society and Culture*, 46-47, 51-52.

38. M. N. Srinivas, *Religion and Society among the Coorgs of South India* (Oxford: Oxford University Press, 1952).

39. Milton Singer provides a wealth of autobiographical information in the various prefaces and introductions included in his *When a Great Tradition Modernizes: An Anthropological Approach to Indian Civilization* (New York: Praeger, 1972; reprint, Chicago: University of Chicago Press, 1980); Singer also offers further perspectives on his own Indian work in the essay he wrote for the David Mandelbaum Festschrift, "David

Mandelbaum and the Rise of South Asian Studies: A Reminiscence," in *Dimensions of Social Life: Essays in Honor of David G. Mandelbaum*, ed. Paul Hockings (Berlin: Mouton de Gruyter, 1987), 1-7.

40. Although still a doctoral candidate at the University of Chicago, Marriott had been hired as a research anthropologist by Berkeley's East Asia Institute.

41. McKim Marriott, ed., *Village India: Studies in the Little Community* (Chicago: University of Chicago Press, 1955).

42. A sense of the excitement *Village India* generated can be gleaned from the reviews it received upon publication; see, especially, Ruth Hill Useem, *American Sociological Review* 21 (February 1956): 100-101; Surajit Sinha, *American Sociological Review* 61 (May 1956): 640-642; Dorothy Spencer, *Annals of the American Academy of Political and Social Science* 303 (Jan 1956): 222-223; Selig Harrison, *New Republic* 133 (12 December 1955): 20; and Maurice Zinkin, *Pacific Affairs* 29 (September 1956): 289-291. *India's Villages*, ed. M. N. Srinivas (Calcutta: West Bengal Government Press, 1955), a similar volume of Indian village studies published in the same year as the Marriott collection did not receive widespread attention because of its limited distribution. Specialists in Indian studies made use of the volume, though, and *India's Villages* should be considered in historical perspective as a companion text to *Village India*.

43. For a history of the conceptualization of the Indian village, see Louis Dumont, "The 'Village Community' from Munro to Maine," *Contributions to Indian Sociology* 9 (1966): 67-89; Bernard S. Cohn, "Notes on the History of the Study of Indian Society and Culture," in *Structure and Change in Indian Society*, ed. Milton Singer and Bernard S. Cohn (Chicago: Aldine Press, 1968), 3-28; and Ronald Inden, *Imagining India* (Cambridge, Mass.: Blackwell, 1990), 131-161.

44. McKim Marriott, "Little Communities in an Indigenous Civilization," in *Village India: Studies in the Little Community*, ed. McKim Marriott (Chicago: University of Chicago Press, 1955), 171; McKim Marriott, interview by author (Chicago, 22 February 1994); Milton Singer, "David Mandelbaum and the Rise of South Asian Studies: A Reminiscence," 1-2.

45. Marriott, "Little Communities," 191-218.

46. Marriott, "Little Communities," 218.

47. Robert Redfield and Milton B. Singer, "The Cultural Role of Cities," *Economic Development and Cultural Change* 3 (October 1954): 53-73.

48. Manning Nash, foreword to *Essays on Economic Development and Cultural Change: In Honor of Bert F. Hoselitz*, ed. Manning Nash (Chicago: University of Chicago Press, 1977), v-vi.

49. Bert F. Hoselitz, "The Role of Cities in the Economic Growth of Underdeveloped Countries," *Journal of Political Economy* 61 (June 1953): 195-208.

50. Bert F. Hoselitz, "Introduction," *Economic Development and Cultural Change* 3 (October 1954): 4-5.

51. Redfield and Singer, "Cultural Role of Cities," 53-63.

52. Redfield and Singer, "Cultural Role of Cities," 58.

53. Redfield and Singer, "Cultural Role of Cities," 59.

54. On the influence of Redfield's and Singer's "Cultural Role of Cities" article, see Gino Germani, "Urbanization, Social Change, and the Great Transformation," in *Modernization, Urbanization, and the Urban Crisis*, ed. Gino Germani (Boston: Little, Brown and Company, 1973), 3-57; Kenneth Moore, "The City as Context: Context as Process,"

Urban Anthropology 3 (Spring 1975): 18-24; Richard G. Fox, *Urban Anthropology: Cities in Their Cultural Settings* (Englewood Cliffs, N.J.: Prentice Hall, 1977), 9-12; and Ulf Hannerz, *Exploring the City: Inquiries toward an Urban Anthropology* (New York: Columbia University Press, 1980), 87-89. For a useful assessment of Redfield's influence on urban anthropology in general, see Thomas Weaver, "From Primitive to Urban Anthropology," in *Crisis in Anthropology: View from Spring Hill, 1980*, ed. E. Adamson Hoebel, Richard Currier, and Susan Kaiser (New York: Garland, 1982), 203-220.

55. Some students of Islamic civilization, especially of mixed Hindu-Buddhist and Islamic societies in the highly diverse cultural matrix of Southeast Asia, have also used Redfield's Great Tradition/Little Tradition as an organizing construct. See Clifford Geertz, *The Religion of Java* (New York: Free Press of Glencoe, 1960). For a recent example, see Fredrik Barth, *Balinese Worlds* (Chicago: University of Chicago Press, 1993).

56. See Gananath Obeyesekere, "The Great Tradition and the Little in the Perspective of Sinhalese Buddhism," *Journal of Asian Studies* 22 (February 1963): 139-153; Michael Ames, "Magical Animism and Buddhism: A Structural Analysis of the Sinhalese Religious System," *Journal of Asian Studies* 23 (June 1964): 21-52; Hans-Dieter Evers, "Buddha and the Seven Gods: The Dual Organization of a Temple in Central Ceylon," *Journal of Asian Studies* 27 (May 1968): 541-550; Melford E. Spiro, *Buddhism and Society: A Great Tradition and Its Burmese Vicissitudes* (New York: Harper and Row, 1970); and Stanley J. Tambiah, *Buddhism and the Spirit Cults in North-East Thailand* (Cambridge: Cambridge University Press, 1970). Terence P. Day provides an invaluable analysis of the influence of the Great Tradition/Little Tradition construct in Buddhist studies in *Great Tradition and Little Tradition in Therevada Buddhist Studies* (Lewiston, N.Y.: Edwin Mellen Press, 1988).

57. The most searching criticisms of Redfield's Great Tradition/Little Tradition construct were those by Louis Dumont and David Pocock, eds., *Contributions to Indian Sociology* 1 (The Hague: Mouton & Co., 1957), 7-41; Dumont, *Contributions to Indian Sociology* 3 (The Hague: Mouton & Co.), 7-54; S. C. Dube, "Indian Village Communities and Social Anthropology," in *Sociology, Social Research and Social Problems in India*, ed. R. N. Saksena (New York: Asia Publishing House, 1961): 119-125; Dube, "Social Anthropology in India," in *Essays in Memory of D. N. Majumdar*, ed. T. N. Madan and Gopala Sarana (New York: Asia Publishing House, 1962): 237-253; and Stanley J. Tambiah, *Buddhism and the Spirit Cults in North-East Thailand*, 367-377.

58. See Redfield's posthumously published "Civilizations as Cultural Structures?" in *The Papers of Robert Redfield*, vol. 1, 392-395.

59. On the state of sociological theory in the early fifties, see Edward Shils, "The Contemplation of Society in America," in *The Calling of Sociology and Other Essays on the Pursuit of Learning* (Chicago: University of Chicago Press, 1980), 125-128.

60. See Edward Shils, *Center and Periphery, Essays in Macrosociology* (Chicago: University of Chicago Press, 1975); Claude Lévi-Strauss, *Structural Anthropology*, trans. Claire Jacobson and Brooke Grundfest Schoepf (New York: Basic Books, 1963); and S. N. Eisenstadt, "The Origins and Diversity of Axial Age Civilizations," in *The Origins and Diversity of Axial Age Civilizations*, ed. S. N. Eisenstadt (Albany: State University of New York Press, 1986), 1-25.

Chapter 6

An Anthropological Approach to Civilizations

In his work on the Great and Little Traditions, Redfield advanced a theoretical rationale for the anthropological study of civilizations. Scholars had traditionally defined civilizations by their philosophical, religious, literary, and artistic expressions. Civilizations, consequently, had been studied largely by humanistic scholars. Redfield proposed, though, that the great world civilizations embraced two distinct sociocultural levels—the level of the literary elite and that of the preliterate and illiterate traditional peoples. Anthropologists were best prepared, he argued, to study these traditional peoples. He offered his Great and Little Traditions notion as a conceptual bridge to connect studies of the literate and nonliterate aspects of the same civilization.

Redfield's Great/Little Traditions notion dealt primarily with theoretical aspects of the anthropological study of complex societies and cultures. Yet Redfield also focused on the practical aspects of these studies. Anthropologists had begun to study complex societies in the early 1940s. Some, such as Margaret Mead and Ruth Benedict, had even gained much acclaim for their wartime studies of national character. But during the late 1940s and early 1950s, many social scientists, particularly sociologists, had come to regard anthropologists' studies of complex societies with grave misgivings. These criticisms mounted sharply, moreover, when anthropologists moved onto what sociologists' considered their turf and began to comment on American culture and civilization. Most serious among charges launched by critics were that: (1) anthropological methods were best suited for study of small, primitive villages and offered little leverage for analysis of more complex social entities; and (2) anthropological methods, particularly those based upon human observation, were insufficiently scientific.[1] As part of his methodology efforts during the early fifties, Redfield attempted to address both of these issues and to provide a sound direction for anthropologists as they undertook the more difficult task of studying complex cultures and societies.

Although in many ways, the argument over whether anthropology was suitable for study of complex societies was little more than an academic struggle over disciplinary boundaries, this argument embodied the deeper philosophical problem of how the discipline of anthropology should be defined. Sociological critics charged that the domain of anthropology should derive from its subject matter and methods. According to sociologist Robert Bierstedt, anthropology's proper focus consisted of the study of primitive, illiterate peoples through such methods as autobiography, life histories, use of informants, and participant and nonparticipant observation. These techniques, Bierstedt emphasized, fell short in analysis of complex literate societies.[2]

Redfield rejected this definition of anthropology. He joined other anthropologists, like A. R. Radcliffe-Brown, Ruth Benedict, Margaret Mead, A. L. Kroeber, and Clyde Kluckhohn, in claiming as anthropology's territory the study of humanity in all its arrangements, primitive or civilized, literate or illiterate. What was distinct about anthropology, Redfield maintained, was not the type of human group chosen for study, or the specific technique employed to collect data, but rather its conceptual outlook, its attempt to conceive social reality—on whatever level—as a whole. Redfield thus directed much effort in his methodological works toward defining and extending the concept of anthropological holism.

The second issue Redfield addressed was the issue of anthropology's status as a science. In the eyes of many social scientists, the controversies that surrounded anthropologists' 1940s studies of American culture and society had cast a shadow over the entire anthropological project. Most critics questioned the nature of anthropological methods; some even suggested that conclusions anthropologists had advanced about culture in primitive societies might be as unreliable as their conclusions about complex societies.[3] In light of the trend in most social sciences during the thirties and forties toward use of more precise statistical methods, anthropologists had begun to appear quaint, indeed unscientific, in their continued use of personal observation as their primary research technique. Critics, like sociologist Jessie Bernard, chided anthropologists for their sluggishness to replace "human sense organs" with more reliable "instruments" for scientific study and pressed them to update their methodology:

> Both the methods of observation and the methods of generalization in cultural anthropology are vulnerable from a scientific point of view when they leave those aspects of culture which may be observed through instruments. What is urgently needed is the invention and application of instruments for purposes of observing . . . nonmaterial and psychosocial aspects of culture.[4]

From the late forties, Redfield had challenged the growing trend toward positivism and scientism in American social science. Although in earlier writings, for example, his Frankfurt lectures, Redfield had spoken of humanism and social science in general; but in his mid-fifties methodological writings, Redfield concentrated upon anthropology. Here he focused explicitly on the core methodology of the discipline, and he offered a reasoned response to those who called for anthropologists to abandon their methods of personal observation in favor of "more objective" research instruments. While Redfield acknowledged that the initial efforts of anthropologists to study complex societies and civilizations had their limitations, he believed that shortcomings in these works reflected problems in research design, and not the failure of anthropologists to gather "hard" data. He was convinced that the way to improve anthropological studies of complex societies was not to drive the personal element out of anthropology but rather to improve the basic design of anthropologists' studies. Redfield thus directed his efforts toward advancing a conceptual approach for anthropologists to use in their studies of complex societies that preserved the personal element but also facilitated sharper, more sophisticated research design. Redfield's methodological works met with positive critical reception and came to provide a theoretical foundation for the anthropological study of complex societies and civilizations that exercised an influence among social scientists for an entire generation.

Community Studies and Anthropological Holism

Redfield's study of anthropological holism formed the cornerstone of his methodological works. He first discussed this issue in the plenary or "inventory" paper, "Relations of Anthropology to the Social Sciences and the Humanities," that he presented in June 1952 at the Wenner-Gren Foundation's International Symposium on Anthropology.[5] In the fall of 1953, Redfield was invited to give the Gottesman Lectures at the University of Uppsala in Sweden, and he used this occasion to expand greatly his consideration of the theory and practice of holism. He subsequently published these lectures as *The Little Community: Viewpoints for a Study of the Human Whole* (1955).[6]

The organized life of humanity could be viewed as a whole, Redfield observed, from only a few distinct perspectives. Among these distinct conceptualizations were the view of humanity from the perspective of an individual person, a community, a people, a nation, or a civilization. Redfield chose to concentrate his analysis of holistic methodology on only one of these perspectives: the community study. Indeed, anthropological holism functioned best, he argued, on the community-study level:

> Of all the conspicuous enduring forms in which humanity occurs, the self-contained community is the most nearly self-sufficient and the most nearly comprehensible in itself alone. Not even a personality is an exception to this, for no person can be understood by himself alone: he is part of his culture and his community. But the community holds those personalities within itself, and is small enough to submit itself to our effort toward total comprehension—

although more and more, as civilization advances, it cannot be understood alone.[7]

Redfield began *The Little Community* by posing a problem: "The point of departure is a certain strain or struggle, so to speak, between the claims of the human whole—person or village or civilization—to communicate to us its nature as a whole, a convincing complex entity, on the one hand, and the disposition of science to take things apart and move toward the precise description of relationships between parts and parts on the other."[8] Holistic conception thus begins in an act of intuition; yet an observer cannot communicate this perceived whole—indeed cannot even think about it—without sacrificing some of its integral aspects. In short, the whole that is more than the sum of its parts tends to collapse into the mere collection of its parts the moment we try to understand, analyze, and describe it. The holistic process requires more from the observer, therefore, than mere intuition. After the whole is intuited, the observer—in Redfield's discussion, the anthropologist—must then analyze the parts and determine their interrelationships; finally, he or she must reassemble these parts, must construct a describable system that recaptures the integral dynamism of the intuited whole. The act of constructing this system, this representation of the intuited whole, rests upon empirical observation but requires imaginative interpretation.

The heart of *The Little Community* consisted of a set of models that Redfield offered to facilitate the analysis of perceived wholes and construction of convincing representations. He intended these models, or "forms of thought," to bring greater sophistication to the design and execution of community studies; he also sought to make community study design more explicit and thereby facilitate greater comparability among different studies. A community could be seen, he suggested, as an ecological system, a social structure, a typical biography, a kind of person, an outlook on life, a life history, a community within communities, and as a combination of opposites. Redfield explored the possibilities offered by these theoretical frameworks and demonstrated how each model offered a different view of a community as a whole. An ethnographic account, he observed, could certainly encompass more than one of these theoretical views; these views simply represented models for conceptualizing the functioning of subsystems within the larger entity of a community.

A book about community studies methodology might be expected to be a rather dry affair. Redfield managed to make his narrative lively and compelling, though, by avoiding discussion of technique in the abstract and by basing his considerations, instead, upon illustrations drawn from actual community studies. In addition to enlivening his text with multiple references to the contemporary anthropological literature, Redfield also illustrated his argument by weaving into his narrative his own experiences as an ethnographer. In fact, his reflections upon his own development, field experiences, and writings occupied such a position within *The Little Community* that this text constituted for Redfield a quasi-intellectual autobiography.

While he considered his anthropological career from several different perspectives, Redfield devoted his greatest attention to discussing Oscar Lewis's critique of his account of Tepoztlán. Redfield used his examination of this controversy as a point of departure for an extended consideration of the issues of objectivity, subjectivity, and verifiability in ethnography. In his celebrated restudy of Tepoztlán, *Life in a Mexican Village: Tepoztlán Restudied* (1951), Lewis had claimed that Redfield had made both factual and interpretative errors in his 1930 study of the village. Lewis believed his own study to be a more accurate representation of life in Tepoztlán than Redfield's.[9] Redfield accepted that Lewis had written a more thorough and in some ways more accurate account of Tepoztlán than he had. Nevertheless, he refused to accept that the issue was simply a matter of a "right" versus a "wrong" account. Instead, he argued that both accounts displayed strengths and weaknesses. He suggested that a "community may have more than one face," and he proposed that differences in values among investigators as well as distinctions between goals of separate studies may indeed produce different, sometimes diametrically opposite accounts. Such variance in ethnographic accounts arose, Redfield argued, because of the element of interpretation that suffused each holistic study:

> An account of a little community is not something that is given one out of a vending machine by putting in the appropriate coins of method and technique. There is no one ultimate and utterly objective account of a human whole. Each account, if it preserves the human quality at all, is a created product in which the human qualities of the creator—the outside viewer and describer—are one ingredient.[10]

Few of Redfield's contemporaries seem to have been convinced, however, by his attempt to defend his account of Tepoztlán versus Lewis's. While they may have resented Lewis's somewhat brazen attack on Redfield, many anthropologists believed that Lewis's claims were not without merit. No reviewer of *The Little Community*, for example, mentioned Redfield's discussion of the Tepoztlán controversy. Yet when viewed from the perspective of almost half a century, one can see in Redfield's efforts an attempt to establish a conception of interpretative ethnography, an attempt to push beyond the limitations of 1950s positivism to an open constructivism or perspectivalism. In short, Redfield was not merely attempting to wriggle out of a difficult personal position; he was advocating, instead, a new, indeed strikingly interpretivist, conception of ethnography.[11]

Yet Redfield recognized that interpretative latitude in ethnographic reporting threatened anthropology with a debilitating perspectivalism. He devoted himself in the last two chapters of *The Little Community* to advancing measures that could help ethnographers transcend the perspectivalism dilemma. He proposed two ways to assist anthropologists dealing with problems presented by variability in ethnographic reporting. First, he suggested that ethnographers conceptually frame their community studies using ideal-typical models, and he described briefly how the use of such models could introduce greater rigor and comparability into ethnographic studies. Redfield had used such models throughout his career and these recommendations did not constitute a drastic shift from his standard approach. He did advance, nevertheless, his final and most sophisticated conception of his own folk-civilization construct in this discussion.

Redfield's second proposal for dealing with variation in ethnographic reporting constituted a much more radical departure. He urged anthropologists to recognize that holistic ethnographic reports would never be equivalent to studies produced in more quantitative social and natural sciences. In essence, he pressed anthropologists to accept that ethnography was not strictly a science and should therefore not be held to the standards of more formalistic disciplines. "The study of human wholes," he observed, "lies today in a borderland between science and art." Most particularly, ethnographers, like novelists, were engaged in the art of "portraiture." However, Redfield did not conceive of the practice of creating such portraits as mere impressionism. While ethnographers resembled novelists, they were not novelists. The villages, towns, and communities they studied were real, and other students could seek to test and verify their conclusions and interpretations.[12]

Most important, Redfield defined the nature of truth claims that should be accorded ethnographic accounts. Here we see Redfield reaching back to his Deweyan pragmatic roots and asserting that truths in ethnographic practice were socially constructed by a community of the competent. The knowledge claims of an ethnographic account were not axiomatic—they emerged by judgment of an informed community. Redfield urged anthropologists to respond to their external critics not by trying to reshape themselves into those critics. Anthropologists needed to preserve and strengthen their own method of practice. He concluded *The Little Community* by reflecting upon the nature and meaning of that practice:

> In the long time between now and some possible clarification of all method for all purposes, we who try to describe such a human whole as a little community need not be too much worried about the relation of what we do to that current halfgod, natural science, or its avatar in the world of the social, the behavioral sciences. For understanding is increased and the needs of mankind are met by any and all honest descriptions, responsible to the facts and intellectually defensible. To see what is there with the perceptions that our own humanity allows; to render our report so as to preserve the significance of these perceptions while submitting them to the questions and tests of our fellows—that is our common duty, whatever the particular means we take to realize it. Understanding, and her apotheosis, wisdom, are the true gods within the temple; science is not; she is only a handmaiden, and serves with others.[13]

From Primitive Isolates to Intermediate Societies

In *The Little Community*, Redfield focused almost exclusively on the study of small isolated communities. He chose this narrow focus in order to concentrate on the essential elements of holistic methodology without having to consider the complicating factors of connections between communities and their surrounding sociocultural matrices. He acknowledged, nevertheless, that such entities rarely could be found in actuality. The "little community" thus represented an abstraction—in short, an ideal type. Redfield understood of course that almost all real communities existed as nodes within complex social and civilizational networks. He saw, moreover, that it was this very connectedness of villages within their surrounding civilizational matrices that allowed village studies to serve as a useful vantage point for the study of complex societies and cultures. Peasant villages, in particular, provided a convenient point of entry into civilizations studies, because peasant communities occupied an intermediate position between tribal societies and modern urban centers. The study of peasant villages thus offered an ideal way to approach the study of complex civilizations.

Redfield had been one of the first anthropologists to study peasant communities, and he had led the way in the effort to develop a distinct body of anthropological theory and methodology for peasant studies. Beginning with his pioneering study of the Mexican village Tepoztlán, Redfield had striven to define peasants in a way that captured their unique status as a hybrid culture, a "type intermediate between the primitive tribe and the modern city." In *Tepoztlán* (1930), he advanced the notion of "folk" society as an abstract description of this intermediate sociocultural position. Redfield sharpened this definition of peasantry in his second ethnographic study, *Chan Kom: A Maya Village* (1934). Here he observed that peasant villages differed from "preliterate tribal communities" specifically through the nature of their relationships to modern society. Whereas the tribal villages were isolated and virtually self-sufficient, peasant villages, he argued, were "politically and economically dependent upon the towns and cities of modern literate civilization"; the villagers, furthermore, were "well aware of the townsmen and city dweller and in part define[d] their position in the world in terms of these."

Redfield's boldest statement during the 1930s on the nature of peasants and, more important, on the significance of peasant studies for social science, came, however, not in his own work but in his introduction to one of his student's books. In the introduction to Horace Miner's *St. Denis: A French-Canadian Parish* (1939), Redfield announced:

> For the comparative study of societies the peasant peoples occupy a strategic position. They form a sort of middle term in the equation of culture and civilization. On the one hand, they resemble the primitive peoples with whom the ethnologist is characteristically acquainted; and on the other, they belong to that modern urbanized world which lies in the foreground of attention of most

American sociologists. To study the peasant peoples is to help to draw into a single field of investigation all the societies of the earth from the simplest to the most complex.[14]

Yet despite his repeated efforts to define the nature of peasantry and the scope of peasant studies, Redfield had not always used his terms consistently. The greatest confusion stemmed from his loose usage during the 1930s and 1940s of the term "folk." Although he had first used the term to describe the culture and society of the Tepoztecans, he later referred to primitive tribal peoples as folk; on some occasions he even lumped together primitive and peasant society and referred to both forms of social organization as folk society. Indeed, in his two major theoretical statements, "The Folk Society and Culture" (1940) and "The Folk Society" (1947), he sometimes applied the term folk to peasants, sometimes to primitives, and sometimes to both.[15] Redfield's colleague Sol Tax and, in a sharper vein, Oscar Lewis both called attention to Redfield's confused usage.[16]

While Redfield briefly clarified the distinction between primitive folk society and peasant society in *The Primitive World and Its Transformations* (1953), he provided a much sharper clarification in a series of lectures he delivered at Swarthmore College in the spring of 1955. Here he offered a more in-depth definition of peasantry and conceptualization of peasant studies. He published these lectures the following year as *Peasant Society and Culture: An Anthropological Approach to Civilization.*[17]

Redfield began his lectures at Swarthmore by briefly reviewing the development of anthropology as a discipline from the late nineteenth to the midtwentieth centuries. As the discipline had first taken shape in the late nineteenth century, he observed, anthropologists "studied culture not cultures, all society but no particular society." In the early decades of the twentieth century, however, a new model emerged, and anthropologists came to define their discipline as the study not of culture but rather of cultures. While this alternative view had a long lineage, one that reached back to the descriptions of native peoples made by nineteenth-century missionaries as well as to Lewis Henry Morgan's 1851 account of the Iroquois, the primary impetus for this change in the conception of culture derived from Franz Boas. Through his own work and the work of his students, Boas engineered the shift in anthropology from concern with culture in general to the focus on individual cultures.

Nevertheless, Redfield asserted, while Boas established the new conceptual outlook of anthropology, Bronislaw Malinowski and A. R. Radcliffe-Brown took the lead in codifying the standard approach to anthropological field research. In 1922, Malinowski published *Argonauts of the Western Pacific* and Radcliffe-Brown *The Andaman Islanders*, and over the next several years these two texts came to define the "model of research in social anthropology." More generally, Malinowski and Radcliffe-Brown established the pattern for ethnographic research that was to hold in the United States and Britain for almost the entire first half of the twentieth century. Through their example, the ethnographic account came to be defined as a "report, by a single investigator, of a whole" that could be "understood as providing for all life's needs in some orderly way that makes sense to the people who live under it." Such an account described, furthermore, "a culture and community" that stood "alone, independent of others." In short, Malinowski and Radcliffe-Brown established the "primitive isolate, the community that is a whole all by itself" as the model of anthropological research.[18]

Ironically, the conception of the primitive isolate was obsolete almost as soon as it took hold among anthropologists. "Just at the time when the primitive isolate as a model of study was being established in anthropology," Redfield observed, sociologists were calling attention to the fact that the world was becoming interconnected into one "great society." Indeed, "the anthropologist himself was one of the instruments of this transformation." By the mid-twentieth century, it became difficult for anthropologists even to find remote isolated communities to study; for most communities existed "in many and complex relationships with other peoples and with histories known or knowable." Following World War II, moreover, American anthropologists shifted predominantly toward the study of complex societies. Nevertheless, Redfield observed, despite the fact that by the mid-fifties most anthropologists studied connected communities situated in complex societies, they still clung to their old body of culture theory. Anthropologists thus continued to use the abstract primitive isolate as a conceptual model to guide the study of anything from a village community, to an urban community, or even an entire nation.[19]

Certainly, Redfield's brief history of anthropology could be challenged from several different angles. His intention, however, was not to provide an authoritative history. Rather, he wanted to explore the implications for the discipline of the shift in focus from the study of primitive isolates to the study of complex societies. He wanted to draw attention, furthermore, to the bad fit that had developed between theory and practice as the scope of inquiry among anthropologists expanded. The shift toward study of complex societies required, he argued, a radical reconstruction in anthropological theory, especially in regard to the notion of culture. It was this reconstruction in cultural theory that he most wanted to address in his discussion of peasant studies. In *Peasant Society and Culture*, Redfield devoted himself, therefore, to constructing a model more suitable than the primitive isolate to guide anthropological study of complex societies.[20]

Redfield began his theoretical considerations by attempting to develop a broader, suppler definition of peasantry than that which existed in common usage. He first suggested that peasants represented a generic social type—a type identifiable across the world, from both contemporary and historical perspectives. Then, he proposed a working definition of peasantry. In the process of presenting this definition, he described how his ideas had been formed through dialogue with several other social scientists interested in the study of peasants;

most influential in helping him to shape his definition were Eric R. Wolf, Gideon Sjoberg, and A. L. Kroeber. From Wolf, Redfield borrowed the view of peasants as agriculturalists whose "agriculture is a livelihood and a way of life, not a business for profit"; from Sjoberg, he adopted the idea that peasants live within a moral system articulated by the elite of the manor or city to which the peasant village is linked; and from Kroeber, Redfield took the conception that peasants constitute "part-societies with part-cultures." Redfield added to these conceptions his own notions that peasants represent the "rural dimensions of old civilizations" and are peculiarly bound through either ownership or simply long-term occupation to a particular parcel of land. Melding these ideas together, Redfield arrived at the conception of peasants as "rural people in old civilizations . . . who control and cultivate their land for subsistence and as a part of a traditional way of life and who look to and are influenced by gentry or townspeople whose way of life is like theirs but in a more civilized form." Redfield cautioned, however, that his was not a definitive conceptualization—he only wanted to suggest enough of a definition of peasantry to support his discussion of anthropological methodology. His was a "type or class loosely defined" he suggested, "a focus of attention rather than a box with a lid."[21]

Following Kroeber's conception of peasants as "part-societies and part-cultures," Redfield discussed first the social structure of peasant communities and then turned to consider their cultural dimensions. The social structure of a community, Redfield proposed, consisted of the "total system of persisting and important relationships" that distinguish one community from another. In a primitive tribal village, he continued, all the critical exchange relationships and the distinctive personal bonds that constitute the social structure of the community are contained within the boundaries of the village. Yet in a peasant community, most of these crucial social relationships extend far beyond the boundaries of the village. The peasant village constitutes a node, for example, in both regional and national political networks; and the villagers participate in an economy that is national or international in scope. Thus, while the social structure of a tribal village could be described solely on the basis of observations made within the village, the social structure of a peasant community could not be represented without describing the "larger and more nearly complete system: the feudal society, the complex region, the national state."[22]

Study of peasant villages represented a substantially more complex undertaking, therefore, than study of isolated tribal villages. Yet two recently proposed models, Redfield observed, offered a way to simplify the process of studying villages situated within complex societies. In *Area Research, Theory and Practice* (1950), Julian Steward had advanced a theoretical approach for conducting community studies that provided a way to view villages and towns within a national context. Steward proposed that national sociocultural systems could be viewed as being composed of three interdependent segments: (1) local "vertical" groups, such as households, neighborhoods, and communities; (2) "horizontal" groups, such as class, occupation, caste, and race, which cut across neighborhoods, communities, and regions; and (3) "formal institutions," such as banking, law, education, and trade systems, which operated on the national level and served to integrate or bind together the horizontal and vertical lattice of local and regional sociocultural levels. Redfield noted that Steward had successfully applied this approach to the modern state of Puerto Rico and suggested that this model appeared to have general use for study of other complex national systems. Another anthropologist, J. A. Barnes, had proposed a similar system in an article on the social system of an island community in Norway. Barnes posited that complex societies could be broken into three distinct "social fields" that represented, like Steward's conceptual groups, discrete but interdependent levels of sociocultural integration. Redfield described these two models in some detail and urged anthropologists to consider both approaches as they strove to move beyond the "local community study" in their analyses of the social structures of peasant communities.[23]

In turning to consider peasant culture, which Kroeber had described as "part-culture," Redfield followed a similar line of logic as he had in his discussion of peasant society. Just as peasant society could not be viewed as an autonomous system, he argued, so also did peasant culture constitute an incomplete system. Much of the culture of a peasant village did not derive from the village but represented, instead, "an aspect or dimension of the civilization" of which the village was a part. The village culture maintained itself, moreover, only "through continual communication to the local community of thought originating outside of it." To understand the intellectual, moral, and religious life of the inhabitants of a peasant village, therefore, the anthropologist needed "to know something of what [went] on in the minds of remote teachers, priests, or philosophers whose thinking affects and is perhaps affected by the peasantry."[24]

Peasants and the Great and Little Traditions

Yet anthropologists could not come to terms with peasant culture merely by traditional ethnographic techniques. For ethnography worked primarily in the present and without attention to the past. The ethnographer studying the culture of a tribal village had not needed to turn to historical study to learn about that culture. The important history existed in the memories and oral lore of the villagers; written accounts did not exist. Peasant villages, on the contrary, could not be studied by such an approach. They had a history. The history of the surrounding civilization was impressed upon the society and culture of the peasant village; indeed, that history was inscribed on the very social institutions of the peasants. "The peasant culture," Redfield noted, "has an evident history; we are called upon to study that history; and the history is not local; it is a history of the civilization of which the village culture is but one local expression." The anthropologist who studied peasant villages needed not only to develop an intimate, on-the-ground understanding of village life, but also to become familiar with the historical, philosophical, and literary scholarship on the civilizational matrix within which the village was situated.[25]

The culture of the peasant village thus represented a compound system between local village culture and the transcendent cultural organization of the surrounding civilization. This compound culture could best be studied, Redfield suggested, through his notion of Great and Little cultural traditions. Redfield advanced in *Peasant Society and Culture* his most complete description of the notion of Great and Little Traditions. He asserted, furthermore, that study of peasant villages offered anthropologists a unique vantage point from which to study the interaction of these two levels of discourse. Peasant studies provided, in short, "an anthropological approach to civilization."

Peasant Society and Culture was to be the last book Redfield ever wrote. This text stood, however, as more than merely his last book; it represented the culmination of his career. For in this book, Redfield managed to bring together into one unified discussion the major themes he had dealt with over the course of his entire career. Here he wove together his concerns with peasant—or intermediate—society, civilized—or urbanized—society and the dialectical process of change that operated between these levels of social organization. As fitting for such a culminating work, this book met with strong critical reception among anthropologists and sociologists in both the United States and Britain.[26]

Peasant Studies: Beginnings of a Movement

Peasant Society and Culture served as a foundational text, moreover, for the anthropology of peasantry, a subfield just emerging during the mid-1950s. Redfield not only offered in this text the first extended effort to describe in theoretical terms the structure and dynamics of peasant society and culture, but he also advanced the first explicit program or charter for an anthropologically oriented approach to peasant studies.

Yet, despite the powerful role he played during the early phase of the peasant studies movement, Redfield's influence declined rapidly during the 1960s. The reason for this decline stemmed from his failure to confront the issue of power in his consideration of peasantry. While he had devoted a full chapter in *Peasant Society and Culture* to discussion of the social structure and dynamics of peasant communities, the obvious emphasis in his book was on the cultural traditions—the Great and Little Traditions—at work in peasant villages. Indeed, from his study of Tepoztlán forward, Redfield had largely concerned himself with the way that a peasant community developed and maintained its body of conventional understandings, its worldview, and its system of meaning—in a word, its culture. Redfield viewed culture from a predominantly structuralist or mentalist perspective. Meaning was constructed in the minds of the villagers, he argued, and it was this inside view that the ethnographer needed to pursue in order to grasp the essence of village life. This concentration upon the cultural elements led Redfield to minimize the political economy of peasant life. He placed little importance, for example, on understanding how the mode of production or political conditions in a peasant village affected the outlook of the villagers. Redfield thus did not seem to appreciate the powerful effect the condition of poverty or serfdom could exercise upon the way in which a peasant constructed his or her sense of meaning.

As peasant studies matured during the 1960s and 1970s, growing into one of the largest subfields within anthropology, the field shifted decisively away from cultural concerns toward the perspective of political economy. While Redfield's cultural ideas continued to hold sway in a limited fashion, particularly in regard to the thorny problem of defining peasantry, his ideas no longer commanded a large audience. Theoretical dominance passed instead to Julian Steward and his Columbia students, especially Eric R. Wolf and Sidney Mintz, who established a materialist, political economy perspective as the central direction of the field. Aside from the work of a few dedicated disciples, Redfield came to be remembered more ceremoniously as one of the principal founders of peasant studies rather than as an enduring intellectual force within the field. [27]

Notes

1. See Robert Bierstedt, "The Limitations of Anthropological Methods in Sociology," *American Journal of Sociology* 54 (July 1948): 22-30; Jesse Bernard, "Observation and Generalization in Cultural Anthropology," *American Journal of Sociology* 50 (January 1945): 284-291; Bernard, "Sociological Mirror for Cultural Anthropologists," *American Anthropologist* 51 (October-December 1949): 671-677; and Alfred R. Lindesmith and Anselm L. Strauss, "A Critique of Culture and Personality Writings," *American Sociological Review* 15 (October 1950): 587-600. Some anthropologists also criticized the excesses of early national character studies; see David G. Mandelbaum's "On the Study of National Character," *American Anthropologist* 55 (April-June 1953): 174-187. Stephen O. Murray offers an insightful account of the relationship between sociology and anthropology during the early to mid-twentieth century in "The Reception of Anthropological Work in Sociology Journals, 1922-1951," *Journal of the History of the Behavioral Sciences* 24 (April 1988): 135-151.

2. Bierstedt, "Limitations of Anthropological Methods in Sociology," 24.

3. Bierstedt, "Limitations of Anthropological Methods in Sociology," 29.

4. Bernard, "Observation and Generalization in Cultural Anthropology," 291.

5. Robert Redfield, "Relations of Anthropology to the Social Sciences and to the Humanities," in *Anthropology Today: An Encyclopedic Inventory*, ed. A. L. Kroeber (Chicago: University of Chicago Press, 1953), 728-738. The Kroeber volume contains all the "inventory" papers presented at the June 1952 International Symposium on Anthropology and represents an encyclopedic survey of the state of the discipline at mid-century.

6. Robert Redfield, *The Little Community: Viewpoints for the Study of a Human Whole* (Chicago: University of Chicago Press, 1955).

7. Redfield, *Little Community*, 157.

8. Redfield, *Little Community*, 1-2.

9. Oscar Lewis, *Life in a Mexican Village: Tepoztlán Restudied* (Urbana: University of Illinois Press, 1951).

10. Redfield, *Little Community*, 136.

11. For an insightful discussion of constructivism in ethnography, see Karl G. Heider, "The Rashomon Effect: When Ethnographers Disagree," *American Anthropologist* 90 (March 1988): 73-80.

12. Redfield, *Little Community*, 163.

13. Redfield, *Little Community*, 168.

14. Robert Redfield, *Tepoztlán, A Mexican Village: A Study of Folk Life* (Chicago: University of Chicago Press, 1930), 217; Robert Redfield and Alfonso Villa Rojas, *Chan Kom: A Maya Village* (Washington, D.C.: Carnegie Institution of Washington, 1934), 1; Robert Redfield, introduction to *St. Denis: A French Canadian Parish*, by Horace Miner (Chicago: University of Chicago Press, 1939), xv.

15. Robert Redfield, "The Folk Society and Culture," *American Journal of Sociology* 45 (March 1940): 731-742; reprinted in *Eleven Twenty-Six: A Decade of Social Science Research*, ed. Louis Wirth (Chicago: University of Chicago Press, 1940); Robert Redfield, "The Folk Society," *American Journal of Sociology* 52 (January 1947): 293-308.

16. Sol Tax, "'Revolutions' and the Process of Civilization," in *Human Origins: An Introductory General Course in Anthropology. Selected Readings, Series 2*, 2d ed. (Chi-

cago: University of Chicago Bookstore, 1946), 234; Oscar Lewis, *Life in a Mexican Village: Tepoztlán Restudied* (Urbana: University of Illinois Press, 1951), 432.

17. Robert Redfield, *Peasant Society and Culture: An Anthropological Approach to Civilization* (Chicago: University of Chicago Press, 1956).

18. Redfield, *Peasant Society and Culture*, 5-9; Bronislaw Malinowski, *Argonauts of the Western Pacific: An Account of Native Enterprise and Adventure in the Archipelagos of Melanesian New Guinea* (London: G. Routledge, 1922); A. R. Radcliffe-Brown, *The Andaman Islanders: A Study in Anthropology* (Cambridge: Cambridge University Press, 1922).

19. Redfield, *Peasant Society and Culture*, 9-11.

20. Redfield pursued this historical train of thought further in his Huxley Memorial Lecture, "Societies and Cultures as Natural Systems," which he presented to the Royal Anthropological Society in March 1956. *Journal of the Royal Anthropological Institute of Great Britain and Ireland* 85 (December-January 1955): 19-32.

21. Redfield, "Societies and Cultures as Natural Systems," 17-20; Eric R. Wolf, "Types of Latin American Peasantry: A Preliminary Discussion, *American Anthropologist* 57 (June 1955): 452-471; Gideon Sjoberg, "Folk and Feudal Societies," *American Journal of Sociology* 58 (November 1952): 231-239; A. L. Kroeber, *Anthropology* (New York: Harcourt, Brace & Co., 1948), 284.

22. Redfield, *Peasant Society and Culture*, 23-24.

23. Julian H. Steward, *Area Research, Theory and Practice* (New York: Social Science Research Council, 1950); Julian Steward et al., *The People of Puerto Rico: A Study in Social Anthropology* (Urbana: University of Illinois Press, 1956); J. A. Barnes, "Class and Committees in a Norwegian Island Parish," *Human Relations* 7, no. 1 (1954): 39-58; Redfield, *Peasant Society and Culture*, 24-35. Ulf Hannerz provides an interesting discussion of the influence that Barnes's ideas exercised upon urban anthropologists, particularly Elizabeth Bott, during the late fifties. Ulf Hannerz, *Exploring the City: Inquiries Toward an Urban Anthropology* (New York: Columbia University Press, 1980), 164-168.

24. Redfield, *Peasant Society and Culture*, 40-41.

25. Redfield, *Peasant Society and Culture*, 41.

26. See reviews by Clyde Kluckhohn, *American Journal of Sociology* 62 (March 1957): 525; Gideon Sjoberg, *American Sociological Review* 21 (October 1956): 643; Robert Paine, *Folk-Lore* 68 (September 1957): 441-442; J. C. Mitchell, *Sociological Review* 4, n.s. (July 1956): 278-280; and Irwin Sanders, *Rural Sociology* 22 (March 1957): 83-84.

27. A sense of the intellectual and social dimensions of the peasant studies movement can be obtained by reviewing a few of the basic texts on peasants that appeared during the mid-1960s and early 1970s. Some of the best known of these texts include Eric R. Wolf, *Peasants* (Englewood Cliffs, N.J.: Prentice Hall, 1966); Jack Potter, May N. Diaz, and George M. Foster, ed. *Peasant Society: A Reader* (Boston: Little, Brown & Company, 1967); and Teodor Shanin, ed., *Peasants and Peasant Society* (Harmondsworth, UK: Penguin, 1971).

Afterword

The Redfield Legacy

In the late 1940s, as Redfield became interested in the study of civilizations, he began to think about returning to the field to test his new ideas about peasants and civilizations. Since these ideas could only be explored within the context of a complex and still-living civilization, he needed to shift his field studies from Latin America to the Old World. The Chinese social anthropologist Fei Xiaotong, who had become known to Chicago sociologists through Robert Park's early 1930s stints of teaching at Chinese universities, had been trying since the mid-1940s to arrange for Redfield to come to China as a visiting professor. After much effort, Redfield secured a Fullbright Fellowship to fund a trip to China, and in the fall of 1948, he, Greta, and their thirteen-year-old son James arrived in Beijing. Redfield planned to teach as a visiting professor at the National Tsinghua University (now Beijing University) and conduct ethnographic studies in a few villages outside Beijing. Redfield was ill, however, with bronchial infections during the first few months he was in China, and in early 1949 the revolution forced the Redfields to flee the country. Redfield's plans to initiate studies in China thus never came to fruition.[1]

In the mid-1950s, Redfield again determined to initiate field studies within an Old World civilization. He and Milton Singer had decided in the early years of their civilizations project that India held the most promise for their proposed anthropological approach. Singer had gone to Madras in early 1955 to begin his studies of the Great Tradition in the city, and Redfield planned to complement his work in India with a study of pilgrimage patterns to sacred cities—a pattern Redfield viewed as a long-standing and important practice within great civilizations. In the fall of 1955, he and Greta traveled to Orissa in eastern India, an important pilgrimage center. Unfortunately, after being in India for only a few months, Redfield became seriously ill. A physician in Calcutta determined that he had an excess of white blood cells and recommended that he return home immediately. Upon returning to Chicago, he found that he had lymphatic leukemia. Over the next three years, Redfield continued to teach and to write, but the illness gradually took its toll. His visits to the hospital became progressively more frequent and longer, and on October 16, 1958, he died at the University of Chicago's Billings Memorial Hospital.

Upon his death, Redfield's colleagues and former students paid tribute to him in several thoughtful obituaries. Everett Hughes wrote a full-page obituary of Redfield for the *American Sociological Review*, and Horace Miner did the same in the *American Journal of Sociology*. Fay-Cooper Cole and Fred Eggan went even further, publishing in the *American Anthropologist* an eleven-page tribute that included a full bibliography of Redfield's work. Milton Singer published a similar lengthy memorial to Redfield in *Man in India*.[2] The authors of all but one of these essays portrayed Redfield as a central figure in the American social science establishment during the 1930s through the 1950s. They focused especially on the official positions Redfield had held, such as president of the American Anthropological Association, chairman of the Department of Anthropology and dean of social sciences at the University of Chicago, and director of the American Council of Learned Societies.

Everett Hughes presented, however, a rather different view of Redfield. Hughes proposed that Redfield was anything but an establishment figure in either anthropology or sociology. He observed that Redfield had throughout his career "ignore[d] the boundaries between the formally separated disciplines," and he suggested that Redfield's lack of loyalty to any single discipline was perhaps the most important characteristic of his career:

> There is a good deal of talk these days of commitment to lines of academic endeavor. I am afraid Redfield would not have qualified as a professional sociologist, perhaps not even as a professional anthropologist, if complete loyalty to the guild and its definitions of proper lines of work be the criterion. He often thought and wrote as a sociologist; but he sometimes wrote as a humanist and a philosopher. Guildwise, he was an uncommitted man; intellectually and morally, he was the most committed man it has been my privilege to know. So committed was he, that early and spectacular success as an administrator did not divert him from his intellectual career.[3]

Redfield had indeed scorned the growing rigidification of disciplinary lines that occurred during the 1930s and 1940s, and he regarded formal departments and disciplines as little more than "trade associations." In portraying Redfield as a liminal figure who chose to spend his career in the borderland between two disciplines, Hughes thus displayed great insight into Redfield's rather complex personal identity.

This liminality was a source of both great strength and weakness for Redfield. In particular, it facilitated his development as a theorist. When he entered the field of anthropology in the mid-1920s, he proposed that anthropologists needed to return to the use of comparative studies. American anthropologists had not engaged in comparative study for almost a quarter of a century—the practice having been stifled largely through the efforts of Franz Boas.[4] Redfield reestablished comparative studies as an accepted technique, however, by shifting the terms of comparison away from the discredited evolutionary model used by nineteenth-century anthropologists toward the conceptual terminology of sociology. The nineteenth-century evolutionary model posited that human societies developed by passing through a fixed set of stages, a progression described most generally as the ascent from savagery to barbarism to civilization. Studies that used the social evolutionary conception as an axis of comparison inevitably ranked societies according to their level of progression toward civilization. Such a comparative scale resulted in little more than a self-congratulatory exercise—a ratings game in which "lesser" societies were ranked against the standard bearer of civilization, white European society.

Redfield's familiarity with sociological theory provided him, however, with an alternative way of viewing social dynamics. He recognized that preliterate "primitive" societies studied by anthropologists were amenable to description in the same terms that sociologists applied to more complex societies; he saw, furthermore, that these terms offered a basis for studying societies and cultures comparatively that was not contaminated with ethnocentric bias. Robert Nisbet has proposed that the "sociological tradition" can be summed up as an extended dialogue over the meaning of five conceptual dichotomies or "linked antitheses": community-society, authority-power, status-class, sacred-secular, and alienation-progress.[5] These conceptual pairs provide a set of continua or a series of comparative axes that can be used to describe the nature and direction of change in virtually any human group. Redfield displayed great originality in introducing this conceptual vocabulary into anthropology and demonstrating its utility for comparative studies. By working on the margins between both sociology and anthropology, Redfield acted as a bridge between the two disciplines and facilitated during the 1930s and 1940s an important transfer of sociological theory into American anthropology.

Redfield's work served as a springboard, moreover, for an entire generation of social change research. His influence stemmed largely from his folk-urban typology. Although American social scientists advanced dozens of such constructs during this period, Redfield's folk-urban notion proved to be one of the most influential. Two reasons can be suggested for the widespread influence of Redfield's typology: (1) Redfield was the first to use a typological scheme as a framework for empirical anthropological research. His Yucatan work gained wide attention and demonstrated the power of a typological scheme for stimulating the construction of testable hypotheses.[6] (2) Anthropologists in the 1930s and 1940s anxiously sought ways to expand their horizons beyond the village. Redfield's folk-urban continuum provided a model that related village studies to the larger sociocultural matrix in which villages were imbedded. The folk-urban continuum construct thus offered mid-century social scientists a valuable methodology for conceptualizing community studies.

Redfield's studies of Tepoztlán and Yucatan derived directly from his connection with the "Chicago School" of urban sociology. And for most of his career, his thought closely paralleled that of his mentor Robert Park. Through the 1930s to the early 1940s, Redfield and fellow Park student Louis Wirth acted as joint spokesmen for the "Chicago" approach to urban theory. Louis Wirth's article "Urbanism as a Way of Life" (1938) and Redfield's "The Folk Society" (1947) provided a tandem summary of the community-society continuum notion that Park had established as the basis of "Chicago" sociology. Nevertheless, in the last decade of his life, Redfield rethought his approach to community-society dynamics. Spurred particularly by Oscar Lewis's challenges to his interpretation of sociocultural dynamics in the village of Tepoztlán, Redfield reexamined his notions of the pattern of cultural breakdown upon urbanization that he described as occurring in Tepoztlán and towns and villages in the Yucatan. These reconsiderations led Redfield to reverse himself and hence go beyond the approach to urban dynamics, which he had espoused along with Park and Wirth, that viewed social change as a zero-sum exchange. In this view, as urbanization increased, community or culture declined as society or civilization came to dominate. In the revisionist view he expressed in *The Little Community*, Redfield posited that while the general pattern of change described by his folk-urban continuum may hold, folk and urban elements could coexist in interpenetrating states within societies. The transition set in motion as the agents of urbanization encroached upon an isolated village could not be described in a predictable unilinear pattern of response but instead involved a dialectic between elements of modernity and tradition that could only be fully apprehended through historical study of the individual village. Redfield thus came in his final years to espouse a historicist approach to the study of cultural dynamics. He transcended his view, moreover, that held the city or civilization as the enemy of the village community. Instead, he came to see villages and cities enmeshed in patterns of mutual influence and development, patterns which taken on a grand scale represent civilizations.[7]

Redfield's reconsiderations about the relationship between tradition and modernity marked a career of thinking about social change. A single overriding theme had linked together all his investigations, namely, the desire to develop a general description of the processes involved in the transformation of culture to civilization. Through the ethnographic studies he conducted from the 1920s through the 1940s, Redfield served as one of the pioneers of modernization theory, a field of study that came to dominate the American social science agenda for a generation following World War II. Yet Redfield demonstrated a distinct approach to modernization studies compared with those who came to dominate the field in the 1950s and 1960s. Specifically, Redfield's work differed from subsequent modernizationists in the area of metaphysical pathos. The theory of change that emerged from Redfield's work bore the unmistakable mark of foreboding; he was certainly not an antimodernist, but his work displayed a pronounced awareness of the high cost in human suffering and dislocation of the modern transformation. The theory of change that lay at the base of the postwar modernizationists' work, however, carried a distinct air of triumph. This sense of triumph derived from the association between the United States—as the world's exemplary modern nation—and the modernizationists themselves as

American scholars. Modernization thought, in its postwar formulation, reflected in other words a self-conscious pro-American bias. Whereas Redfield viewed social change with an air of detachment, even remorse—with a sense that no nation was exempt from the dislocations stemming from the spread of world capitalism—the postwar modernizationists adopted a decidedly optimistic approach to world social change. They depicted the United States of the late fifties as the model for world transformation—a model most sharply drawn in the work of Walt Rostow—and viewed change that led in the direction of this model as progress. Redfield shared with other modernizationists great enthusiasm for the potential of a predictive model of social change, but he avoided linking the modernizing impulse with Americanization.[8]

Contrary to many of his contemporaries, Redfield did not conceive America's role to be that of a tutor to the world. Indeed, Redfield argued that in order to fit into the community of nations, the United States needed to learn to talk less and listen more. Writing in September 1953, as the Cold War became increasingly heated, Redfield asked "would it be untactful to suggest that America needs a hearing aid?" Americans needed to learn to listen not only to what other peoples in the world were saying, but also to the messages that we ourselves sent out constantly to the rest of the world. Social science had a role to play, Redfield believed, in transforming the way Americans related to other nations and peoples. In this essay written toward the end of his life, Redfield summarized his entire conception of social science. Although he recognized social science had instrumentalist aims, he believed the highest aims of social science were moral. The ultimate purpose of social science, in Redfield's conception, was not to prepare social technicians but citizens. And from his vantage point in 1953, Redfield saw that Americans needed most to become citizens of the world. He dismissed the Cold War arms buildup that was well under way by 1953 and asserted that national strength and security came not from arms but from mutual understandings—mutual understandings that could come only through dialogue and engagement. Redfield saw in social science a means of making connections and reaching understandings with the many peoples of the world, and he saw in that process a means to lasting world security. Similar efforts are required today. Robert Redfield's life and work provide a compelling model for us to follow as we go forward into the twenty-first century.[9]

Notes

1. Robert Redfield, China travel diary, box 1, folder 14, Robert Redfield Papers, Special Collections, Joseph Regenstein Library, University of Chicago, Chicago; Burton Pasternak, "A Conversation with Fei Xiaotong," *Current Anthropology* 29 (August-October 1988): 643.

2. Everett C. Hughes, "Robert Redfield, 1897-1958," *American Sociological Review* 24 (April 1959): 256-257; Horace Miner, "Robert Redfield, 1897-1958," *American Journal of Sociology* 64 (January 1959): 405; Fay-Cooper Cole and Fred Eggan, "Robert Redfield (1897-1958)," *American Anthropologist* 61 (August 1959): 652-662; Milton Singer, "Robert Redfield: Anthropologist, 1897-1958," *Man in India* 39 (April-June 1959): 81-91.

3. Hughes, "Robert Redfield, 1897-1958," 257.

4. Boas presented his argument against the comparative method most forcefully in his widely read article "The Limitations of the Comparative Method of Anthropology," *Science*, n.s. 4 (18 December 1896): 901-908.

5. Robert Nisbet, *The Sociological Tradition* (New York: Basic Books, 1966; reprint, New Brunswick, N.J.: Transaction Books, 1993), 3-7.

6. In the early 1960s, Ralph L. Beals surveyed the use of typologies in anthropology, specifically within studies of Latin American communities, and assessed the impact of various typologies proposed during the 1930s through the 1950s. He judged Redfield's folk-urban notion, despite its numerous conceptual shortcomings, to have been the "most productive" of all such typologies. See Ralph L. Beals, "Community Typologies in Latin America," *Anthropological Linguistics* 3, no. 1 (1961): 8-16.

7. Robert Redfield, "The Folk Society," *American Journal of Sociology* 52 (January 1947): 293-308; Louis Wirth, "Urbanism as a Way of Life," *American Journal of Sociology* 44 (July 1938): 1-24; Robert Redfield, *The Little Community: Viewpoints for the Study of a Human Whole* (Chicago: University of Chicago Press, 1955). Thomas Bender offers an insightful discussion of Redfield's revised theoretical stance in *Community and Social Change in America* (New Brunswick, N.J.: Rutgers University Press, 1978; reprint, Baltimore: Johns Hopkins University Press, 1982), 40-43.

8. Howard Brick has suggested that two major interpretive streams can be seen within postwar modernizationist thought, one influenced largely by theorists from the University of Chicago, and the other shaped by theorists working within the orbit of Harvard University. The key difference between the Chicago and Harvard orientations, Brick argues, lay in the way theorists defined the relationship between tradition and modernity. Drawing upon the works of Dewey, Park, and Redfield, the Chicago camp "studied transitional phenomena on the way to modernity." Where the "transitional emphasis of the Chicago school encouraged attention to the commingling of tradition and modernity, the Harvard school, based upon Talcott Parsons's formal scheme of 'pattern variables' saw sharper disjunctions." Texts by the Chicago modernizationists that most clearly demonstrate Redfield's influence include Milton Singer's *When a Great Tradition Modernizes: An Anthropological Approach to Indian Civilization* (1972), Lloyd I. Rudolph and Susanne Hoeber Rudolph's, *The Modernity of Tradition: Political Development in India* (1967), and Donald N. Levine's, *Wax and Gold: Tradition and Innovation in Ethiopian Culture* (1965). Howard Brick, *Age of Contradiction: American Thought and Culture in the 1960s* (New York: Twayne Publishers, 1998; reprint, Ithaca, N.Y.: Cornell University Press, 2000), 44-52.

9. Robert Redfield, "Does America Need a Hearing Aid?" *Saturday Review* 36 (September 26, 1953): 11-45; reprinted in *The Social Uses of Social Science: The Papers of Robert Redfield*, vol. 2, ed. Margaret Park Redfield (Chicago: University of Chicago Press, 1963), 232-240.

Bibliography

Manuscript Collections

American Philosophical Society, Philadelphia, Pennsylvania.
    Anne Roe Papers.

Ford Foundation Archives, New York, New York.
    Robert Redfield, University of Chicago Civilizations Project Papers.

Harvard University Archives, Harvard University, Cambridge, Massachusetts.
    Alfred Vincent Kidder Papers.
    Clyde Kluckhohn Papers.
    Gordon Willey Papers.

Peabody Museum of Archaeology and Ethnology, Harvard University, Cambridge, Massachusetts.
    Carnegie Institution of Washington Papers.

Joseph Regenstein Library, University of Chicago, Chicago, Illinois.
    Ernest Burgess Papers.
    Committee on Social Thought Papers.
    Department of Anthropology Papers.
    Department of Sociology Papers.
    Fred Eggan Papers.
    Everett C. Hughes Papers.
    Robert M. Hutchins Papers.
    Frank H. Knight Papers.
    Charles M. Leslie Papers.
    Fred H. Matthews Papers.
    Charles Merriam Papers.
    John U. Neff Papers.
    Robert E. Park Papers.
    President's Papers, 1929-1951.
    Margaret Park Redfield Papers.
    Robert Redfield Papers.

Robert Redfield, Ford Foundation Papers.
Milton Singer Papers.
University of Chicago Press Papers.
Louis Wirth Papers.

Rockefeller Archive Center, Sleepy Hollow, New York.
Laura Spelman Rockefeller Memorial Archives.

Bentley Historical Library, University of Michigan, Ann Arbor, Michigan.
Leslie A. White Papers.

Primary Sources

Interviews

Taped Interviews
Cohn, Bernard, 22 February 1994, Chicago, Ill.
Foster, George M., 27 May 1994, Berkeley, Calif.
Gutmann, David, 5 October 1994, Chicago, Ill.
Gutmann, Joanna Redfield, 9 September 1994, Chicago, Ill.
Leslie, Charles M., 1 August, 1994, Newark, Del.
Levine, Donald N., 4 April 1994, 10 November 1994, Chicago, Ill.
Marriott, McKim, 5 April 1994, Chicago, Ill.
McNeill, William H., 2 August 1994, Colebrook, Conn.
Paul, Benjamin, 2 June 1994, Stanford, Calif.
Peattie, Lisa Redfield, 2 August 1994, Boston, Mass.
Redfield, James M., 6 October 1994, Chicago, Ill.
Singer, Milton, 5 April 1994, Chicago, Ill.

Untaped Conversations
Adams, Robert McCormick, 13 April 1995, telephone.
Bell, Daniel, 27 August 1994, telephone.
Braidwood, Robert, 7 September 1994, Chicago, Ill.
Braidwood, Linda, 7 September 1994, Chicago, Ill.
Bruner, Edward, 24 July 1994, telephone.
Fallers, Margaret, 5 May 1994, Chicago, Ill.
Gourevitch, Victor, 14 September 1995, telephone.
Griffin, James, 15 April 1995, telephone.
Gusfield, Joseph, 11 August 1995, telephone.
Marriot, McKim, 22 February 1994, Chicago, Ill.
McQuown, Norman, 28 August 1996, Chicago, Ill.
Miner, Agnes, 16 March 1994, Ann Arbor, Mich.
Mintz, Sidney W., 29 June 1995, Baltimore, Md.

Murra, John, 6 March 1994, telephone.
Peattie, Lisa Redfield, 1 May 1995, Boston, Mass.
Peattie, Mark, 20 March 1995, telephone.
Riesman, David, 20 August 1994, telephone.
Shils, Edward, 6 May 1994, Chicago, Ill.
Siegel, Bernard J., 30 March 1995, telephone.
Singer, Milton, 22 February 1994, 4 May 1994, Chicago, Ill.
Tarn, Nathaniel, 3 September 1994, telephone.
Vogt, Evon Z., 2 May 1995, Cambridge, Mass.
Washburn, Sherwood, 27 May 1994, Berkeley, Calif.
Wax, Murray, 12 September 1994, 17 June 1995, telephone.
Willey, Gordon, 2 May 1995, telephone.
Wolf, Eric R., 18 July 1994, telephone; 26 April 1994, Tarrytown, N.Y.

(All tapes and typed notes for untaped conversations are in author's possession.)

Books and Articles

Adams, Robert McCormick. *The Evolution of Urban Society: Early Mesopotamia and Prehispanic Mexico*. Chicago: Aldine, 1966.
Alpert, Harry. Review of *The Folk Culture of Yucatan*, by Robert Redfield. *American Sociological Review* 6 (December 1941): 896-898.
Ames, Michael M. "Magical Animism and Buddhism: A Structural Analysis of the Sinhalese Religious System." *Journal of Asian Studies* 23 (June 1964): 21-52.
Aurbach, Herbert A. "An Empirical Study in the Application of the Folk-Urban Typology to the Classification of Social Systems." Ph.D. diss., University of Kentucky, 1960.
Barnes, J. A. "Class and Committees in a Norwegian Island Parish." *Human Relations* 7 (May 1954): 39-58.
Barth, Fredrik. *Balinese Worlds*. Chicago: University of Chicago Press, 1993.
Bates, Ralph. "There Is Yucatan!" Review of *The Folk Culture of Yucatan*, by Robert Redfield. *Nation* 153 (20 September 1941): 258-260.
Beals, Carleton. "Mexico's Middletown." Review of *Tepoztlán, A Mexican Village: A Study of Folk Life*, by Robert Redfield. *Saturday Review of Literature* 6 (19 July 1930): 1201-1202.
Beals, Ralph L. "Urbanism, Urbanization and Acculturation." *American Anthropologist* 53 (January-March 1951): 1-10.
_____. "Community Typologies in Latin America." *Anthropological Linguistics* 3, no. 1 (1961): 8-16.
Beck, Lewis White. "The 'Natural Science Ideal' in the Social Sciences." *Scientific Monthly* 68 (June 1949): 386-394.

Benedict, Ruth. "Folk Life in Mexico." Review of *Tepoztlán, A Mexican Village: A Study of Folk Life*, by Robert Redfield. *New York Herald Tribune Books* (2 November 1930), 24.

_____. *Patterns of Culture*. Boston: Houghton Mifflin, 1934.

_____. Review of *Chan Kom: A Maya Village*, by Robert Redfield and Alfonso Villa Rojas. *American Anthropologist* 39 (April-June 1937): 340-342.

_____. *The Chrysanthemum and the Sword*. Boston: Houghton Mifflin, 1946.

_____. "Anthropology and the Humanities." *American Anthropologist* 50 (October-December 1950): 585-593.

Bennett, John W. "The Interpretation of Pueblo Culture: A Question of Values." *Southwestern Journal of Anthropology* 2 (Winter 1946): 361-374.

Bernard, Jesse. "Observation and Generalization in Cultural Anthropology." *American Journal of Sociology* 50 (January 1945): 284-291.

_____. "Sociological Mirror for Cultural Anthropology." *American Anthropologist* 51 (October-December 1949): 671-677.

Bierstedt, Robert. "The Limitations of Anthropological Methods in Sociology." *American Journal of Sociology* 54 (July 1948): 22-30.

Boas, Franz. "The Limitations of the Comparative Method of Anthropology." *Science*, n.s., 4 (18 December 1896): 901-908.

_____. *Anthropology: A Lecture Delivered at Columbia University, December 18, 1907*. New York: Columbia University Press, 1908.

_____. "History and Science in Anthropology: A Reply." *American Anthropologist* 38 (January-March 1936): 137-141.

_____. *The Mind of Primitive Man*. Rev. ed. New York: Macmillan, 1938.

_____. *Race, Language, and Culture*. New York: Free Press, 1940.

Boskoff, Alvin. "Structure, Function, and the Folk Society." *American Sociological Review* 14 (December 1949): 749-758.

Braidwood, Robert J. "Near Eastern Prehistory." *Science* 127 (20 June 1958): 1419-1430.

Braidwood, Robert J., and Linda Braidwood. "Jarmo: A Village of Early Farmers in Iraq." *Antiquity* 24 (December 1950): 189-195.

Bruner, Edward M. "Urbanization and Ethnic Identity in North Sumatra." *American Anthropologist* 63 (June 1961): 508-521.

Bunzel, Ruth. *Introduction to Zuni Ceremonialism* and *Zuni Origin Myths*. In *Forty-seventh Annual Report of the Bureau of American Ethnology, 1929-1930*, 467-544; 547-609. Washington, D.C.: Smithsonian Institution, 1932; reprinted in *Zuni Ceremonialism*, Albuquerque: University of New Mexico Press, 1992.

Burke, Kenneth, "The Downfall of Western Civilization," *Dial* 77 (November 1924): 361-378; *Dial* 77 (December 1924): 482-504; *Dial* 78 (January 1925): 9-26.

Chase, Stuart. "Corn and Fiestas." Review of *Tepoztlán, A Mexican Village: A Study of Folk Life*, by Robert Redfield. *New Republic* 64 (24 September 1930): 160.

_____. Review of *Chan Kom: A Maya Village*, by Robert Redfield and Alfonso Villa Rojas. *New Republic* 82 (20 February 1935): 51.

Chase, Stuart, with Marian Tyler. *Mexico: A Study of Two Americas*. New York: Macmillan, 1931.

Childe, V. Gordon. *Man Makes Himself*. London: Watts & Co., 1936.

_____. "Archaeology and Anthropology." *Southwestern Journal of Anthropology* 2 (Autumn 1946): 243-251.

_____. "The Urban Revolution." *Town Planning Review* 21 (April 1950): 3-17.

_____. *Prehistoric Migrations in Europe*. Oslo: Aschebourg; Cambridge, Mass.: Harvard University Press, 1950.

Cline, Howard. "Mexican Community Studies." *Hispanic American Historical Review* 32 (May 1952): 212-242.

Cohn, Bernard S., and McKim Marriott. "Networks and Centres in the Integration of Indian Civilisation." *Journal of Social Research* 1 (September 1958): 1-9.

Dewey, John. "Progress." *International Journal of Ethics* 26 (April 1916): 311-322.

Dube, S. C. "Approaches to the Study of Complex Cultures." *Journal of Social Research* 1 (September 1958): 10-23.

_____. "Indian Village Communities and Social Anthropology." In *Sociology, Social Research and Social Problems in India*, edited by R. N. Saksena, 119-125. New York: Asia Publishing House, 1961.

_____. "Social Anthropology in India." In *Essays in Memory of D. N. Majumdar*, edited by T. N. Madan and Gopala Sarana, 237-253. New York: Asia Publishing House, 1962.

Dumont, Louis. "The 'Village Community' from Munro to Maine," *Contributions to Indian Sociology* 9 (1966): 67-89.

Dumont, Louis, and David Pocock, eds. *Contributions to Indian Sociology*. 5 vols. The Hague: Mouton & Co., 1957-1961.

Durkheim, Émile. *The Division of Labor in Society*. Translated by W. D. Halls. New York: Free Press, [1893] 1984.

Edel, Abraham. "Some Relations of Philosophy and Anthropology." *American Anthropologist* 55 (December 1953): 649-660.

Eliot, T. S. *The Waste Land* in *The Waste Land and Other Poems*. New York: Harcourt, Brace & World, 1934.

Evers, Hans-Dieter. "Buddha and the Seven Gods: The Dual Organization of a Temple in Central Ceylon." *Journal of Asian Studies* 27 (May 1968): 541-550.

Fei, Hsiao-tung, and Chih-i Chang. *Earthbound China: A Study of Rural Economy in Yunnan*. Chicago: University of Chicago Press, 1945.

Fitzgerald, F. Scott. *The Great Gatsby*. New York: Charles Scribner's Sons, 1925.

Foster, George M. "What Is Folk Culture?" *American Anthropologist* 55 (January-March 1953): 159-173.

_____. "Interpersonal Relations in Peasant Society." *Human Organization* 19 (Winter 1960-1961): 174-178.

_____. "Peasant Society and the Image of the Limited Good." *American Anthropologist* 67 (April 1965): 293-315.

Frankfort, Henri. *The Birth of Civilization in the Near East*. Bloomington: Indiana University Press, 1951.

Freedman, Ronald, Amos H. Hawley, Werner S. Landecker, Gerhard E. Lenski, and Horace M. Miner. *Principles of Sociology: A Text with Readings*. Rev. ed. New York: Henry Holt and Co., 1956.

Freeman, Linton C. "An Empirical Test of Folk-Urbanism." Ph.D. diss, Northwestern University. 1957.

Garrett, Henry E. "Negro-White Differences in Mental Ability in the United States." *Scientific Monthly* 65 (October 1947): 329-333.

Geertz, Clifford. *The Religion of Java*. New York: Free Press of Glencoe, 1960.

Griaule, Marcel. *Conversations with Ogotemmeli: An Introduction to Dogon Religious Ideas*. London: Oxford University Press, 1965.

Gruening, Earnest. "The Mexican." Review of *Tepoztlán, A Mexican Village: A Study of Folk Life*. *Nation* 131 (15 October 1930): 417.

Guiteras-Holmes, Calixta. *Perils of the Soul: The World View of a Tzotil Indian*. New York: Free Press of Glencoe, 1961.

Hansen, Asael T. "The Ecology of a Latin American City." In *Race and Culture Contacts*, edited by E. B. Reuter. New York: McGraw-Hill, 1934.

Hartung, Frank E. Review of *The Primitive World and Its Transformations*, by Robert Redfield. *Ethics* 64 (April 1954): 234-236.

Haskell, Thomas. *The Emergence of Professional Social Science: The American Social Science Association and the Nineteenth-Century Crisis of Authority*. Urbana: University of Illinois Press, 1977.

Herskovits, Melville J. "The Significance of the Study of Acculturation for Anthropology." *American Anthropologist* 39 (January-March 1937): 259-264.

_____. *Acculturation: The Study of Culture Contact*. New York: J. J. Augustin, 1938; reprint, Gloucester, Mass.: Peter Smith, 1958.

_____. "Some Comments on the Study of Cultural Contact." *American Anthropologist* 43 (January-March 1941): 1-10.

_____. *Man and His Works: The Science of Cultural Anthropology*. New York: Alfred A. Knopf, 1948.

_____. "Some Further Comments on Cultural Relativism." *American Anthropologist* 60 (April 1958): 266-273.

Hocking, William, Robert Hutchins, Reinhold Niebuhr, and Robert Redfield. "The Crisis of Our Time." *The University of Chicago Roundtable* 353 (24 December 1944): 1-17.

Hoijer, Harry, ed. *Language in Culture: Conference on the Interrelations of Language and Other Aspects of Culture*. Chicago: University of Chicago Press, 1954.

Holmberg, Allan R. *Nomads of the Long Bow: The Siriono of Eastern Bolivia*. Washington, D.C.: Smithsonian Institution, 1950.

Hoselitz, Bert F. "The Role of Cities in the Economic Growth of Underdeveloped Countries." *Journal of Political Economy* 61 (June 1953): 195-208.

Hutchins, Robert M. "Address of Dedication." In *The New Social Science*, edited by Leonard D. White, 1-3. Chicago: University of Chicago Press, 1930.

_____. *The Higher Learning in America*. New Haven, Conn.: Yale University Press, 1936.

_____. "Address." In *Eleven Twenty-Six: A Decade of Social Science Research*, edited by Louis Wirth, 1-4. Chicago: University of Chicago Press, 1940; reprint, New York: Arno Press, 1974.

_____. "Civilization of the Dialogue." *University of Chicago Magazine* 41 (March 1949): 3-6.

Jacobsen, Thorkild. "The Relative Roles of Technology and Literacy in the Development of Old World Civilizations." In *University of Chicago, Anthropology 220, Human Origins: An Introductory General Course in Anthropology; Selected Readings, Series II*. 2d ed., 241-255. Chicago: University of Chicago Bookstore, 1946.

_____. "Appraisal of Breasted and Childe on Mesopotamia." In *University of Chicago, Anthropology 220, Human Origins: An Introductory General Course in Anthropology; Selected Readings, Series II*. 2d ed., 250-255. Chicago: University of Chicago Bookstore, 1946.

Johnson, Charles S. Review of *The Folk Culture of Yucatan*, by Robert Redfield. *American Journal of Sociology* 48 (1942): 430-431.

Kluckhohn, Clyde. Review of *The Primitive World and Its Transformations*, by Robert Redfield. *American Anthropologist* 56 (April 1954): 295-297.

_____. "The Conceptual Structure of Middle American Studies." In *The Maya and Their Neighbors*, edited by Clarence L. Hay et al. New York: Appleton-Century, 1940; reprint, Salt Lake City: University of Utah Press, 1962.

Kroeber, A. L. "The Culture-Area and Age-Area Concepts of Clark Wissler." In *Methods in Social Science: A Case Book*, edited by Stuart A. Rice, 248-265. Chicago: University of Chicago Press, 1931.

_____. Review of *Tepoztlán, A Mexican Village: A Study of Folk Life*, by Robert Redfield. *American Anthropologist* 33 (April-June 1931): 236-238.

_____. *Anthropology*. New York: Harcourt, Brace and Company, 1948.

_____, ed. *Anthropology Today: An Encyclopedic Inventory*. Chicago: University of Chicago Press, 1953.

_____. "The Delimitation of Civilizations." *Journal of the History of Ideas* 14 (April 1953): 264-275.

Lasswell, Harold D. "The Policy Orientation." In *The Policy Sciences: Recent Developments in Scope and Method*, edited by Daniel Lerner and Harold D. Lasswell, 3-15. Stanford, Calif.: Stanford University Press, 1951.

Lawrence, D. H. "New Mexico." *Survey Graphic* 19 (May 1931): 153-155.

Leighton, Alexander H. *The Governing of Men: General Principles and Recommendations Based on Experience at a Japanese Relocation Camp*. Princeton, N.J.: Princeton University Press, 1945.

Lerner, Daniel, and Harold D. Lasswell, eds. *The Policy Sciences: Recent Developments in Scope and Method*. Stanford, Calif.: Stanford University Press, 1951.

Leslie, Charles M. *Now We Are Civilized: A Study of the World View of the Zapotec Indians of Mitla, Oaxaca*. Detroit: Wayne State University Press, 1960.

Lesser, Alexander. *History, Evolution, and the Concept of Culture: Selected Papers by Alexander Lesser*. Edited by Sidney W. Mintz. Cambridge: Cambridge University Press, 1985.

Lewis, Oscar. *Life in a Mexican Village: Tepoztlán Restudied*. Urbana: University of Illinois Press, 1951.

_____. "Urbanization without Breakdown: A Case Study." *Scientific Monthly* 75, no. 1 (1952): 31-41.

_____. "Controls and Experiments in Field Work." In *Anthropology Today: An Encyclopedic Inventory*, edited by A. L. Kroeber, 452-475. Chicago: University of Chicago Press, 1953.

_____. "Tepoztlán Restudied: A Critique of the Folk-Urban Conceptualization of Social Change." *Rural Sociology* 18, no. 2 (1953): 121-136.

Lindesmith, Alfred R., and Anselm L. Strauss. "A Critique of Culture and Personality Writings." *American Sociological Review* 15 (1950): 587-600.

Linton, Ralph. *The Study of Man: An Introduction*. New York: D. Appleton-Century Co., 1936; reprint, New York: Appleton-Century-Crofts, 1964.

Lippmann, Walter. *A Preface to Morals*. New York: Macmillan, 1929.

Lundberg, George A. "The Proximate Future of American Sociology: The Growth of Scientific Method." *American Journal of Sociology* 50 (May 1945): 502-513.

Lynd, Robert S. Review of *Tepoztlán, A Mexican Village: A Study of Folk Life*, by Robert Redfield. *American Journal of Sociology* 36 (1930): 823.

Macdonald, Dwight. *The Ford Foundation: The Men and the Millions*. New York: Reynal & Company, 1956.

Maine, Henry Sumner. *Ancient Law*. New York: Holt, 1864; reprint, Tucson: University of Arizona Press, 1986.

Malinowski, Bronislaw. *Argonauts of the Western Pacific: An Account of Native Enterprise and Adventure in the Archipelagos of Melanesian New Guinea*. London: G. Routledge, 1922.

Mandelbaum, David G. "On the Study of National Character." *American Anthropologist* 55 (April-June 1953): 174-187.

_____. "The Study of Complex Civilizations." In *Current Anthropology: A Supplement to Anthropology Today*, edited by W. H. Thomas, 203-225. Chicago: University of Chicago Press, 1956.

Marriott, McKim, ed. *Village India: Studies in the Little Community*. Chicago: University of Chicago Press, 1955.

_____. "Little Communities in an Indigenous Civilization." In *Village India: Studies in the Little Community*, edited by McKim Marriott, 171-222. Chicago: University of Chicago Press, 1955.

Martin, Paul S., and John Rinaldo. "Archaeological Work in Ackmen-Lowry Area, Southwestern Colorado, 1937." *Anthropological Series, Field Museum of Natural History* 23, no. 2 (1938): 229-304.

McCarthy, Raphael C., Halvdan Koht, Gerhardus Van Der Leeu, Ernst Simon, and Robert Redfield. "Ethics and Politics." In *Goethe and the Modern Age: The International Convocation at Aspen, Colorado, 1949*, edited by Arnold Bergstraesser, 365-381. Chicago: Henry Regnery, 1950.

McKinney, John C. "The Role of Constructive Typology in Scientific Sociological Analysis." *Social Forces* 28 (March 1950): 235-240.

Mead, Margaret. *Coming of Age in Samoa*. New York: William Morrow & Co., 1928.

Means, P. A. "Yucatan: Its Living Present and Its Records of the Past." Review of *The Folk Culture of Yucatan*, by Robert Redfield." *New York Times Book Review* (28 September 1941), 11, 29.

Mendelson, E. Michael. "Religion and World-view in Santiago Atitlan." Ph.D. diss., University of Chicago, 1957.

_____. "The King, the Traitor, and the Cross: An Interpretation of Highland Maya Religious Conflict." *Diogenes* 21 (Spring 1958): 1-10.

_____. "A Guatemalan Sacred Bundle," *Man* 58 (August 1958): 121-126.

_____. *Los Escandalos de Maximon*, Seminario de Intregracion Social, Publication No. 19 (Guatemala City: Ministerio de Educacion, 1965).

Mills, C. Wright. "The Professional Ideology of Social Pathologies." *American Journal of Sociology* 49 (September 1943): 165-180.

_____. *The Sociological Imagination*. New York: Oxford University Press, 1959.

Miner, Horace. "The Folk-Urban Continuum." *American Sociological Review* 17 (October 1952): 529-537.

_____. *St. Denis: A French-Canadian Parish*. Chicago: University of Chicago Press, 1939; reprint, Chicago: University of Chicago Press, Phoenix Books, 1963.

_____. *The Primitive City of Timbuctoo*. Princeton, N.J.: Princeton University Press, 1954.

Mintz, Sidney W. "Canamelar: The Culture of a Rural Puerto Rican Proletariat." Ph.D. diss., Columbia University, 1951.

_____. "The Folk-Urban Continuum and the Rural Proletarian Community." *American Journal of Sociology* 59 (July 1953): 136-143.

_____. "On Redfield and Foster." *American Anthropologist* 56 (February 1954): 87-92.

Moore, Wilbert E. *Industrialization and Labor: Social Aspects of Economic Development*. Ithaca, N.Y.: Cornell University Press, 1951.

Mumford, Lewis. "Spengler's 'The Decline of the West.'" In *Books That Changed Our Minds*, edited by Malcolm Cowley and Bernard Smith, 217-235 (New York: Doubleday, Doran 1939).

Murdock, George Peter. Review of *The Folk Culture of Yucatan*, by Robert Redfield. *American Anthropologist* 45 (January-March 1943): 133-136.

Myrdal, Gunnar. *An American Dilemma*. New York: Harper and Row, 1944.

Nef, John U. "The American Universities and the Future of Western Civilization." *Review of Politics* 1 (July 1939): 241-260.

____. "A Social Science Objective." *University of Chicago Magazine* 31 (November 1939): 10-11, 27-28.

____. "On the Future of American Civilization." *Review of Politics* 2 (July 1940): 261-282.

____. "Civilization at the Crossroads." *Review of Politics* 3 (July 1941): 283-299.

____. "Civilization at the Crossroads-II." *Review of Politics* 3 (October 1941): 451-478.

____. "Philosophical Values and American Learning." *Review of Politics* 4 (July 1942): 257-270.

____. *The United States and Civilization*. Chicago: University of Chicago Press, 1942.

____. "Philosophical Values and the Future of Civilization." *Review of Politics* 5 (April 1943): 156-176.

____. "The University of Chicago and the World, 1929-1951." *Review of Politics* 13 (October 1951): 399-429.

____. *The Universities Look for Unity: An Essay on the Responsibilities of the Mind to Civilization in War and Peace*. New York: Pantheon, 1953.

____. *Search for Meaning: The Autobiography of a Noncomformist*. Washington, D.C.: Public Affairs Press, 1973.

Obeyesekere, Gananath. "The Great Tradition and the Little in the Perspective of Sinhalese Buddhism." *Journal of Asian Studies* 22 (February 1963): 139-153.

Ogburn, William Fielding. *Social Change: With Respect to Culture and Original Nature*. New York: B. W. Huebsch, 1922; reprint, New York: Viking Press, 1936.

____. "Sociology and the Atom." *American Journal of Sociology* 51 (January 1946): 267-275.

Park, Robert E. "The City: Suggestions for the Investigation of Human Behavior in the Urban Environment." *American Journal of Sociology* 20 (March 1915): 577-612.

____. *The Immigrant Press and Its Control*. New York: Harper & Brothers, 1922.

____. "Magic, Mentality, and City Life." *Publications of the American Sociological Society* 18 (September 1924): 102-115.

____. "Culture and Cultural Trends." *Publications of the American Sociological Society* 19 (December 1925): 24-36.

____. "The Urban Community as a Spatial Pattern and a Moral Order." In *The Urban Community*, edited by Ernest W. Burgess, 3-18. Chicago: University of Chicago Press, 1926.

____. "Our Racial Frontier on the Pacific." *Survey Graphic* 9 (May 1926): 192-196.

_____. "Human Migration and the Marginal Man." *American Journal of Sociology* 33 (May 1928): 881-893.

_____. "The City as Social Laboratory." In *Chicago: An Experiment in Social Science Research*, edited by T. V. Smith and Leonard D. White, 1-19. Chicago: University of Chicago Press, 1929.

_____. "Society." In *Research in the Social Sciences*, edited by Wilson Gee, 3-49. New York: Macmillan, 1929.

_____. "The Sociological Methods of William Graham Sumner, and of William I. Thomas and Florian Znaniecki." In *Methods in Social Science: A Case Book*, edited by Stuart A. Rice, 154-175. Chicago: University of Chicago Press, 1931.

_____. Introduction to *Shadow of the Plantation*, by Charles S. Johnson. Chicago: University of Chicago Press, 1934.

_____. "Methods of Teaching: Impressions and a Verdict." *Social Forces* 20 (October 1941): 36-46.

_____. *Race and Culture*. Edited by Everett Cherrington Hughes. Glencoe, Ill.: Free Press, 1950.

_____. "The Problem of Cultural Differences." In *Race and Culture*, 3-14. Glencoe, Ill.: Free Press, 1950.

_____. "Culture and Civilization." In *Race and Culture*, 15-23. Glencoe, Ill.: Free Press, 1950.

_____. "The City and Civilization." In *Human Communities: The City and Human Ecology*, edited by Everett Cherrington Hughes, 128-144. Glencoe, Ill.: Free Press, 1952.

_____. "Reflections on Communication and Culture." *American Journal of Sociology* 54 (September 1938): 187-205.

_____. *Human Communities: The City and Human Ecology*. Edited by Everett Cherrington Hughes. Glencoe, Ill.: Free Press, 1952.

_____. *The Crowd and the Public and Other Essays*. Chicago: University of Chicago Press, 1972.

Park, Robert E., and Ernest W. Burgess. *Introduction to the Science of Sociology*. Chicago: University of Chicago Press, 1921.

Park, Robert E., Ernest W. Burgess, and Roderick D. McKenzie. *The City*. Chicago: University of Chicago Press, 1925.

Park, Robert E., Herbert A. Miller, and [William I. Thomas]. *Old World Traits Transplanted*. New York: Harper and Brothers, 1921.

Parker, Richard A. "Appraisal of Breasted and Childe on Egypt." In *University of Chicago, Anthropology 220, Human Origins: An Introductory General Course in Anthropology; Selected Readings, Series II*. 2d ed., 256-257. Chicago: University of Chicago Bookstore, 1946.

Parsons, Elsie Clews. *Mitla, Town of the Souls: And Other Zapoteco-Speaking Peoples of Oaxaca*. Chicago: University of Chicago Press, 1936.

Poore, C. G. "From Sun-Up to Bedtime in a Village of Old Mexico." Review of *Tepoztlán, A Mexican Village: A Study of Folk Life,* by Robert Redfield. *New York Times Book Review* (27 July 1930), 10.

Radcliffe-Brown, A. R. *The Andaman Islanders: A Study in Anthropology.* Cambridge: Cambridge University Press, 1922.

Ray, Verne F., ed. *Intermediate Societies, Social Mobility, and Communication: Proceedings of the 1959 Annual Spring Meeting of the American Ethnological Society.* Seattle: University of Washington Press, 1959.

Redfield, Robert. "War Sketches." *Poetry* 12 (August 1918): 242-243.

____. "Anthropology, A Natural Science?" *Social Forces* 4 (June 1926): 715-721.

____. "A Plan for the Study of Tepoztlán, Morelos." Ph.D. diss., University of Chicago, 1928.

____. "Among the Middle Americans." *University of Chicago Magazine* 20 (March 1928): 242-247.

____. *Tepoztlán, A Mexican Village: A Study of Folk Life.* Chicago: University of Chicago Press, 1930.

____. "The Regional Aspect of Culture." *Publications of the American Sociological Society* 24, no. 2 (1930): 33-41.

____. "Sociological Investigation in Yucatan." In *Carnegie Institution Year Book 30,* 122-124. Washington, D.C.: Carnegie Institution of Washington, 1931.

____. "Ethnological Research." In *Carnegie Institution of Washington Year Book 31,* 111-114. Washington, D.C.: Carnegie Institution of Washington, 1932.

____. "Sociological Study." In *Carnegie Institution of Washington Year Book 32,* 100-104. Washington, D.C.: Carnegie Institution of Washington, 1933.

____. "Culture Changes in Yucatan." *American Anthropologist* 36 (January-March 1934): 57-69.

____. "The Long Road Back." *University of Chicago Magazine* 27 (February 1935): 131-134.

____. "The Place of the Social Sciences in a General Education." In *Growth and Development: The Basis for Educational Programs,* 145-151. New York: Progressive Education Association, 1936.

____. "The Second Epilogue to Maya History." *Hispanic American Historical Review* 17 (May 1937): 170-181.

____. Review of *Man and Culture,* 6th ed., by Clark Wissler. *American Journal of Sociology* 44 (November 1938): 477.

____. Introduction to *St. Denis: A French Canadian Parish,* by Horace Miner. Chicago: University of Chicago Press, 1939.

____. "Primitive Merchants of Guatemala." *Quarterly Journal of Inter-American Relations* 1 (October 1939): 42-56.

____. "The Folk Society and Culture." *American Journal of Sociology* 45 (March 1940): 731-742.

____. *The Folk Culture of Yucatan.* Chicago: University of Chicago Press, 1941.

_____. "Consequences of Atomic Energy." *Phi Delta Kappan* 8 (April 1946): 221-224.

_____. "The Folk Society." *American Journal of Sociology* 52 (January 1947): 293-308.

_____. "Social Science in the Atomic Age." *Journal of General Education* 1 (January 1947): 120-124.

_____. "The Study of Culture in General Education." *Social Education* 11 (October 1947): 259-264.

_____. "The Art of Social Science." *American Journal of Sociology* 54 (November 1948): 181-190.

_____. "Visit to China." *University of Chicago Magazine* 42 (1949): 13, 19-20.

_____. *A Village That Chose Progress: Chan Kom Revisited*. Chicago: University of Chicago Press, 1950.

_____. "Social Science among the Humanities." *Measure* 1 (Winter 1950): 60-74.

_____. "Social Science in Our Society." *Phylon* 11, no. 1 (1950): 31-41.

_____. "The Patriot." *Common Cause* 3 (June 1950): 566.

_____. Interview by Anne Roe, 1950, Anne Roe Papers, American Philosophical Library, Philadelphia.

_____. "The Frontier of Underdeveloped Areas." In *Frontiers for Freedom*, edited by R. Gordon Hoxie. Denver: University of Denver Press, 1952.

_____. "Social-Science Research in General Education." *Journal of General Education* 6 (January 1952): 81-91.

_____. "The Primitive World View." *Proceedings of the American Philosophical Society* 96 (February 1952): 30-36.

_____. *The Primitive World and Its Transformations*. Ithaca, N.Y.: Cornell University Press, 1953.

_____. "Relations of Anthropology to the Social Sciences and to the Humanities." In *Anthropology Today: An Encyclopedic Inventory*, edited by A. L. Kroeber, 728-738. Chicago: University of Chicago Press, 1953.

_____. "Integration: High and Low." In *An Introduction to Social Science*, edited by Arthur Naftalin, Benjamin N. Nelson, Mulford Q. Sibley and Donald C. Calhoun, 353-355. Chicago: J. B. Lippincott, 1953.

_____. "The Natural History of the Folk Society." *Social Forces* 31 (March 1953): 224-229.

_____. "Does America Need a Hearing Aid?" *Saturday Review* 36 (26 September 1953): 11-45.

_____. "Community Studies in Japan and China: A Symposium." *Far Eastern Quarterly* 14 (November 1954): 3-10.

_____. *The Little Community: Viewpoints for the Study of a Human Whole*. Chicago: University of Chicago Press, 1955.

_____. "The Social Organization of Tradition." *Far Eastern Quarterly* 15 (November 1955): 13-21.

_____. "Societies and Cultures as Natural Systems." *Journal of the Royal Anthropological Institute of Great Britain and Ireland* 85 (January-December 1955): 19-32.

_____. *Peasant Society and Culture: An Anthropological Approach to Civilization.* Chicago: University of Chicago Press, 1956.

_____. "The Relations between Indians and Ladinos in Agua Escondida, Guatemala." *America Indigena* 16 (October 1956): 253-276.

_____. *The Papers of Robert Redfield: Human Nature and the Study of Society,* vol. 1. Edited by Margaret Park Redfield. Chicago: University of Chicago, 1962.

_____. *The Papers of Robert Redfield: The Social Uses of Social Science,* vol. 2. Edited by Margaret Park Redfield. Chicago: University of Chicago Press, 1963.

Redfield, Robert, Ralph Linton, and Melville J. Herskovits. "Memorandum for the Study of Acculturation." *American Anthropologist* 38 (January-March 1936): 149-152.

Redfield, Robert, et al. "The Hutchins Influence." *University of Chicago Magazine* 43 (June 1951): 9-15.

Redfield, Robert, and Milton Singer. Foreword to *Studies in Chinese Thought,* edited by *Arthur F. Wright,* v-viii. Chicago: University of Chicago Press, 1953.

_____. "The Cultural Role of Cities." *Economic Development and Cultural Change* 3 (October 1954): 53-73.

_____. Foreword to *Village India: Studies in the Little Community,* edited by McKim Marriott. Chicago: University of Chicago Press, 1955.

Redfield, Robert, and Alfonso Villa Rojas. *Chan Kom: A Maya Village.* Washington, D.C.: Carnegie Institution of Washington, 1934; reprint, Chicago: University of Chicago Press, 1962.

Reed, Stephen W. Review of *The Primitive World and Its Transformations,* by Robert Redfield. *Yale Review* 43 (Autumn 1953): 152-154.

Riesman, David, and with Nathan Glazer and Reuel Denney. *The Lonely Crowd: A Study of the Changing American Character.* New Haven, Conn.: Yale University Press, 1950.

Rivers, W. H. R. "The Pyschological Factor." In *Essays on the Depopulation of Melanesia,* edited by W. H. R. Rivers, 84-113. Cambridge: Cambridge University Press, 1922.

Saksena, R. N. "Sociology, Social Research, and Social Problems in India." In *Sociology, Social Research, and Social Problems in India,* edited by R. N. Saksena, 7-19. New York: Asia Publishing House, 1961.

Sapir, Edward. "Civilization and Culture." *Dial* 67 (20 September 1919): 233-236.

_____. "Culture, Genuine and Spurious," *Dalhousie Review* 2 (1922): 358-368.

_____. "Culture, Genuine and Spurious." *American Journal of Sociology* 29 (January 1924): 401-429.

Simmel, Georg. "The Metropolis and Mental Life." Translated by Hans Gerth and C. Wright Mills. In *The Sociology of Georg Simmel*, edited by Kurt H. Wolff, 409-424. New York: Free Press, [1903] 1950.

_____. "The Stranger." Translated by Kurt H. Wolff. In *The Sociology of Georg Simmel*, edited by Kurt H. Wolff, 402-408. New York: Free Press, [1908] 1950.

Singer, Milton. "How the American Got His Character." *Ethics* 60 (October 1949): 62-66.

_____. "The Cultural Pattern of Indian Civilization." *Far Eastern Quarterly* 15 (November 1955): 23-36.

_____, ed. *Introducing India in Liberal Education*. Chicago: University of Chicago Press, 1957.

_____, ed. *Traditional India: Structure and Change*. Philadelphia: American Folklore Society, 1959.

_____. "A Survey of Culture and Personality Theory and Research." In *Studying Personality Cross-Culturally*, edited by Bert Kaplan, 9-90. New York: Harper & Row, 1961.

_____. *When a Great Tradition Modernizes: An Anthropological Approach to Indian Civilization*. New York: Praeger, 1972; reprint, Chicago: University of Chicago Press, 1980.

Singer, Milton, and Bernard S. Cohn, eds. *Structure and Change in Indian Society*. Chicago: Aldine, 1968.

Sjoberg, Gideon. "Folk and Feudal Societies." *American Journal of Sociology* 58 (November 1952): 231-239.

_____. Review of *The Primitive World and Its Transformations*, by Robert Redfield. *American Journal of Sociology* 59 (November 1953): 277-278.

Spengler, Oswald. *The Decline of the West*. Translated by Charles Francis Atkinson, 2 vols. New York: Alfred A. Knopf, 1926.

Spicer, Edward H. *Pascua: A Yaqui Village in Arizona*. Chicago: University of Chicago Press, 1940; reprint, Tucson: University of Arizona Press, 1984.

_____. Review of *The Folk Culture of Yucatan*, by Robert Redfield. *Annals of the American Academy of Political and Social Science* 219 (January 1942): 201-202.

Spiro, Melford E. *Buddhism and Society: A Great Tradition and Its Burmese Vicissitudes*. New York: Harper and Row, 1970.

Srinivas, M. N. *Religion and Society among the Coorgs of South India*. Oxford: Oxford University Press, 1952.

_____, ed. *India's Villages*. Calcutta: West Bengal Government Press, 1955.

Staal, J. F. "Sanskrit and Sanskritization." *Journal of Asian Studies* 22 (May 1963): 261-275.

Steward, Julian H. Review of *The Folk Culture of Yucatan*, by Robert Redfield. *Journal of American Folklore* 57 (April-June 1944): 146-148.

_____. *Area Research: Theory and Practice*. New York: Social Science Research Council, 1950.

Steward, Julian H., Robert A. Manners, Eric R. Wolf, Elena Padilla Seda, Sidney W. Mintz, and Raymond L. Scheele. *The People of Puerto Rico: A Study in Social Anthropology.* Urbana: University of Illinois Press, 1956.

Stewart, W. K. "The Decline of Western Culture: Oswald Spengler's 'Downfall of Western Civilization' Explained," *Century* 108 (September 1924): 589-598.

Supreme Court. "Sweatt V. Painter, et al. 339 U.S. 629, Record and Briefs." *Supreme Court Record and Briefs* 339 (October 1949): 189-208 (RR).

Tambiah, S. J. *Buddhism and the Spirit Cults in North-East Thailand.* Cambridge: Cambridge University Press, 1970.

Tax, Sol. "The Municipios of the Midwestern Highlands of Guatemala." *American Anthropologist* 39 (July-September 1937): 423-444.

_____. "Culture and Civilization in Guatemalan Societies." *Scientific Monthly* 48 (May 1939): 463-467.

_____. "World View and Social Relations in Guatemala." *American Anthropologist* 43 (January-March 1941): 27-42.

_____. "'Revolutions' and the Process of Civilization." In *University of Chicago, Anthropology 220, Human Origins: An Introductory General Course in Anthropology; Selected Readings, Series II.* 2d ed., 228-239. Chicago: University of Chicago Bookstore, 1946.

_____, ed. *Heritage of Conquest: The Ethnology of Middle America.* Glencoe, Ill.: Free Press, 1952; reprint, New York: Cooper Square Publishers, 1968.

Teggart, Frederick J. *The Processes of History.* New Haven, Conn.: Yale University Press, 1918; reprinted in *Theory and Processes of History*, Berkeley: University of California Press, 1977.

_____. *Theory of History.* New Haven, Conn.:Yale University Press, 1925; reprinted in *Theory and Processes of History*, Berkeley: University of California Press, 1977.

Tepoztlán, A Mexican Village: A Study of Folk Life, by Robert Redfield, anonymous review, *Times Literary Supplement* (24 July 1930), 613.

Thomas, William I. *Source Book for Social Origins.* Chicago: University of Chicago Press, 1909.

_____. "Race Psychology: Standpoint and Questionnaire, with Particular Reverence to the Immigrant and the Negro." *American Journal of Sociology* 17 (May 1912): 725-775.

Thomas, William I., and Florian Znaniecki. *The Polish Peasant in Europe and America,* 5 vols. Boston: Badger, 1918-1919; reprint, 2 vols., New York: Alfred A. Knopf, 1927.

Toennies, Ferdinand. *Community and Association.* Translated by Charles P. Loomis. London: Routledge & Kegan Paul, [1887] 1955.

Toynbee, Arnold J., abridgement by D. C. Somervell. *A Study of History.* New York: Oxford University Press, 1946.

Toynbee, Arnold J. *The World and the West.* New York: Oxford University Press, 1953.

Tumin, Melvin. "Culture, Genuine and Spurious: A Reevaluation." *American Sociological Review* 10 (February 1945): 199-207.

von Grunebaum, Gustave E., ed. *Unity and Variety in Muslim Civilization.* Chicago: University of Chicago Press, 1955.

Wallas, Graham. *The Great Society: A Psychological Analysis.* London: Macmillan, 1914.

Whitehead, Alfred North. *The Adventure of Ideas.* New York: Macmillan, 1933.

Willey, Gordon R. "The Structure of Ancient Maya Society: Evidence from the Southern Lowlands." *American Anthropologist* 58 (October 1956): 777-782.

Wilson, Edmund. *Axel's Castle: A Study in the Imaginative Literature of 1870 to 1930.* New York: Charles Scribner's Sons, 1931.

Wilson, Godfrey, and Monica Wilson. *The Analysis of Social Change: Based on Observations in Central Africa.* Cambridge: Cambridge University Press, 1954.

Wirth, Louis. "Urbanism as a Way of Life." *American Journal of Sociology* 44 (July 1938): 1-24.

_____, ed. *Eleven Twenty-Six: A Decade of Social Science Research.* Chicago: University of Chicago Press, 1940; reprint, New York: Arno Press, 1974.

_____. "The Urban Society and Civilization." *American Journal of Sociology* 45 (March 1940): 743-755.

_____. "Responsibility of Social Science." *Annals of American Academy of Political and Social Science* 249 (January 1947): 143-151.

_____. "American Sociology, 1915-47." *American Journal of Sociology* index to volumes 1-52, 1895-1947 (1947): 273-281.

_____. "Rural-Urban Differences." In *Louis Wirth, On Cities and Social Life,* edited by Albert J. Reiss, Jr., 221-225. Chicago: University of Chicago Press, 1964.

Wissler, Clark. *Man and Culture.* New York: Thomas Y. Crowell, 1923; reprint, New York: Johnson Reprint Corporation, 1965.

_____. Review of *Chan Kom: A Maya Village,* by Robert Redfield and Alfonso Villa Rojas. *American Journal of Sociology* 41 (September 1935): 266.

Wolf, Eric R. "Types of Latin American Peasantry: A Preliminary Discussion." *American Anthropologist* 57 (June 1955): 452-471.

Wolfe, Bertram D. "Studies of Amerindians." Review of *The Folk Culture of Yucatan,* by Robert Redfield. *New York Herald Tribune Books* (5 October 1941), 29.

Wright, Arthur F., ed. *Studies in Chinese Thought.* Chicago: University of Chicago Press, 1953.

Young, Kimball. *Sociology: A Study of Society and Culture.* 2d ed. New York: American Book Company, 1949.

Secondary Sources

Abbott, Andrew, and Emanuel Gaziano. "Transition and Tradition: Departmental Faculty in the Era of the Second Chicago School." In *A Second Chicago School? The Development of a Postwar American Sociology*, edited by Gary Alan Fine, 221-272. Chicago: University of Chicago Press, 1995.

Allen, James Sloan. *The Romance of Commerce and Culture: Capitalism, Modernism, and the Chicago-Aspen Crusade for Cultural Reform*. Chicago: University of Chicago Press, 1983.

Allison, John Victor. "Robert Redfield's Folk-Urban Construct." M.A. thesis, San Francisco State University, 1967.

Apter, David E. *Rethinking Development: Modernization, Dependency, and Postmodern Politics*. Newbury Park, Calif.: Sage Publications, 1987.

Arensberg, Conrad M., and Solon T. Kimball. *Culture and Community*. New York: Harcourt, Brace & World, 1963.

Ashmore, Harry S. *Unseasonable Truths: The Life of Robert Maynard Hutchins*. Boston: Little, Brown and Company, 1989.

Audhuy, Letha. "The *Waste Land* Myth and Symbols in *The Great Gatsby*." In *F. Scott Fitzgerald's The Great Gatsby*, edited by Harold Boom, 109-122. New York: Chelsea House, 1986.

Avila, Manuel. *Tradition and Growth: A Study of Four Mexican Villages*. Chicago: University of Chicago Press, 1969.

Baldwin, David A. *Foreign Aid and American Foreign Policy: A Documentary Analysis*. New York: Praeger, 1966.

Bannister, Robert C. *Sociology and Scientism: The Quest for American Objectivity, 1880-1940*. Chapel Hill: University of North Carolina Press, 1987.

Banton, Michael. "The Folk Society and Civilization." *Race* 6 (July 1964): 27-33.

———. "The Folk Society and Civilization." Review of *Human Nature and the Study of Society* and *The Social Uses of Social Science: The Papers of Robert Redfield*, vols. 1 and 2. Edited by Margaret Park Redfield. *Race* 6 (July 1964): 27-33.

Beals, Alan R. Review of *Human Nature and the Study of Society: The Papers of Robert Redfield*, vol. 1. Edited by Margaret Park Redfield. *American Anthropologist* 66, no. 2 (1964): 430-432.

Becker, Ernest. *The Lost Science of Man*. New York: George Braziller, 1971.

Beeman, Richard R. "The New Social History and the Search for 'Community' in Colonial America." *American Quarterly* 29 (Fall 1977): 422-443.

Bell, Colin, and Howard Newby. *Community Studies: An Introduction to the Sociology of the Local Community*. New York: Praeger, 1972.

Bell, Daniel. *The Reforming of General Education: The Columbia College Experience in Its National Setting*. New York: Columbia University Press, 1966.

Bender, Thomas. *Community and Social Change in America*. New Brunswick, N.J.: Rutgers University Press, 1978; reprint, Baltimore: Johns Hopkins University Press, 1982.

Bendix, Reinhard. "Tradition and Modernity Reconsidered." *Comparative Studies in Society and History* 9 (April 1967): 292-346.

Benet, Francisco. "Sociology Uncertain: The Ideology of the Rural-Urban Continuum." *Comparative Studies in Society and History* 6 (October 1963): 1-23.

Bennett, John W. "A Course in Comparative Civilizations." In *The Teaching of Anthropology*, edited by David G. Mandelbaum, Gabriel W. Lasker, and Ethel M. Albert, 191-212. Berkeley: University of California Press, 1963.

_____. *The Ecological Transition: Cultural Anthropology and Human Adaptation*. New York: Pergamon Press, 1976.

_____. "Anthropology and Development: The Ambiguous Development." In *Production and Autonomy: Anthropological Studies and Critiques of Development*, edited by John W. Bennett and John R. Bowen. Lanham, Md.: University Press of America, 1988.

_____. "Walks on the Dark Side: 'Sick Societies,' Interpersonal Violence, and Anthropology's Love Affair with the Folk Society." *Reviews in Anthropology* 24 (1995): 145-158.

Berger, Peter L. *Invitation to Sociology: A Humanistic Perspective*. New York: Anchor Books, 1963.

Berman, Marshall. *All That Is Solid Melts into Air: The Experience of Modernity*. New York: Simon and Schuster, 1982; reprint, New York: Penguin Books, 1988.

Berry, Brian J. L. *The Human Consequences of Urbanization: Divergent Paths in the Urban Experience of the Twentieth Century*. New York: St. Martin's Press, 1973.

Beteille, Andre. *Essays in Comparative Sociology*. Delhi: Oxford University Press, 1987.

Bharati, Agehananda. *Great Tradition and Little Traditions: Indological Investigations in Cultural Anthropology*. Varansi: Chowkhamba Sanskrit Series Office, 1978.

_____. "Peasant Society and Redfield's Fields." *Reviews in Anthropology* 7 (Summer 1980): 303-322.

Bierstedt, Robert. "Sociology and Humane Learning." *American Sociological Review* 25 (February 1960).

Binford, Lewis R. "Archaeological Systematics and the Study of Culture Process." *American Antiquity* 31 (October 1965): 203-210.

Blanchard, Margaret. "The Hutchins Commission, the Press, and the Responsibility Concept." *Journalism Monographs* 47 (May 1977): 1-59.

Bock, Kenneth. "Theories of Progress, Development, Evolution." In *A History of Sociological Analysis*, edited by Tom Bottomore and Robert Nisbet, 39-79. New York: Basic Books, 1978.

Bock, Philip K. "Tepoztlán Reconsidered." *Journal of Latin American Lore* 6 (Summer 1980): 129-150.

Boyer, Paul. *By the Bomb's Early Light: American Thought and Culture at the Dawn of the Atomic Age*. New York: Pantheon, 1985.

Boylan, James. "The Hutchins Report: A Twenty-Year View." *Columbia Journalism Review* 6 (Summer 1967): 5-8.

Braidwood, Robert J. "Prehistoric Investigations in Southwestern Asia." *Proceedings of the American Philosophical Society* 116 (August 1972): 310-320.

____. "Robert J. Braidwood." In *The Pastmasters: Eleven Modern Pioneers of Archaeology*, edited by Glyn Daniel and Christopher Chippindale, 89-99. New York: Thames and Hudson, 1989.

Bramson, Leon. *The Political Context of Sociology*. Princeton: Princeton University Press, 1961.

Brick, Howard. *Age of Contradiction: American Thought and Culture in the 1960s*. New York: Twayne Publishers, 1998; reprint, Ithaca, N.Y.: Cornell University Press, 2000.

Britton, John A. *Carleton Beals: A Radical Journalist in Latin America*. Albuquerque: University of New Mexico Press, 1987.

Bulmer, Martin. "Chicago Sociology and the Society for Social Research: A Comment." *Journal of the History of the Behavioral Sciences* 19 (October 1983): 353-357.

____. *The Chicago School of Sociology: Institutionalization, Diversity, and the Rise of Sociological Research*. Chicago: University of Chicago Press, 1984.

Cahnman, Werner J. "The Rise of Civilization as a Paradigm of Cultural Change." In *Sociology and History: Theory and Research*, edited by Werner J. Cahnman and Alvin Boskoff, 537-559. New York: Free Press, 1964.

____. "Tönnies in America." *History and Theory* 16, no. 1 (1977): 147-167.

Cappetti, Carla. *Writing Chicago: Modernism, Ethnography, and the Novel*. New York: Columbia University Press, 1993.

Cardoso, Lawrence A. *Mexican Emigration to the United States, 1897-1931*. Tucson: University of Arizona Press, 1980.

Carey, James. *Sociology and Public Affairs: The Chicago School*. Beverly Hills, Calif.: Sage, 1975.

Carter, Paul A. *The Twenties in America*. 2d ed. Arlington Heights, Ill.: AHM Publishing, 1975.

Castells, Manuel. *The Urban Question: A Marxist Approach*. Translated by Alan Sheridan. Cambridge, Mass.: MIT Press, 1977.

Chodak, Szymon. *Societal Development: Five Approaches with Conclusions from Comparative Analysis*. New York: Oxford University Press, 1973.

Clifford, James. *The Predicament of Culture: Twentieth Century Ethnography, Literature, and Art*. Cambridge, Mass.: Harvard University Press, 1988.

Cohen, Anthony P. *The Symbolic Construction of Community*. Chichester, Sussex, England: Ellis Horwood, 1985.

Cohn, Bernard S. *India: The Social Anthropology of a Civilization*. Englewood Cliffs, N.J.: Prentice Hall, 1971.

_____. *An Anthropologist among the Historians and Other Essays*. Delhi: Oxford University Press, 1987.

Cole, Fay-Cooper, and Fred Eggan. "Robert Redfield, 1897-1958." *American Anthropologist* 61 (August 1959): 652-662.

Collins, June, Everett C. Hughes, James B. Griffin, and Margaret Mead, discussants. "American Ethnology: The Role of Redfield." In *American Anthropology: The Early Years, 1974 Proceedings of the American Ethnological Society*, edited by John V. Murra, 139-145. St. Paul, Minn.: West Publishing, 1974.

Cousins, Albert N., and Hans Nagpual. *Urban Life: The Sociology of Cities and Urban Society*. New York: John Wiley and Sons, 1979.

Cowell, Bainbridge, Jr. "Model Building and Data Gathering in Latin American Urban History." *Journal of Urban History* 2 (August 1976): 487-498.

Cowley, Malcolm. *Exile's Return: A Literary Odyssey of the 1920s*. New York: Norton, 1934; revised edition, New York: Viking Press, 1951; reprint, New York: Penguin, 1976.

Cowley, Malcolm, and Bernard Smith, eds. *Books That Changed Our Minds*. New York: Doubleday, Doran, 1939; reprint, Freeport, N.Y.: Books for Libraries Press, 1970.

Darnell, Regna. "Personality and Culture: The Fate of the Sapirian Alternative." In *History of Anthropology, vol. 4: Malinowski, Rivers, Benedict and Others: Essays on Culture and Personality*, edited by George W. Stocking, Jr., 156-183. Madison: University of Wisconsin Press, 1986.

_____. *Edward Sapir: Linguist, Anthropologist, Humanist*. Berkeley: University of California Press, 1990.

Davis, Richard H. *South Asia at Chicago: A History*. Chicago: Committee on Southern Asian Studies, University of Chicago, 1985.

Day, Terence P. *Great Tradition and Little Tradition in Theravada Buddhist Studies*. Lewiston, N.Y.: Edwin Mellen Press, 1988.

Delpar, Helen. *The Enormous Vogue of Things Mexican: Cultural Relations between the United States and Mexico, 1920-1935*. Tuscaloosa: University of Alabama Press, 1992.

Despres, Leo A. "An Interview with John W. Bennett." *Current Anthropology* 35 (December 1994): 653-664.

Devore, Irven. "An Interview with Sherwood Washburn." *Current Anthropology* 33 (August-October 1992): 411-423.

De Waal Malefijt, Annemarie. *Images of Man: A History of Anthropological Thought*. New York: Alfred A. Knopf, 1974.

Diamond, Stanley, ed. *Primitive Views of the World*. New York: Columbia University Press, 1964.

_____. *In Search of the Primitive: A Critique of Civilization*. New Brunswick, N.J.: Transaction Books, 1974.

Dumond, D. E. "Competition, Cooperation, and the Folk Society." *Southwestern Journal of Anthropology* 26 (Autumn 1970): 261-286.

Dzuback, Mary Ann. *Robert M. Hutchins: Portrait of an Educator.* Chicago: University of Chicago Press, 1991.

Edmondson, Munro S. "The Anthropology of Values." In *Culture and Life: Essays in Memory of Clyde Kluckhohn,* edited by Walter W. Taylor, John L. Fischerand, and Evon Z. Vogt, 157-197. Carbondale.: Southern Illinois University Press, 1973.

Eggan, Fred. "Social Anthropology and the Method of Controlled Comparison." *American Anthropologist* 56 (October 1954): 743-763.

Eisenstadt, S. N. *Tradition, Change, and Modernity.* New York: Wiley, 1973.

_____. "Studies of Modernization and Sociological Theory." *History and Theory* 13, no. 3 (1974): 225-252.

_____. ed. *The Origins and Diversity of Axial Age Civilizations.* Albany: State University of New York Press, 1986.

_____. "The Axial Age Breakthroughs—Their Characteristics and Origins." In *The Origins and Diversity of Axial Age Civilizations,* edited by S. N. Eisenstadt, 1-25. Albany: State University of New York Press, 1986.

_____. "A Reappraisal of Theories of Social Change and Modernization." In *Social Change and Modernity,* edited by Hans Haferkamp and Neil J. Smelser. Berkeley: University of California Press, 1992.

Entin, Jonathan L. *Sweatt v. Painter,* the End of Segregation, and the Transformation of Education Law." *Review of Litigation* 5 (Winter 1986): 3-71.

Evans, Paul M. *John Fairbank and the American Understanding of China.* New York: Basil Blackwell, 1988.

Fairbank, John K., ed. *Chinese Thought and Institutions.* Chicago: University of Chicago Press, 1957.

Fairbank, John King. *Chinabound: A Fifty-Year Memoir.* New York: Harper & Row, 1982.

Farberman, Harvey A. "The Chicago School: Continuities in Urban Sociology." *Studies in Symbolic Interaction: A Research Annual,* edited by Norman K. Denzin (Greenwich, Conn.) 2 (1979): 3-20, JAI Press.

Faris, Robert E. L. *Chicago Sociology, 1920-1932.* San Francisco: Chandler, 1967; reprint, Chicago: University of Chicago Press, 1970.

Fenton, Charles A. "Ambulance Drivers in France and Italy: 1914-1918," *American Quarterly* 3 (Winter 1951): 326-343.

Fischer, Claude G. "The Study of Urban Community and Personality." *Annual Review of Sociology* 1 (1975): 67-89.

Fischer, Claude S. "'Urbanism as a Way of Life': A Review and an Agenda." *Sociological Methods and Research* 1 (November 1972): 187-242.

_____. "Toward a Subcultural Theory of Urbanism." *American Journal of Sociology* 80 (May 1975): 1319-1341.

Fisher, Berenice M., and Anselm L. Strauss. "Interactionism." In *A History of Sociological Analysis,* edited by Tom Bottomore and Robert Nisbet. New York: Basic Books, 1978.

____. "The Chicago Tradition and Social Change: Thomas, Park, and Their Successors." *Symbolic Interaction* 1 (Spring 1978): 5-23.

Fox, Richard G. *Urban Anthropology: Cities in Their Cultural Settings.* Englewood Cliffs, N.J.: Prentice Hall, 1977.

Freed, Stanley A., and Ruth S. Freed. "Clark Wissler and the Development of Anthroplogy in the United States." *American Anthropologist* 87 (December 1983): 800-825.

French, Robert Mills, ed. *The Community in Perspective.* Itasca, Ill.: F. E. Peacock, 1969.

Friedrichs, Robert W. *A Sociology of Sociology.* New York: Free Press, 1970.

Gamst, Frederick C. *Peasants in Complex Society.* New York: Holt, Rinehart and Winston, 1974.

Geertz, Clifford. "Studies in Peasant Life: Community and Society." In *Biennial Review of Anthropology* 2, edited by Bernard J. Siegel, 1-41. Stanford, Calif.: Stanford University Press, 1962.

Gendzier, Irene L. *Managing Political Change: Social Scientists and the Third World.* Boulder, Colo.: Westview Press, 1985.

Germani, Gino. "Urbanization, Social Change, and the Great Transformation." In *Modernization, Urbanization, and the Urban Crisis*, edited by Gino Germani, 3-57. Boston: Little, Brown and Company, 1973.

Gibbon, Guy. *Anthropological Archaeology.* New York: Columbia University Press, 1984.

Gilkeson, John S., Jr. "The Domestication of 'Culture' in Interwar America, 1919-1941." In *The Estate of Social Knowledge*, edited by JoAnne Brown and David K. van Keuren, 153-174. Baltimore: Johns Hopkins University Press, 1991.

Gillette, Michael L. "Heman Marion Sweatt: Civil Rights Plaintiff." In *Black Leaders: Texans for Their Times*, edited by Alwyn Barr and Robert A. Calvert, 157-188. Austin: Texas State Historical Association, 1981.

____. "Blacks Challenge the White University." *Southwestern Historical Quarterly* 86 (October 1982): 321-344.

Givens, Douglas R. *Alfred Vincent Kidder and the Development of Americanist Archaeology.* Albuquerque: University of New Mexico Press, 1992.

Gleason, Philip. "World War II and the Development of American Studies." *American Quarterly* 36, no. 3 (1984): 343-358.

Godoy, Ricardo. "Franz Boas and His Plans for an International School of American Archaeology and Ethnology in Mexico." *Journal of the History of the Behavioral Sciences* 13 (July 1977): 228-242.

____. "The Background and Context of Redfield's *Tepoztlán.*" *Journal of the Steward Anthropological Society* 10 (Fall 1978): 47-79.

Goist, Park Dixon. "City and 'Community': The Urban Theory of Robert Park." *American Quarterly* 23 (Spring 1971): 46-59.

Goldkind, Victor. "Social Stratification in the Peasant Community: Redfield's Chan Kom Reinterpreted." *American Anthropologist* 67 (August 1965): 863-884.

_____. "Class Conflict and Cacique in Chan Kom." *Southwestern Journal of Anthropology* 22 (Winter 1966): 325-345.

Goldschmidt, Walter. "The Cultural Paradigm in the Post-War World." In *Social Contexts of American Ethnology, 1840-1984, 1984 Proceedings of the American Ethnological Society*, edited by June Helm, 164-176. Washington, D.C.: American Ethnological Society, 1984.

Goodwin, Paul, Hugh M. Hamill, Jr., and Bruce M. Stave. "A Conversation with Richard M. Morse." *Journal of Urban History* 2 (May 1976): 331-356.

Gorman, Paul R. *Left Intellectuals and Popular Culture in Twentieth-Century America*. Chapel Hill: University of North Carolina Press, 1996.

Gossen, Gary H. "Mesoamerican Ideas as a Foundation for Regional Synthesis." In *Symbol and Meaning beyond the Closed Community: Essays in Mesoamerican Ideas*, edited by Gary H. Gossen, 1-8. Albany: Institute for Mesoamerican Studies, the University at Albany, State University of New York, 1986.

Greenfeld, Liah, and Michel Martin. *Center: Ideas and Institutions*. Chicago: University of Chicago Press, 1988.

Grew, Raymond. "Modernization and Its Discontents." *American Behavioral Scientist* 21 (November-December 1977): 289-312.

_____. "More on Modernization." *Journal of Social History* 14 (Fall 1980): 179-187.

Gulick, John. "The City as Microcosm of Society." *Urban Anthropology* 3 (Spring 1975): 5-15.

Gusfield, Joseph R. "Tradition and Modernity: Misplaced Polarities in the Study of Social Change." *American Journal of Sociology* 72 (January 1967): 351-362.

Handler, Richard. "Anti-Romantic Romanticism: Edward Sapir and the Critique of American Individualism." *Anthropological Quarterly* 62 (October 1988): 1-13.

_____. "Boasian Anthropology and the Critique of American Culture." *American Quarterly* 42 (June 1990): 252-273.

Hannerz, Ulf. *Exploring the City: Inquiries toward an Urban Anthropology*. New York: Columbia University Press, 1980.

Hansen, Asael T. "Robert Redfield, the Yucatan Project, and I." In *American Anthropology: The Early Years, 1974 Proceedings of the American Ethnological Society*, edited by John V. Murra, 167-186. St. Paul, Minn.: West Publishing, 1976.

Harris, David R., ed. *The Archaeology of V. Gordon Childe: Contemporary Perspectives*. London: University College of London Press, 1994.

Harris, Marvin. *The Rise of Anthropological Theory: A History of Theories of Culture*. New York: Thomas Y. Crowell, 1968.

Harrison, David. *The Sociology of Modernization and Development.* London: Unwyn Hyman, 1988.

Hart, C. W. M. "Cultural Anthropology and Sociology." In *Modern Sociological Theory in Continuity and Change,* edited by Howard Becker and Alvin Boskoff, 528-549. New York: Holt, Rinehart and Winston, 1957.

Harvey, Lee. *Myths of the Chicago School of Sociology.* Aldershot, England: Avebury, 1987.

Hatch, Elvin. *Culture and Morality: The Relativity of Values in Anthropology.* New York: Columbia University Press, 1983.

Hauser, Philip M., and Leo F. Schnore, eds. *The Study of Urbanization.* New York: John Wiley & Sons, 1965.

Hawkins, John. "Robert Redfield's Culture Concept and Mesoamerican Anthropology." In *Heritage of Conquest: Thirty Years Later,* edited by Carl Kendall, John Hawkins, and Laura Bossen. Albuquerque: University of New Mexico Press, 1983.

Heider, Karl G. "The Rashomon Effect: When Ethnographers Disagree." *American Anthropologist* 90 (March 1988): 73-80.

Helm, June, ed. *Social Contexts of American Ethnology, 1840-1984, 1984 Proceedings of the American Ethnological Society.* Washington, D.C.: American Anthropological Association, 1985.

Herman, Ellen. *The Romance of American Psychology: Political Culture in the Age of Experts.* Berkeley: University of California Press, 1995.

Hewitt de Alcántara, Cynthia. *Anthropological Perspectives on Rural Mexico.* London: Routledge & Kegan Paul, 1984.

Higham, John A. *Strangers in the Land: Patterns of American Nativism, 1860-1925.* 2d ed. New Brunswick, N.J.: Rutgers University Press, 1963; reprint, New York: Atheneum, 1963.

Hoebel, E. Adamson, Richard Currier, and Susan Kaiser, eds. *Crisis in Anthropology: View from Spring Hill, 1980.* New York: Garland, 1982.

Hoffman, Frederick J. *The Twenties: American Writing in the Postwar Decade.* Rev. ed. New York: Free Press, 1962.

Hogbin, H. Ian. *Social Change.* London: Watts, 1958.

Hollinger, David A. *In the American Province: Studies in the History and Historiography of Ideas.* Bloomington: Indiana University Press, 1985; reprint, Baltimore: Johns Hopkins University Press, 1989.

Honigmann, John J. *The Development of Anthropological Ideas.* Homewood, Ill.: Dorsey Press, 1976.

Hoover, Dwight. "The Long Ordeal of Modernization Theory." *Prospects* 11 (1986): 407-451.

Hovenkamp, Herbert. "Social Science and Segregation before *Brown.*" *Duke Law Journal* 1985 (June-September 1985): 624-672.

Hsu, Francis L. K. *The Study of Literate Civilizations.* New York: Holt, Rinehart, and Winston, 1969.

Hughes, Everett C. *French Canada in Transition*. Chicago: University of Chicago Press, 1943.

_____. "The Cultural Aspect of Urban Research." In *The State of the Social Sciences*, edited by Leonard D. White. Chicago: University of Chicago Press, 1956.

_____. "French Canada: The Natural History of a Research Project." In *Reflections on Community Studies*, edited by Joseph Bensman, Maurice R. Stein, and Arthur J. Vidich, 71-83. New York: John Wiley and Sons, 1964.

Hughes, H. Stuart. *Oswald Spengler: A Critical Estimate*. New York: Charles Scribner's Sons, 1952; reprint, Westport, Conn.: Greenwood Press, 1975.

_____. *Consciousness and Society: The Reconstruction of European Social Thought, 1890-1930*. New York: Alfred A. Knopf, 1958; reprint, New York: Vintage Books, 1961.

Huntington, Samuel P. "The Change to Change." *Comparative Politics* 3 (April 1971): 283-322.

_____. *The Clash of Civilizations and the Remaking of World Order*. New York: Simon and Schuster, 1996.

Inden, Ronald. *Imagining India*. Cambridge, Mass.: Blackwell, 1990.

Jackson, Peter. "Social Disorganization and Moral Order in the City." *Transactions, Institute of British Geographers* 9, no. 1 (1984): 169-180.

Janowitz, Morris. Introduction to *W. I. Thomas, On Social Organization and Social Personality: Selected Papers*, edited by Morris Janowitz. Chicago: University of Chicago Press, 1966.

Joseph, Gilbert M. *Rediscovering the Past at Mexico's Periphery: Essays on the History of Modern Yucatan*. Tuscaloosa: University of Alabama Press, 1986.

Kadel, Kathryn Jean. "Little Community to the World: The Social Vision of Robert Redfield, 1897-1958." Ph.D. diss., Northern Illinois University, DeKalb, Ill., 2000.

Kazin, Alfred. *On Native Grounds: An Interpretation of Modern American Prose Literature*. New York: Reynal & Hitchcock; reprint, San Diego: Harcourt Brace Jovanovich, 1982.

Kearney, Michael. *World View*. San Francisco: Chandler & Sharp Publishers, 1984.

Keen, Benjamin. *The Aztec Image in Western Thought*. New Brunswick, N.J.: Rutgers University Press, 1971.

Kett, Joseph F. *The Pursuit of Knowledge under Difficulties: From Self-Improvement to Adult Education in America, 1750-1990*. Stanford, Calif.: Stanford University Press, 1994.

King, Arden R. "Civilization." In *A Dictionary of the Social Sciences*, edited by Julius Gould and William L. Kolb. New York: Free Press of Glencoe, 1964.

Klausner, Samuel Z., and Victor M. Lidz, eds. *The Nationalization of the Social Sciences*. Philadelphia: University of Pennsylvania Press, 1986.

Kleiman, Jordan. "Modernization." In *A Companion to American Thought*, edited by Richard W. Fox and James T. Kloppenberg. Cambridge, Mass.: Blackwell, 1995.

Kluger, Richard. *The History of Brown vs. Board of Education and Black America's Struggle for Equality*. New York: Alfred A. Knopf, 1976; reprint, New York: Vintage, 1977.

Knight, Alan. "Racism, Revolution, and Indigenismo: Mexico, 1910-1940." In *The Idea of Race in Latin America, 1870-1940*, edited by Richard Graham. Austin: University of Texas Press, 1992.

König, René. *The Community*. Translated by Edward Fitzgerald. London: Routledge & Kegan Paul, 1968.

Kraeling, Carl H., and Robert M. Adams. *City Invincible: A Symposium on Urbanization and Cultural Development in the Ancient Near East*. Chicago: University of Chicago Press, 1958.

Kress, Paul F. *Social Science and the Idea of Process: The Ambiguous Legacy of Arthur F. Bentley*. Urbana: University of Illinois Press, 1970.

Kroeber, A. L., and Clyde Kluckhohn. *Culture: A Critical Review of Concepts and Definitions*. Cambridge, Mass.: Papers of the Peabody Museum of American Archaeology and Ethnology, Harvard University, 47, no. 1, 1952; reprint, New York: Vintage Books, 1963.

Kuklick, Bruce. *Puritans in Babylon: The Ancient Near East and American Intellectual Life, 1880-1930*. Princeton, N.J.: Princeton University Press, 1996.

Kuklick, Henrika. "A 'Scientific Revolution': Sociological Theory in the United States, 1930-1945." *Sociological Inquiry* 43, no. 1 (1973): 3-22.

____. "Boundary Maintenance in American Sociology: Limitations to Academic 'Professionalization." *Journal of the History of the Behavioral Sciences* 16 (July 1980): 201-219.

Kurtz, Lester R. *Evaluating Chicago Sociology: A Guide to the Literature with an Annotated Bibliography*. Chicago: University of Chicago Press, 1984.

Lal, Barbara Ballis. *The Romance of Culture in an Urban Civilization: Robert E. Park on Race and Ethnic Relations in Cities*. London: Routledge, 1990.

Latham, Michael E. *Modernization as Ideology: American Social Science and "Nation Building" in the Kennedy Era*. Chapel Hill: University of North Carolina Press, 2000.

Leeds, Anthony. *Cities, Classes, and the Social Order*. Edited by Roger Sanjek. Ithaca, N.Y.: Cornell University Press, 1994.

Lehan, Richard. *The City in Literature: An Intellectual and Cultural History*. Berkeley: University of California Press, 1998.

Leis, Philip E. "Palm Oil, Illicit Gin, and the Moral Order of the Ijaw." *American Anthropologist* 66 (August 1964): 828-838.

Lerner, Daniel. *The Passing of Traditional Society: Modernizing the Middle East*. New York: Free Press, 1958.

Leslie, Charles M. "Redfield, Robert." In *International Encyclopedia of the Social Sciences*, edited by David L. Sills. New York: Macmillan and Free Press, 1968.

_____. "The Hedgehog and the Fox in Robert Redfield's Work and Career." In *American Anthropology: The Early Years, 1974 Proceedings of the American Ethnological Society*, edited by John V. Murra, 146-166. St. Paul, Minn.: West Publishing, 1976.

Lessa, W. A. "Folk Culture." In *A Dictionary of the Social Sciences*, edited by Julius Gould and William L. Kolb. New York: Free Press of Glencoe, 1964.

Levine, Donald N. *Wax and Gold: Tradition and Innovation in Ethiopian Culture*. Chicago: University of Chicago Press, 1965.

_____. *Visions of the Sociological Tradition*. Chicago: University of Chicago Press, 1995.

_____. "Challenging Certain Myths about the 'Hutchins' College." *University of Chicago Magazine* 77 (Winter 1985): 36-39, 51.

Levine, Donald, and Ellwood B., Gorman, Eleanor Miller Carter. "Simmel's Influence on American Sociology." *American Journal of Sociology* 81 (January-March 1976): 813-845, 1112-1132.

Lévi-Strauss, Claude. *Structural Anthropology*. Translated by Claire Jacobson and Brooke Grundfest Schoepf. New York: Basic Books, 1963.

Lewis, Oscar. "Further Observations on the Folk-Urban Continuum and Urbanization, with Special Reference to Mexico City." In *The Study of Urbanization*, edited by Philip M. Hauser and Leo F. Schnore, 491-502. New York: John Wiley & Sons, 1965.

_____. *Anthropological Essays*. New York: Random House, 1970.

Liebersohn, Harry. *Fate and Utopia in German Sociology, 1870-1923*. Cambridge, Mass.: MIT Press, 1988.

Lingeman, Richard. "A Consonance of Towns." In *Making America: The Society and Culture of the United States*, edited by Luther S. Luedtke. Chapel Hill: University of North Carolina Press, 1992.

Lofland, Lyn H. "Reminiscences of Classic Chicago: The Blumer-Hughes Talk." *Urban Life* 9 (October 1980): 251-281.

Lynd, Robert S., and Helen Merrill Lynd. *Middletown: A Study of Contemporary Culture*. New York: Harcourt, Brace & Co., 1929.

MacAloon, John J., ed. *General Education in the Social Sciences: Centennial Reflections on the College of the University of Chicago*. Chicago: University of Chicago Press, 1992.

Macias, Anna. *Against All Odds: The Feminist Movement in Mexico to 1940*. Westport, Conn.: Greenwood Press, 1982.

MacNeish, Richard S. *The Science of Archaeology?* North Scituate, Mass.: Duxbury Press, 1978.

Madge, John. *The Origins of Scientific Sociology*. New York: Free Press of Glencoe, 1962.

Mahale, Prabha. "Relevance of Folk-Urban Continuum in Studies of Complex Societies." *Man in India* 63 (June 1983): 197-205.

Marcus, George, and Michael M. J. Fischer. *Anthropology as Cultural Critique: An Experimental Moment in the Human Sciences*. Chicago: University of Chicago Press, 1986.

Marriott, McKim. "Anthropology Courses in Regions and Civilizations: An Indian Civilization Course." In *The Teaching of Anthropology*, edited by David G. Mandelbaum, Gabriel W. Lasker, and Ethel M. Albert, 203-216. Berkeley: University of California Press, 1963.

Martin, Paul S. "Early Development in Mogollon Research." In *Archaeological Researches in Retrospect*, edited by Gordon R. Willey, 3-32. Cambridge, Mass.: Winthrop, 1974.

Matthews, Fred H. "The Revolt against Americanism: Cultural Pluralism and Cultural Relativism as an Ideology of Liberation." *Canadian Review of American Studies* 1 (Spring 1970): 4-31.

_____. *Quest for an American Sociology: Robert E. Park and the Chicago School*. Montreal: McGill-Queen's University Press, 1977.

_____. "Louis Wirth and American Ethnic Studies: The Worldview of Enlightened Assimilationism, 1925-1950." In *The Jews of North America*, edited by Moses Rischin, 123-143. Detroit: Wayne State University, 1987.

_____. "Social Scientists and the Culture Concept, 1930-1950: The Conflict between Processual and Structural Approaches." *Sociological Theory* 7 (Spring 1989): 106-120.

May, Henry F. *The End of American Innocence: A Study of the First Years of Our Own Time, 1912-1917*. New York: Alfred A. Knopf, 1959; reprint, Chicago: Quadrangle Books, 1964.

Mazlish, Bruce. *A New Science: The Breakdown of Connections and the Birth of Sociology*. New York: Oxford University Press, 1989.

McArthur, Benjamin. "Revisiting Hutchins and the Higher Learning in America." *History of Higher Education Annual* 7 (1987): 9-28.

_____. "A Gamble on Youth: Robert M. Hutchins and the Politics of Presidential Selection." *History of Education Quarterly* 30 (Summer 1990): 161-186.

McCaughey, Robert A. *International Studies and Academic Enterprise*. New York: Columbia University Press, 1984.

McKinney, John C., and Charles P. Loomis. "The Typological Tradition." In *Contemporary Sociology*, edited by Joseph S. Roucek, 557-582. New York: Philosophical Library, 1958.

McMillan, Robert Lee. "The Study of Anthropology, 1931-1937, at Columbia University and the University of Chicago." Ph.D. diss., York University, 1986.

McNeill, William H. *Arnold J. Toynbee: A Life*. New York: Oxford University Press, 1989.

_____. *Hutchins' University: A Memoir of the University of Chicago*. Chicago: University of Chicago Press, 1991.

Mencher, Joan P. "Discussion." In *Social Anthropology of Peasantry*, edited by Joan P. Mencher. Bombay: Somaiya, 1983.

Mendelson, E. M. "World View." In *International Encyclopedia of the Social Sciences*, edited by David L. Sills. New York: Macmillan and Free Press, 1968.

Miller, Donald L. *Lewis Mumford: A Life*. New York: Weidenfield & Nicolson, 1989.

Miner, Horace, ed. *The City in Modern Africa*. New York: Frederick A. Praeger, 1967.

____. "Community-Society Continua." In *International Encyclopedia of the Social Sciences*, edited by David L. Sills. New York: Macmillan and Free Press, 1968.

Mintz, Sidney W. "A Note on the Definition of Peasantries." *Journal of Peasant Studies* 1 (October 1973): 90-106.

Moore, Kenneth. "The City as Context: Context as Process." *Urban Anthropology* 3 (Spring 1975): 17-26.

Murphy, Robert F. "A Quarter Century of American Anthropology." In *Selected Papers from the American Anthropologist, 1946-1970*, edited by Robert F. Murphy, 1-22. Washington, D.C.: American Anthropological Association, 1976.

____. "Anthropology at Columbia: A Reminiscence." *Dialectical Anthropology* 16, no. 1 (1991): 65-81.

Murray, Stephen O. "Edward Sapir in 'The Chicago School' of Sociology." In *New Perspectives in Language, Culture, and Personality: Proceedings of the Edward Sapir Centenary Conference*, Ottawa, 1-3 October 1984, edited by William Cowan, Michael K. Foster, and Konrad Koerner, 241-291. Amsterdam: John Benjamins, 1986.

____. "The Reception of Anthropological Work in the Sociology Journals, 1922-1951." *Journal of the History of the Behavioral Sciences* 24 (April 1988): 135-151.

____. "Anthropologists Discover Peasants." Manuscript, personal collection of the author, 1995.

Nash, Manning. Foreword to *Essays on Economic Development and Cultural Change: In Honor of Bert F. Hoselitz*, edited by Manning Nash. Chicago: University of Chicago Press, 1977.

Nash, Roderick. *The Nervous Generation: American Thought, 1917-1930*. Chicago: Rand McNally & Company, 1970.

Nisbet, Robert A. *The Sociological Tradition*. New York: Basic Books, 1966; reprint, New Brunswick, N. J.: Transaction Publishers, 1993.

____. *Social Change and History: Aspects of the Western Theory of Development*. New York: Oxford University Press, 1969.

____. *Sociology as an Art Form*. New York: Oxford University Press, 1976.

____. *History of the Idea of Progress*. New York: Basic Books, 1980.

____. *The Making of Modern Society*. New York: New York University Press, 1986.

Norbeck, Edward. "Peasant Society." In *A Dictionary of the Social Sciences*, edited by Julius Gould and William L. Kolb. New York: Free Press of Glencoe, 1964.

Oleson, Alexandra, and John Voss, eds. *The Organization of Knowledge in Modern America, 1860-1920*. Baltimore: Johns Hopkins University Press, 1979.

Olson, Keith W. *The G.I. Bill, the Veterans, and the Colleges*. Lexington: University of Kentucky Press, 1974.

Packenham, Robert A. *Liberal America and the Third World: Political Development Ideas in Foreign Aid and Social Science*. Princeton, N.J.: Princeton University Press, 1973.

Paine, Robert. "A Critique of the Methodology of Robert Redfield: 'Folk Culture' and Other Concepts." *Ethnos* 31, no. 1 (1966): 161-172.

Pasternak, Burton. "A Conversation with Fei Xiatong." *Current Anthropology* 29 (August-October 1988): 637-662.

Peace, William J. "Vere Gordon Childe and American Anthropology." *Journal of Anthropological Research* 44 (Winter 1988): 417-433.

Pells, Richard H. *Radical Visions and American Dreams: Culture and Social Thought in the Depression Years*. New York: Harper & Row, 1973; reprint, Middletown, Conn.: Wesleyan University Press, 1984.

Persons, Stow. *Ethnic Studies at Chicago, 1905-45*. Urbana: University of Illinois Press, 1987.

Pike, Frederick B. *The United States and Latin America: Myths and Stereotypes of Civilization and Nature*. Austin: University of Texas Press, 1992.

Poplin, Dennis E. *Communities: A Survey of Theories and Methods of Research*. 2d ed. New York: Macmillan, 1979.

Potter, Jack, May N. Diaz, and George M. Foster, eds. *Peasant Society: A Reader*. Boston: Little, Brown & Company, 1967.

Powell, John Duncan. "On Defining Peasants and Peasant Society." *Peasant Studies Newsletter* 1, no. 3 (1972): 94-99.

Purcell, Edward A., Jr. *The Crisis of Democratic Theory: Scientific Naturalism and the Problem of Value*. Lexington: University Press of Kentucky, 1973.

Quandt, Jean B. *From the Small Town to the Great Community: The Social Thought of Progressive Intellectuals*. New Brunswick, N.J.: Rutgers University Press, 1970.

Redfield, James. "Redfield, Robert." In *Thinkers of the Twentieth Century*, edited by Roland Turner. 2d ed. Chicago: St. James Press, 1987.

Reissman, Leonard. *The Urban Process: Cities in Industrial Societies*. New York: Free Press, 1964.

Riesman, David. "Becoming an Academic Man." In *Authors of Their Own Lives: Intellectual Biographies by Twenty American Sociologists*, edited by Bennett M. Berger, 22-74. Berkeley: University of California Press, 1990.

Rigdon, Susan M. *The Culture Facade: Art, Science, and Politics in the Work of Oscar Lewis*. Urbana: University of Illinois Press, 1988.

Roberts, J. Timmons, and Amy Hite, eds. *From Modernization to Globalization: Perspectives on Development and Social Change*. Malden, Mass.: Blackwell, 2000.

Roseberry, William. *Anthropologies and Histories: Essays in Culture, History, and Political Economy*. New Brunswick, N.J.: Rutgers University Press, 1989.

Ross, Dorothy. "American Social Science and the Idea of Progress." In *The Authority of Experts*, edited by Thomas L. Haskell, 157-179. Bloomington: Indiana University Press, 1984.

____. *The Origins of American Social Science*. Cambridge: Cambridge University Press, 1991.

____, ed. *Modernist Impulses in the Human Sciences, 1870-1930*. Baltimore: Johns Hopkins Press, 1994.

Rostow, W. W. *The Stages of Economic Growth: A Non-Communist Manifesto*. Cambridge: Cambridge University Press, 1960.

Rubinstein, Robert A., ed. *Fieldwork: The Correspondence of Robert Redfield and Sol Tax*. Boulder, Colo.: Westview Press, 1991.

Rudolph, Lloyd I., and Susanne Hoeber Rudolph. *The Modernity of Tradition: Political Development in India*. Chicago: University of Chicago Press, 1967.

Ruiz, Ramon Eduardo. *Mexico: The Challenge of Poverty and Illiteracy*. San Marino, Calif.: Huntington Library, 1963.

Rundell, John, and Stephen Mennell. *Classical Readings in Culture and Civilization*. London: Routledge, 1998.

Ryan, Bryce F. *Social and Cultural Change*. New York: Ronald Press, 1969.

Sanderson, Stephen K. *Social Evolutionism: A Critical History*. Cambridge, Mass.: Basil Blackwell, 1990.

Sartori, Andrew. "Robert Redfield's Comparative Civilizations Project and the Political Imagination of Postwar America." *Positions* 6, no. 1 (1998): 33-65.

Schmidt, Henry C. "The American Intellectual Discovery of Mexico in the 1920s." *South Atlantic Quarterly* 77 (Summer 1978): 335-351.

____. *The Roots of Lo Mexicano: Self and Society in Mexican Thought, 1900-1934*. College Station: Texas A&M University Press, 1978.

Schudson, Michael. *Discovering the News: A Social History of American Newspapers*. New York: Basic Books, 1982.

Shanin, Teodor, ed. *Peasants and Peasant Society*. Harmondsworth, UK: Penguin, 1971.

____. *Defining Peasants: Essays Concerning Rural Societies, Expolary Economies, and Learning from Them in the Contemporary World*. Oxford: Basil Blackwell, 1990.

Sherratt, Andrew. "V. Gordon Childe: Archaeology and Intellectual History." *Past and Present* 125 (November 1989): 151-185.

Shils, Edward. "The Calling of Sociology." In *Theories of Society: Foundations of Modern Sociological Theory*, edited by Talcott Parsons et al., 1405-1448. New York: Free Press, 1961.

_____. *Center and Periphery: Essays in Macrosociology*. Chicago: University of Chicago Press, 1975.

_____. "Learning and Liberalism." In *The Calling of Sociology and Other Essays on the Pursuit of Learning*. Chicago: University of Chicago Press, 1980.

_____. "The Contemplation of Society in America." In *The Calling of Sociology and Other Essays on the Pursuit of Learning*. Chicago: University of Chicago Press, 1980.

_____. "Robert Maynard Hutchins." *American Scholar* 59 (Spring 1990): 211-235.

Shiner, L. E. "Tradition/Modernity: An Ideal Type Gone Astray." *Comparative Studies in Society and History* 17 (July 1975): 245-252.

Sica, Alan. "The Rhetoric of Sociology and Its Audience." In *Sociology and Its Publics: The Forms and Fates of Disciplinary Organization*, edited by Terrence C. Halliday and Morris Janowitz. Chicago: University of Chicago Press, 1992.

Silverman, Sydel. "The Peasant Concept in Anthropology." *Journal of Peasant Studies* 7 (1979): 49-69.

_____, ed. *Totems and Teachers: Perspectives on the History of Anthropology*. New York: Columbia University Press, 1981.

Singal, Daniel Joseph. *The War Within: From Victorian to Modernist Thought in the South, 1919-1945*. Chapel Hill: University of North Carolina Press, 1982.

_____, ed. *Modernist Culture in America*. Belmont, Calif.: Wadsworth, 1991.

Singer, Milton. "Robert Redfield: Anthropologist." *Man in India* 39 (April-June 1959): 81-91.

_____. "Robert Redfield's Development of a Social Anthropology of Civilizations." In *American Anthropology: The Early Years,* 1974 Proceedings of the American Ethnological Society, edited by John V. Murra, 187-260. St. Paul, Minn.: West Publishing, 1976.

_____. "David Mandelbaum and the Rise of South Asian Studies: A Reminiscence." In *Dimensions of Social Life: Essays in Honor of David G. Mandelbaum*, edited by Paul Hockings, 1-7. Berlin: Mouton de Gruyter, 1987.

_____. "Robert Redfield." In *Remembering the University of Chicago*, edited by Edward Shils, 413-429. Chicago: University of Chicago Press, 1991.

_____. "A Conversation of Cultures: The United States and Southern Asia." In *Semiotics of Cities, Selves, and Cultures: Explorations in Semiotic Anthropology*. Berlin: Mouton de Gruyter, 1991.

_____. "Redfield, Robert." In *International Dictionary of Anthropologists*, edited by Christopher Winters. New York: Garland, 1991.

Sinha, Surajit. "Changes in the Cycle of Festivals in a Bhumji Village." *Journal of Social Research* 1 (September 1958): 24-53.

Sitton, Salomon Nahmad, and Thomas Weaver. "Manuel Gamio, El Primer An-
tropologo Aplicado y Su Relacion Con la Antropologica Norteamericana."
America Indigena 50, no. (October-December 1990): 291-321.

Sjoberg, Gideon. "The Rural-Urban Dimension in Preindustrial, Transitional,
and Industrial Societies." In *Handbook of Modern Sociology*, edited by
Robert E. L. Faris, 127-159. Chicago: Rand McNally, 1964.

Smith, Alice Kimball. *A Peril and a Hope: The Scientists' Movement in America*. Chicago: University of Chicago Press, 1965.

Smith, Dennis. *The Chicago School: A Liberal Critique of Capitalism*. New
York: St. Martin's Press, 1988.

Smith, Mark C. *Social Science in the Crucible: The American Debate over Objectivity and Purpose, 1918-1941*. Durham, N.C.: Duke University Press,
1994.

Sollors, Werner. *Beyond Ethnicity: Consent and Descent in American Culture*.
New York: Oxford University Press, 1986.

_____. "Anthropological and Sociological Tendencies in American Literature of
the 1930s and 1940s: Richard Wright, Zora Neale Hurston, and American
Culture." In *Looking Inward, Looking Outward: From the 1930s through
the 1940s*. European Contributions to American Studies 18, edited by Steve
Ickringill, 22-75. Amsterdam: VU University Press, 1990.

Spicer, Edward H. "Acculturation." In *International Encyclopedia of the Social
Sciences*, edited by David L. Sills. New York: Macmillan and Free Press,
1968.

Steel, Ronald. *Walter Lippmann and the American Century*. New York: Vintage
Books, 1981.

Stein, Maurice R. *The Eclipse of Community: An Interpretation of American
Studies*. Princeton, N.J.: Princeton University Press; reprint, New York:
Harper & Row, 1964.

Steward, Julian H. *Theory of Culture Change: The Methodology of Multilinear
Evolution*. Urbana: University of Illinois Press, 1963.

_____. Review of *Human Nature and the Study of Society: The Papers of Robert
Redfield*, vol. 1. Edited by Margaret Park Redfield. *Science* 141 (August 2
1963): 419.

Stocking, George W., Jr. "The History of Anthropology: Where, Whence,
Whither?" *Journal of the History of the Behavioral Sciences* 2 (October
1966): 281-290.

_____. *Race, Culture, and Evolution: Essays in the History of Anthropology*.
New York: Free Press, 1968.

_____. "Boas, Franz." In *Dictionary of American Biography*, supplement 3. Ed-
ited by Edward T. James. New York: Charles Scribner's Sons, 1973.

_____. "Introduction: The Basic Assumptions of Boasian Anthropology." In *The
Shaping of American Anthropology, 1883-1911: A Franz Boas Reader*, edited by George W. Stocking, Jr., 1-20. New York: Basic Books, 1974.

_____. "Clio's Fancy: Documents to Pique the Historical Imagination." *History
of Anthropology Newsletter* 2 (1978): 10.

____. "Pedants and Potentates: Robert Redfield at the 1930 Hanover Conference." *History of Anthropology Newsletter* 5, no. 2 (1978): 10-13.

____. "Die Geschichtlichkeit der Wilden und die Geschichte der Ethnologie." *Geschichte und Gesellschaft* 4 (1978): 520-535.

____. *Anthropology at Chicago: Tradition, Discipline, Department.* Chicago: Joseph Regenstein Library of the University of Chicago, 1979.

____. "Redfield, Robert." In *Dictionary of American Biography,* supplement 6. Edited by John A. Garraty. New York: Charles Scribner's Sons, 1980.

____. "Philanthropoids and Vanishing Cultures: Rockefeller Funding and the End of the Museum Era in Anglo-American Anthropology." In *History of Anthropology,* vol. 3, *Objects and Others: Essays on Museums and Material Culture,* edited by George W. Stocking, Jr., 112-145. Madison: University of Wisconsin Press, 1985.

____. "Ideal Types and Aging Glands: Robert Redfield's Response to Oscar Lewis's Critique of Tepoztlán." *History of Anthropology Newsletter* 16 (June 1989): 3-10.

____. *The Ethnographer's Magic and Other Essays in the History of Anthropology.* Madison: University of Wisconsin Press, 1992.

Strauss, Anselm. Introduction to *George Herbert Mead on Social Psychology: Selected Papers,* edited by Anselm Strauss. Chicago: University of Chicago Press, 1964.

Strickon, Arnold. "Hacienda and Plantation in Yucatan: An Historical-Ecological Consideration of the Folk-Urban Continuum in Yucatan." *America Indigena* 25 (January 1965): 35-63.

Sullivan, Paul. *Unfinished Conversations: Mayas and Foreigners between Two Wars.* New York: Alfred A. Knopf, 1989.

____. Review of *Fieldwork: The Correspondence of Robert Redfield and Sol Tax,* by Robert A. Rubinstein, ed. In *Man* 28 (March 1993): 191-192.

Susman, Warren I. *Culture as History: The Transformation of American Society in the Twentieth Century.* New York: Pantheon, 1984.

Sutton, Francis X. "The Ford Foundation: The Early Years." *Daedalus* 116 (Winter 1987): 41-92.

Tarn, Nathaniel. "The Literate and the Literary: Notes on the Anthropological Discourse of Robert Redfield." In *Views from the Weaving Mountain: Selected Essays in Poetics and Anthropology.* Albuquerque: University of New Mexico Press, 1991.

Tent, James F. *Mission on the Rhine: Reeducation and Denazification in America-Occupied Germany.* Chicago: University of Chicago Press, 1982.

Tipps, Dean C. "Modernization Theory and the Comparative Study of Societies: A Critical Perspective." *Comparative Studies in Society and History* 15 (March 1973): 199-226.

Trigger, Bruce G. *Gordon Childe: Revolutions in Archaeology.* New York: Columbia University Press, 1980.

_____. *A History of Archaeological Thought*. Cambridge: Cambridge University Press, 1989.

Turner, Ralph H. Introduction to *Robert E. Park: On Social Control and Collective Behavior*, edited By Ralph H. Turner. Chicago: University of Chicago Press, 1967.

Tushnet, Mark V. *The NAACP's Legal Strategy against Segregated Education, 1925-1950*. Madison: University of Wisconsin Press, 1987.

Vidich, Arthur J., and Stanford M. Lyman. *American Sociology: Worldly Rejections of Religion and Their Directions*. New Haven, Conn.: Yale University Press, 1985.

Villa Rojas, Alfonso. "Fieldwork in the Mayan Region of Mexico." In *Long-Term Field Research in Social Anthropology*, edited by George M. Foster, Thayer Scudder, Elizabeth Colson, and Robert V. Kemper, 45-64. New York: Academic Press, 1979.

Vincent, Joan. *Anthropology and Politics: Visions, Traditions, and Trends*. Tucson: University of Arizona Press, 1990.

Voget, Fred W. "Anthropology and Sociology." In *Contemporary Sociology*, edited by Joseph S. Roucek, 453-487. New York: Philosophical Library, 1958.

_____. *A History of Ethnology*. New York: Holt, Rinehart, and Winston, 1975.

Vogt, Evon Z. "Culture Change." In *International Encyclopedia of the Social Sciences*, edited by David L. Sills. New York: Macmillan and Free Press, 1968.

_____. *Fieldwork among the Maya: Reflections on the Harvard Chiapas Project*. Albuquerque: University of New Mexico Press, 1994.

Vonnegut, Kurt, Jr. "Address to the National Institute of Arts and Letters, 1971." In *Wampeters, Foma, and Granfalloons*. New York: Delacorte, 1974.

_____. *Fates Worse Than Death: An Autobiographical Collage of the 1980s*. New York: G. P. Putnam's Sons, 1991.

Wagley, Charles, and Marvin Harris. "A Typology of Latin American Subcultures." *American Anthropologist* 57 (April 1955): 428-451.

Ward, F. Champion, ed. *The Idea and Practice of General Education: An Account of the College of the University of Chicago*. Chicago: University of Chicago Press, 1950.

Washburn, Sherwood L. "Evolution of a Teacher." *Annual Review of Anthropology* 12 (1983): 1-24.

Westbrook, Robert B. "Tribune of the Technostructure: The Popular Economics of Stuart Chase." *American Quarterly* 32 (Fall 1980): 387-408.

White, Morton. *Social Thought in America: The Revolt against Formalism*. New York: Viking Press, 1949; reprint, New York: Oxford University Press, 1975.

Willey, Gordon R. "Vogt at Harvard." In *Ethnographic Encounters in Southern Mesoamerica: Essays in Honor of Evon Zartman Vogt, Jr.*, edited by Victoria R. Bricker and Gary H. Gossen, 21-31. Albany: Institute for Mesoamerican Studies, the University at Albany, State University of New York, 1989.

Williams, Raymond. *Culture and Society, 1780-1950*. New York: Columbia University Press, 1958; reprint, New York: 1966.

Wittner, Lawrence S. *The Struggle against the Bomb*. Vol. 1: *One World or None: A History of the World Nuclear Disarmament Movement through 1953*. Stanford, Calif.: Stanford University Press, 1993.

Wolf, Eric R. *Anthropology*. Englewood Cliffs, N.J.: Prentice Hall; reprint, New York: W. W. Norton, 1973.

_____. *Peasants*. Englewood Cliffs, N.J.: Prentice Hall, 1966.

_____. "Understanding Civilizations: A Review Article." *Comparative Studies in Society and History* 9 (July 1967): 446-465.

_____. "Summing Up." In *Social Anthropology of Peasants*, edited by Joan P. Mencher, 345-351. Bombay: Somaiya, 1983.

_____. "Reply to Alan R. Beals' Eric Wolf and the North Berkeley Gang." *Current Anthropology* 29 (April 1988): 306-307.

Woodbury, Richard B. *Alfred V. Kidder*. New York: Columbia University Press, 1973.

Wooley, Wesley T. *Alternatives to Anarchy: American Supranationalism since World War II*. Bloomington: Indiana University Press, 1988.

Yans-McLaughlin, Virginia. "Science, Democracy, and Ethics: Mobilizing Culture and Personality for World War II." In *History of Anthropology*. Vol. 4: *Malinowski, Rivers, Benedict and Others: Essays on Culture and Personality*, edited by George W. Stocking, Jr., 184-217. Madison: University of Wisconsin Press, 1986.

Young, Frank W. "Durkheim and Development Theory." *Sociological Theory* 12 (March 1994): 73-82.

Zaretsky, Eli. Introduction to *The Polish Peasant in Europe and America*, by William I. Thomas and Florian Znaniecki. Edited and abridged by Eli Zaretsky. Urbana: University of Illinois Press, 1984.

Index

About the Author

Clifford Wilcox earned a Ph.D. in American intellectual history from the University of Michigan, Ann Arbor. He taught briefly at Eastern Michigan University in Ypsilanti, Michigan, and the Bolles School in Jacksonville, Florida and is now Director of Information Technology for Somera Communications in Santa Barbara, California. In addition to this study, he has also published articles on 1960s student activism and the history of American higher education.